JAZZ GUITAR
SOLOING CONCEPTS
A PENTATONIC MODAL APPROACH TO IMPROVISATION

ISBN 978-1-4234-2013-2

HAL•LEONARD®
CORPORATION

7777 W. BLUEMOUND RD. P.O. BOX 13819 MILWAUKEE, WI 53213

In Australia Contact:
Hal Leonard Australia Pty. Ltd.
4 Lentara Court
Cheltenham, Victoria, 3192 Australia
Email: ausadmin@halleonard.com.au

Visit Hal Leonard Online at
www.halleonard.com

ACKNOWLEDGMENTS

I would like to thank everyone at Hal Leonard Corporation for all their hard work throughout the development of this book.

I would like to acknowledge my brother, Dean Lemos, for all that he has taught me about jazz music and jazz guitar. I consider Dean to be the greatest "unknown" jazz guitarist on the planet. His artistry, particularly as a solo jazz guitarist, continues to inspire me.

I would also like to dedicate this book to the memory of the great jazz guitarist John Collins (1912–2001). While John had worked with many jazz legends, including Art Tatum, Billie Holiday, and Dizzy Gillespie, he is best known as Nat "King" Cole's guitarist for 14 years. John was also my teacher in the early seventies. In addition to being one of the great jazz guitarists of our time, John was also a wonderful person who is deeply missed by all who knew him. Thank you, John, for your wisdom, inspiration, patience, and graciousness.

Lastly, I would like to thank Sylvia for her love and inspiration to be the best that I can be in all facets of my life.

Ron Lemos
December 2008

TABLE OF CONTENTS

INTRODUCTION

The goal of this book is to dramatically improve your ability to solo over virtually any chord progression. The pentatonic-modal system presented in the following chapters will work with any genre of music, including jazz, rock, pop, Latin, and even country. However, the focus is on jazz because that is where you find music with the richest and most complex chord changes.

The Pentatonic Approach

Soloing over chords and chord progressions is very challenging. Many formulas and methods for navigating chord changes exist, including:

- Major, minor, and other scales

- Arpeggios

- Scale sequences

- Bebop scales (Baker, 1987)

- Four-note scale patterns (Bergonzi, 1992)

- Omitting the 4th degree of the scale (i.e., six-note patterns)

- Substituting the ♭4th for the natural 4th scale tone (Russell, 1959)

- Chromatic notes

- Licks

- Transcribed/memorized patterns

All of the preceding methods are useful. However, each method requires a different approach to the fretboard and musical facility in order to utilize it effectively. Some of the aforementioned devices work best for other instruments (like piano or sax) and are difficult to implement on guitar. Knowledge of these devices is most useful for technique practice and for analyzing favorite solos.

The system presented in this book is based exclusively on pentatonic (five-note) scales, optimized specifically for the unique physical attributes of the guitar fretboard. Moreover, each pentatonic scale is optimized for a specific chord and chord family, and most accurately reflects the sound, or "color," of each chord.

The basic minor/major pentatonic scale is discussed in most books on jazz and rock improvisation, a few of which are listed in the bibliography at the back of this book (Ricker, 1978; Saunders, 2004; Bergonzi, 1994; Roikinger, 1987). While all of these books are very good, especially their exercises, they do not provide a comprehensive approach to soloing, nor do they take advantage of the inherent guitaristic device of playing two-notes-per-string pentatonic scales. Finally, none of them take a modal approach to linking pentatonic scales to chords and chord families. A modal approach is very important because modes provide the link between chords and scales.

The system described in this book has many advantages, including the following:

- It will work with *any* chord progression, from simple to complex.

- The strict two-notes-per-string convention works particularly well for guitar.

- Unlike other scale systems, there are *no* notes to avoid.

- Solos can start or stop on any note and sound good.

- Any note can be sustained.

- The system works best with jazz but can be used for Latin, pop, funk, rock, etc.

- The system works on *any* chord extension.

- The system works on *any* chord substitution.

- Solos are inherently melodic because each note in the scale is "right," and the emphasis is on the relationship of the scale to the "sweet notes" of the associated chords.

- Complex chords can be covered with basic or substitute pentatonic scales.

- The system will work for a beginner, as well as for intermediate and even advanced players.

- The system will work at any tempo.

- The system will work using any desired note patterns.

- The system will work no matter how many beats there are for each chord.

- The system can be used exclusively, selectively, or in combination with any other system for playing solos.

- The system can seamlessly augment, complement, or even transform your current soloing style.

- The scales can be used with different degrees of consonance/dissonance.

- Different scales can be used for different chord types or extensions.

- All scales/modes are in proximity to basic chords.

- The system fits perfectly with other pattern-based soloing devices such as:
    Arpeggios
    One-, two-, three-, or four-note patterns/sequences
    Six-note scales (e.g., blues or whole tone)
    Seven-note scales (major or minor)
    Eight-note scales (bebop or diminished)
    Twelve-note scales (chromatic)

- Chromatic notes can be used freely to connect notes in the scales.

- The system works equally well in major or minor tonalities.

- Each set of five scales per chord covers the entire fretboard.

- Finger movement is minimized once all scale inversions are learned.

- Virtually any chord progression/song can be played in one position, if desired.

- In some cases, one pentatonic scale can be used for an entire progression.

- It is not mandatory that scales be changed for every chord change.

- Finally, while learning all five modes for each scale would be best, you can get by only learning one or two modes. Many well-known guitarists are successful using only two positions of the blues scale. In this system, you can add positions at your own speed and based on your own interests and needs.

This is a lot to promise. However, I believe that this system delivers on these promises. The system is theoretically sound, designed specifically for guitar, easy to implement, and sounds good over any chord or chord progression.

OVERVIEW OF THE BOOK

This book is divided into six sections. A brief overview of each section is described below.

Section 1: The Eleven Pentatonic Scales (key of C)

Eleven pentatonic scales are described in relationship to the seven modes of the major scale, one additional mode from the harmonic-minor scale, one additional mode from the melodic-minor scale, the standard minor/major pentatonic scale, and a pentatonic blues scale. This adds up to eleven. However, two major modes and two minor modes from the major scale use the same pentatonic scales. Additionally, one of the minor modes uses the basic minor/major pentatonic scale, and the pentatonic blues scale uses a mode from the major scale. Consequently, only seven modes need to be learned. Even better, you already know one of these modes—the basic minor/major pentatonic scale. Thus, by learning only six additional pentatonic scales, you will be able to solo effectively on virtually any chord or chord progression.

Section 2: Substituting Pentatonic Scales

This section describes how you can use the pentatonic scales from Section 1 as substitute scales for different chords, giving you many more soloing options for any particular chord without having to learn any new scales.

Section 3: The Symmetrical Pentatonic Scales

This section provides the appropriate pentatonic scales for soloing over chords that are built from symmetrical diminished or whole tone scales. These pentatonic scales also provide useful "color" alternatives for soloing over chord changes. The chapter on diminished chords will be particularly useful, since no new scale is introduced.

Section 4: Other Pentatonic Scales

Five additional pentatonic scales are provided, each offering additional scale color options.

Section 5: Chord Progressions

This section includes approaches to using the pentatonic scales in common jazz chord progressions. These include: ii–V progressions, ii–V–I progressions, iim7♭5–V7–i progressions, blues changes, Rhythm Changes, jazz standards, and Coltrane Changes.

Section 6: Appendices

Six appendices are provided that contain important background and supplemental material. These appendices include: Overview of Modes, Overview of Roman Numeral Systems, Overview of Roman Numeral Pentatonic Scale Modes, Enharmonic Notes and Intervals, and an Annotated List of Resources for Soloing Over "Giant Steps."

Bibliography

Suggested supplemental readings are referenced.

This book was designed to flow sequentially from one chapter to another. However, an important feature of the book is that you do not have to follow this sequence to derive full benefit of the concepts; you can skip around the book in any order that you feel is useful. For example, if you have an immediate need to deal with a dominant flat five chord, it is perfectly fine to skip to the chapter on the Lydian Dominant Pentatonic Scale (Chapter 10). However, you should gain familiarity with the scales in Section 1, since many of the chapters in the other sections refer to scales covered in that section.

IMPORTANT NOTES

Note 1: Transposing the Examples

It is important to be able to incorporate these concepts in any key. To supplement the text in each chapter, examples of the pentatonic chord scales are provided in three forms: musical notation, tab, and fretboard diagrams. Most of these examples are presented in the key of C; however, it is important that you are able to transpose them to other keys as needed—especially "jazz" keys like E♭, B♭, F, and A♭. Notating all of the examples in this book in all 12 keys would not be practical. However, one advantage of the guitar is that it is relatively easy to transpose patterns up and down the fretboard by simply shifting your left hand. Toward that end, a very good exercise is for you to write out your own examples in keys in which you want to work. A real strength of this book, though, is that it is based on patterns, and patterns are easy to transpose on the guitar.

Note 2: Using All Four Fingers

It is highly recommended that you use all four fingers of the fretting hand while learning these scales. This will pay big dividends in the development of your technique. All of the scales (except the basic pentatonic scale) use finger stretches of no more than four frets. Some of the stretches are up, and some are down. If you have always wanted to learn to use your pinky finger for soloing, now would be a good time to start. That said, all of the patterns can be played with only three or even two (like Django Reinhardt) fingers.

Note 3: Picking Style

Picking style is left up to the guitarist. The two-notes-per-string approach shown in this method works very well with strict alternate picking. However, any comfortable picking pattern will be effective. Also, this system is very compatible with common pentatonic devices like hammer-ons, pull-offs, slides, and bends. All of these devices lend a more "vocal" quality to solos.

Note 4: How to Practice Scales

Specific exercises have not been written out; this is not a book of "licks" or patterns. The pentatonic scales are presented as frameworks for you to build your own soloing patterns and melodies. However, for those who would like to practice the scales in a formal manner, the following approach is suggested.

First, practice using steady streams of eighth notes. Use a metronome to ensure that you are keeping good time. This is *very important*. Start at a slow speed (e.g., 100 beats per minute) and stay there until you can perfectly execute steady streams of eighth notes. Then, gradually increase the speed, playing your exercise routine over and over again until you can once again play it cleanly.

Once you have eighth-note patterns down, practice with triplet patterns. Next, try sixteenth-note patterns. Then, practice patterns with a combination of note values. This will be important practice for making your solos more melodic and "vocal-like." While it is fun to "shred" sixteenth notes, it is more important to make your solos sound like melodies.

The aforementioned practice routines can be played in various ways, as described below.

Strum the chord and then:

- Run the scale, from the lowest note to the highest.
- Run the scale, from the highest note to the lowest.
- Run the scale, from the lowest note to highest and then back.

- Run the scale, from the highest note to lowest and then back.
- Run different combinations of four-note patterns.
- Run different combinations of eight-note patterns.
- Use upward or downward slides when notes on the same string are one fret apart.
- Use hammer-ons when notes on the same string are one fret apart.
- Use hammer-ons when notes on the same string are more than one fret apart.
- Use pull-offs when notes on the same string are one fret apart.
- Use pull-offs when notes on the same string are more than one fret apart.
- Use bends when notes on the same string are one fret apart.

Finally, the best way to learn these scales is to start applying them to real songs. Practice using the scales on songs:

- That you already are playing.
- That you have tried before but could not get the results you wanted.
- That have only a few chords, like modal tunes.
- That have complex chord changes.

Also, try applying the scales to different genres of music, besides jazz. Try the scales on pop, Latin, country, or original tunes.

Note 5: How to Practice Songs and Chord Progressions

Specific examples have been written out for practicing various chord progressions. However, if you would like to practice the scales in a formal manner, the following approaches are suggested:

- Learn the chords to the progression, making sure that you can play them cleanly.
- Record the progression on a sequencer, practicing the scale over the changes. (I strongly recommend Band-In-A-Box by PG Music.)
- Make sure that you are able to play the song's melody. This is *very* important. Your solo should have something in common with the melody of the song. Once you can play the melody, try using the pentatonic scales to "fill up" the space between the melody notes. This will have a tremendously positive affect on your solos. Now you are ready to simply focus on your solo.
- Pay attention to the transitions between pentatonic scales. Ideally, the switch should sound seamless.

Tip: Try to start the new scale close to the last note that you played in the previous scale. For example, practice switching scales while maintaining an ascending pattern of notes. Then, try switching scales while maintaining a descending pattern of notes.

- Let your solos "breathe." The reason why horn players sound so good is that their phrasing mimics the human voice (i.e., they have to breathe). Guitarists are notorious for playing constant streams of rapid sixteenth notes. After a while, this is *not* fun for the listener. Use your speed as an accent to your solo. It is the silence between the notes that is the most important. Many great musicians sing their solos while they are playing (e.g., George Benson).

Note 6: What Are Modes?

This book is based on a modal approach to soloing that uses only pentatonic scales. Appendix A gives background information on modes and how they are used in this book.

Note 7: What is the Roman Numeral System?

This book uses the Roman numeral system in three distinct ways. The first two ways are described in Appendix B. The third is described in Appendix C.

First, this book describes chords in Roman numerals (vi, ii, V, etc.) instead of lettered chords (Am7, Dm7, G7, etc.). The Roman numeral system is very useful because it allows you to describe chords in terms of chord relationships within the key, chord quality, and chord extensions.

Second, this book describes chord *progressions* using the Roman numeral system. The Roman numeral system is designed to represent chord progressions, independent of the key from which they are derived. This is of great help in transposing (especially in jazz) since you can focus on the entire song as opposed to transposing chords individually.

Third, this book uses Roman numerals to identify the five modes of the pentatonic scales. The Roman numerals represent the starting pentatonic-scale step/note on the guitar's sixth string. This is detailed in Appendix C.

Note 8: What Does "Position" Mean?

The term "position" is used in this book to refer to the fretboard position of your fret hand for each pattern (i.e., which fret your index finger starts at for each pattern). For example, the fifth position means your index finger is covering the fifth fret, your middle finger is covering the sixth fret, your ring finger is covering the seventh fret, and your pinky is covering the eighth fret. Some patterns will require your index finger to stretch down one fret on some of the strings and your pinky to stretch up one fret on some of the strings. However, you should think of these stretches as temporary movements. Your hand should always come back to the pattern's original position—unless, of course, you are intentionally moving to a new pattern position.

In conclusion, I am confident that you will be amazed by the musical doors that this book will open for you.

Best wishes,
Ron Lemos

TUNING   TRACK 59   NOTES

SECTION 1

The Eleven Pentatonic Scales (Key of C)

Eleven pentatonic scales are presented in this section. Nine are based on

the diatonic major scale, including the basic pentatonic scale and the blues

scale; one is based on the harmonic-minor scale; and one is based on the melodic-

minor scale. These eleven scales enable you to use two-notes-per-string pentatonic

patterns to play over any chord or chord progression that you find in jazz, pop,

Latin, or even country music. Additionally, these same scales will be used in

subsequent sections as substitute scales for different chords and as

scales that can be used to reharmonize chord progressions.

CHAPTER 1
THE BASIC MINOR/MAJOR PENTATONIC SCALE

One of the greatest joys in learning how to play guitar solos is the discovery of the pentatonic scale. All of a sudden, the whole history of rock, pop, and blues lead-guitar playing becomes available to the aspiring guitar player.

This chapter presents a brief review of the basic minor/major pentatonic scales that you probably already know. Subsequent chapters show how only a few additional pentatonic scales can be used to cover virtually any chord progression in jazz, rock, pop, or Latin. The advantage of this system is that new techniques and/or complicated theory do not need to be learned. Also, these new scales can easily be incorporated into the individual playing style that you have already developed.

Minor, Major, and Blues Pentatonic Scales

Minor Pentatonic Scale: Probably the greatest "*a-ha!*" experience when learning how to play lead guitar is the discovery of the minor pentatonic scale. This "magical" scale allows us to emulate all of our rock and blues heroes. With the minor pentatonic scale under one's fingers, even a beginning guitar player can solo over any blues-based song. For blues songs, the problem of chord changes is solved: using the minor pentatonic scale, the changes can be ignored. This is also true for many other rock and pop songs, especially those in a minor tonality (e.g., "Light My Fire" solo, "Moondance," "Summertime").

The great thing about the minor pentatonic scale is that you can play pretty decent solos by only learning one pentatonic position (e.g., the Am pentatonic scale in fifth position). As you learn additional positions, the entire fretboard opens up to you for soloing. This scale really has no end with respect to what can be accomplished with it. In the hands of an exceptional guitarist like Eric Johnson, the pentatonic scale can always sound fresh and musical.

Major Pentatonic Scale: Another "*a-ha!*" moment is when one learns that the minor pentatonic scale can actually be used in two different situations. By moving the minor pentatonic scale patterns down three half steps, you get a parallel major pentatonic scale. This scale uses the exact same patterns and adds some very important color possibilities to a solo. In other words, the major and minor pentatonic scales can be used interchangeably to add harmonic depth to a solo.

Also, the major pentatonic scale is a better choice for major tonality chord progressions such as the following. (Note: See Appendix B for more on the Roman numeral system.)

à la "Stand By Me"...

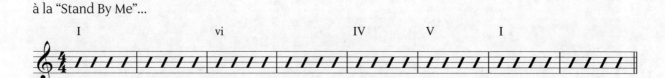

Turnarounds in jazz or pop songs...

à la "La Bamba" and "Twist and Shout"...

Blues Scales: Another great discovery is the addition of the ♭5th to the minor pentatonic scale (i.e., blues scale). Now a solo can be significantly enriched and really start to sound "bluesy" and more sophisticated. Just as importantly, the ♭5th can also be added to the major pentatonic scale . These two blues scales offer additional note-color options.

Since this book focuses on pentatonic scales, the six-note blues scales are not covered. For an excellent reference on major and minor blues scales, pick up a copy of Dan Greenblatt's *The Blues Scales: Essential Tools for Jazz Improvisation* (Sher Music Co, 2004). However, pentatonic (five-note) versions of the two blues scales will be covered in Chapter 11.

Am Minor/C Major Pentatonic Scale Description

Fig. 1A shows the five fingerings for the A minor/C major pentatonic scale in music and tab notation, along with a fretboard diagram. Each pattern follows the two-notes-per-string rule. The initial chords are suggested voicings that are a good fit for each of the five patterns with respect to sound and proximity.

Fig. 1A
A Minor/C Major Pentatonic Scale

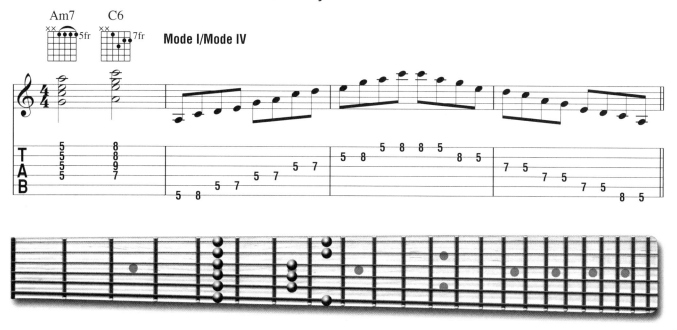

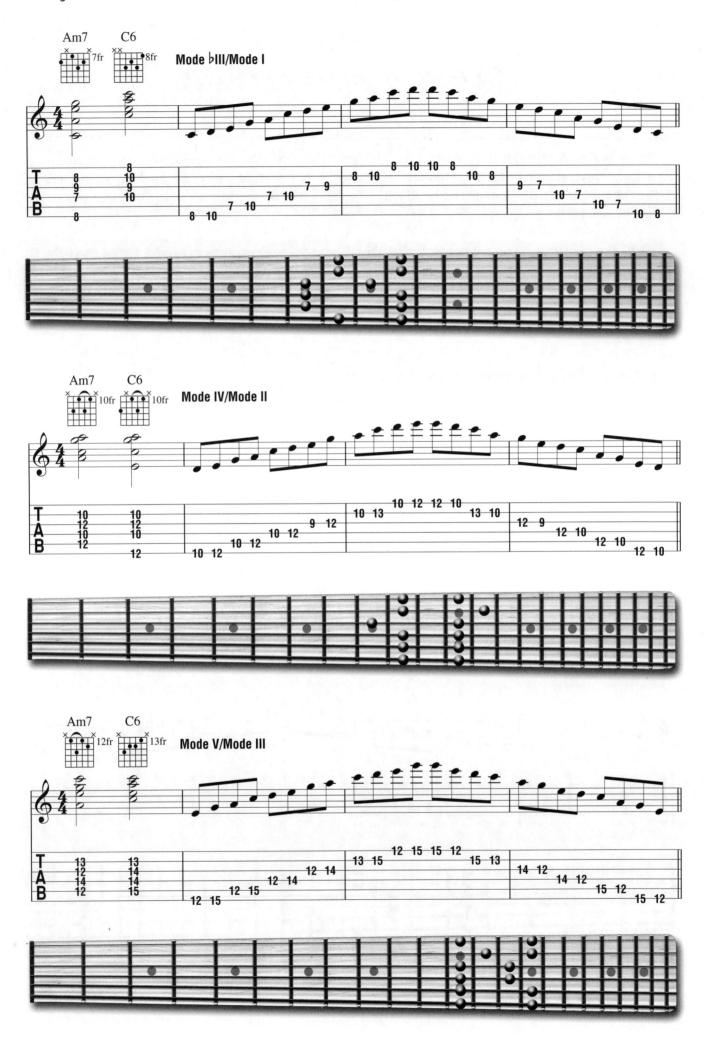

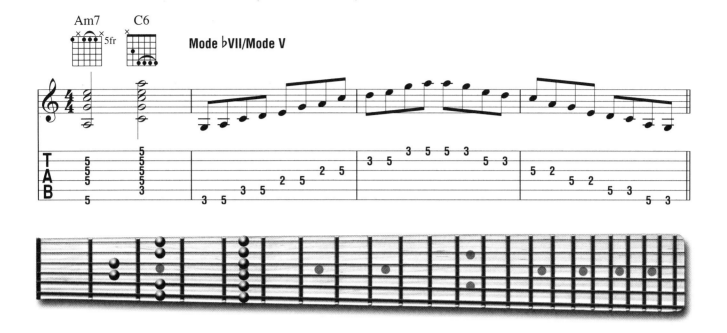

Both scales consist of the same five notes. However, each note plays a different "color tone" role in the two related scales. For example, the note C is the ♭3rd in the A minor pentatonic scale; the same note, C, is the root in the C major pentatonic scale.

NOTES	A	C	D	E	G
A Minor:	root	♭3rd	4th	5th	♭7th
C Major:	6th	root	2nd/9th	3rd	5th

Mode I of the minor pentatonic scale (equivalent to Mode VI of the major pentatonic scale) is the familiar "box" pattern that most guitar players learn first.

The fingerings are exactly the same for both scales. The only difference is position on the fretboard (i.e., the fret at which your index finger is placed for each pattern). The following chart maps the positions for both the A minor pentatonic scale and the C major pentatonic scale:

KEY	A Minor	C Major
Fifth Position:	Mode I	Mode VI
Seventh Position:	Mode ♭III	Mode I
Ninth & Tenth Position:	Mode IV	Mode II
Twelfth Position:	Mode V	Mode III
Second Position:	Mode ♭VII	Mode V

Once again, even though the mode names are different, the five fretboard patterns are the same for both the minor pentatonic scale and its relative major pentatonic scale. For example, there is no difference between the A minor pentatonic scale and the relative C major pentatonic scale. Both scales use the exact same fretboard patterns and positions.

A good example of using both scales in a very basic, descending solo is shown below, played over this simple blues progression in the key of C:

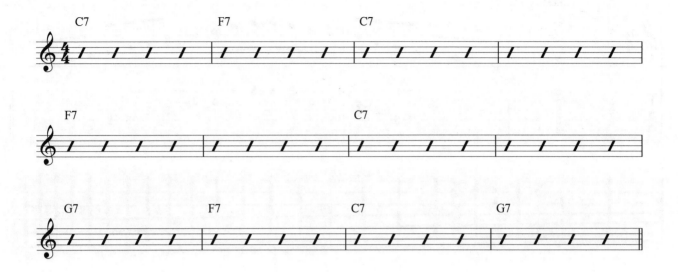

The C minor pentatonic scale can be used for the entire progression, ignoring the chord changes [**Fig. 1B**]. While many blues solos use this approach, the C minor pentatonic scale is missing some important notes, particularly with respect to the 3rd (E) of the C7 chord. By using the C major pentatonic scale (or A minor pentatonic scale) for the C7 chord and the C minor pentatonic scale for the other chords, you get a much wider range of melodic movement without having to learn any new scale patterns [**Fig. 1C**].

Fig. 1B
C Minor Pentatonic Blues

Track 1

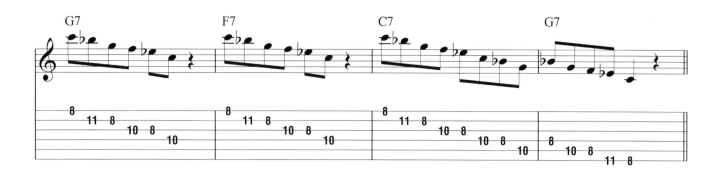

Fig. 1C
C Major Pentatonic Blues

Track 1 (cont.)

Subsequent chapters will introduce new pentatonic scales that give you many more options for soloing over blues progressions, static chord vamps, or virtually any chord progression.

Figs. 1D–E show two examples of eight-bar solos that use only the A minor pentatonic scale. **Figs. 1F–G** show two examples of eight-bar solos that use only the relative C major pentatonic scale.

Fig. 1D
A Minor Pentatonic Song 1

Fig. 1E
A Minor Pentatonic Song 2

Fig. 1F
C Major Pentatonic Song 1

Track 1 (cont.)

C Major - Mode VI

Fig. 1G
C Major Pentatonic Song 2

Track 1 (cont.)

C Major - Mode I

*Outside scale form

I strongly recommend that you create your own eight-bar solos with a focus on trying to create melodic phrases as opposed to just running streams of eighth or sixteenth notes. I believe that focusing on pentatonic scales will support your efforts to create more melodic lines that will sound good at any speed.

CHAPTER 2
IONIAN (Imaj7) PENTATONIC SCALE

Imaj7 Chord Description

The sound of the major seventh (Imaj7) chord is extremely important in jazz. It has a beautiful, lush sound, and it establishes the basic key of a song or signals temporary or permanent key changes.

The Ionian scale is built on the first degree of the major scale. In the key of C, for example, the Ionian scale is:

C–D–E–F–G–A–B

The Imaj7 chord is built on the following degrees of the Ionian major scale:

1–3–5–7

In the key of C, the notes are: C–E–G–B

Almost any Imaj7 chord voicing or inversion that you use will sound good.

Other related major chords are 6ths and 9ths (e.g., C6, Cmaj9, C6/9). They can be substituted freely, subject to desired bass leading and chord voicing movements.

The Imaj7 chord is notated in several different ways. You may come across any of the following:

Cmaj7 CM7 Cma7 CΔ7

Note from the Editor: Though Ionian is usually referred to as a "mode," as is Dorian, Lydian, etc., in this text they're used as scale sources from which to derive specific pentatonic forms. Therefore, the terms "scale" and "mode" will be used interchangeably throughout.

C Ionian Pentatonic Scale Description

Fig. 2A shows the five fingerings for the C Ionian (Imaj7) pentatonic scale in music and tab notation, along with a fretboard diagram. Each pattern follows the two-notes-per-string rule. The initial chords are suggested voicings that are a good fit for each of the five patterns with respect to sound and proximity.

The C Ionian pentatonic scale consists of the following five scale tones (notes):

1–2–3–5–7 (C–D–E–G–B)

Fig. 2A
C Ionian Pentatonic Scale

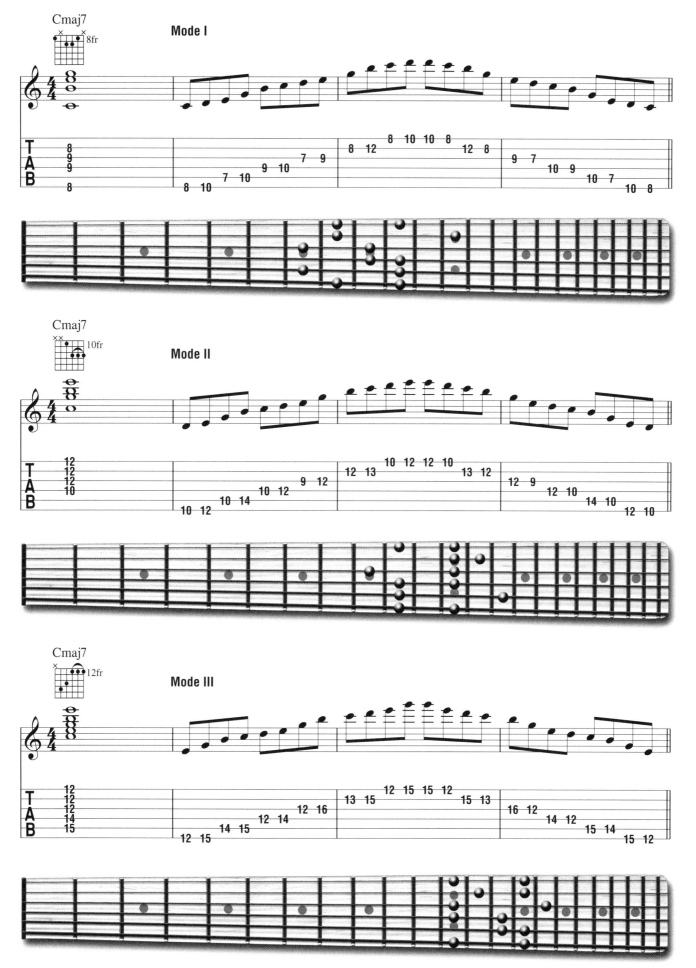

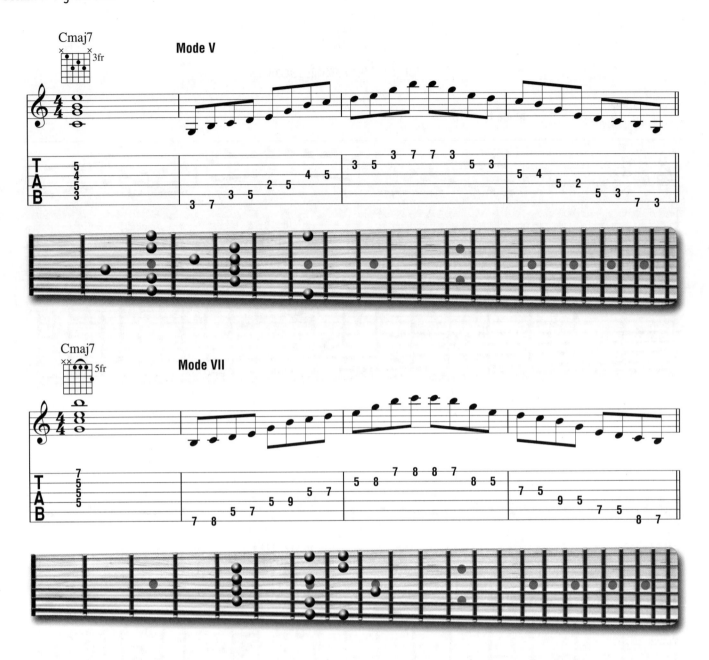

Soloing on the Ionian major seventh-chord is very challenging. It is easy to just run the C major scale (or any other melodic devices). However, it will become boring very quickly, especially if the chord lasts more than one measure. The Ionian pentatonic scale is much more resistant to this problem since it closely models the soloing approach with which you are currently comfortable. It is much easier to just play the music and not be concerned with specific note choices or hitting wrong notes.

Important Note: A common suggestion for pentatonic soloing over the Imaj7 chord is to use the major pentatonic scale (1–2–3–5–6). In the key of C, the notes would be C–D–E–G–A. This pattern can work, as will be discussed later. However, the subtle change of the one note makes a big difference in:

- The sound of the scale (the Ionian pentatonic scale sounds more "jazzy" since it focuses on the major 7th note as opposed to the major 6th).

- The versatility of the scale with respect to playing different maj7 chords in a measure or song and always sounding "right." (Try to play different combinations of major seventh chords and the related scales to see how nicely they sound together.)

- Clearly distinguishing a modal center contrast to any other modal or non-modal chords in a chord sequence (i.e., it sounds good with any chord sequence).

Fig. 2B contains four four-bar solos that use the C Ionian pentatonic scale. Notice that the first and fourth examples use chromatic notes to add additional "jazziness" to the solos. Chromatic notes can be used freely in any of the pentatonic scales described in this book. However, with the "pentatonic-modal approach", chromatic notes are completely optional. This means that the pentatonic-modal approach can be used exclusively, if you desire. For example, try replacing the chromatic notes in Fig. 2C with neighboring notes from the C Ionian pentatonic scale. The solos will still sound good. In fact, the further away the replacement note is from the original scale tone, the more "outside" your solo will sound.

Fig. 2B
Improvising with the Ionian Pentatonic Scale

*Chromatic passing tone

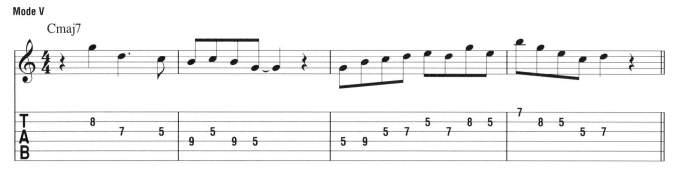

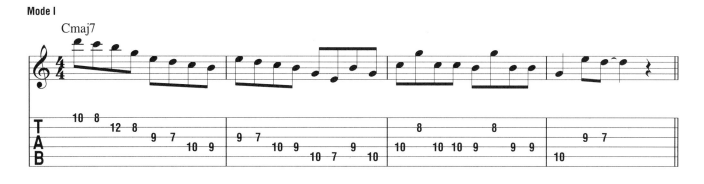

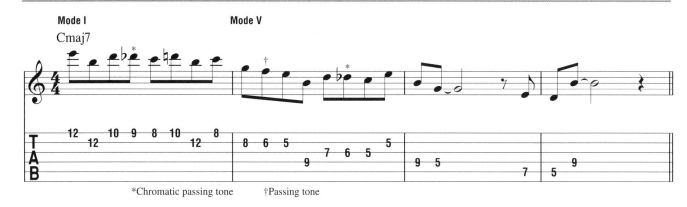

*Chromatic passing tone   †Passing tone

There are several approaches to soloing over the major seventh chord that are taught in various jazz texts. For a Cmaj7 chord, these include:

- Ionian major scale (C–D–E–F–G–A–B)

- Lydian major scale (C–D–E–F♯–G–A–B)

- Major pentatonic scale, starting at the root of the chord (C–D–E–G–A)

- Major pentatonic scale, starting at the 5th of the chord (G–A–B–D–E)

- Major pentatonic scale, starting at the 2nd of the chord (D–E–F♯–A–B)

- Major bebop scale, starting at the root of the chord (C–D–E–F–G–G♯–A–B)

- Major blues scale, starting at the root of the chord (C–D–D♯/E♭–E–G–A)

- Minor blues scale, starting at the root of the chord (C–E♭–F–G♭–G–B♭)

- Minor pentatonic scale, starting at the root of the chord (C–E♭–F–G–B♭).

Several of these will be discussed in later chapters as additional choices for soloing over the major seventh chord. However, the best choice for soloing over a major seventh chord is the Ionian pentatonic scale. It emphasizes the important color tones of the chord (3rd, 7th, 9th, etc.) and includes the root note, which serves to "anchor" the scale and clearly define the major seventh tonality.

CHAPTER 3
DORIAN (iim7) PENTATONIC SCALE

iim7 Chord Description

The sound of the Dorian minor seventh (iim7) chord is very important. As a stand-alone chord, it has a signature minor sound that is very modern. For jazz, it has a Miles Davis/John Coltrane sound over static minor seventh chords. For Latin rock music, it has a sound that suggests the playing of Carlos Santana.

Even more importantly, it's a basic component of the iim7–V7 and iim7–V7–Imaj7 chord progressions that form the basis of jazz, Latin, and popular music. Mastering this chord progression is absolutely critical and essential for soloing effectively over jazz songs and chord progressions (see Chapters 26–27).

The Dorian scale is built on the 2nd degree of the major scale. In the key of C, for example, the Dorian scale is:

$$D–E–F–G–A–B–C$$

The iim7 chord is built on the following degrees of the Dorian scale:

$$1–{}^\flat 3–5–{}^\flat 7$$

In the key of C, the notes for a Dm7 are: D–F–A–C

Almost any iim7 chord voicing or inversion that you use will sound good.

Other related minor chords are 6ths, 9ths, and 11ths (e.g., Dm9, Dm6/9, Dm6, and Dm11). They can be substituted freely, subject to desired bass leading and chord voicing movements.

Below are several ways that a iim7 chord might be notated (sometimes the "7" is incorrectly omitted):

Dm7	D–7	Dmin7	Dmi7	D–	Dm	Dmin	Dmi

D Dorian Pentatonic Scale Description

Fig. 3A shows the five fingerings for the D Dorian (iim7) pentatonic scale in music and tab notation, along with a fretboard diagram. Each pattern follows the two-notes-per-string rule. The initial chords are suggested voicings that are a good fit for each of the five patterns with respect to sound and proximity.

The D Dorian pentatonic scale consists of the following five scale tones (notes):

$$1–2–{}^\flat 3–5–{}^\flat 7 \quad (D–E–F–A–C)$$

Fig. 3A
D Dorian Pentatonic Scale

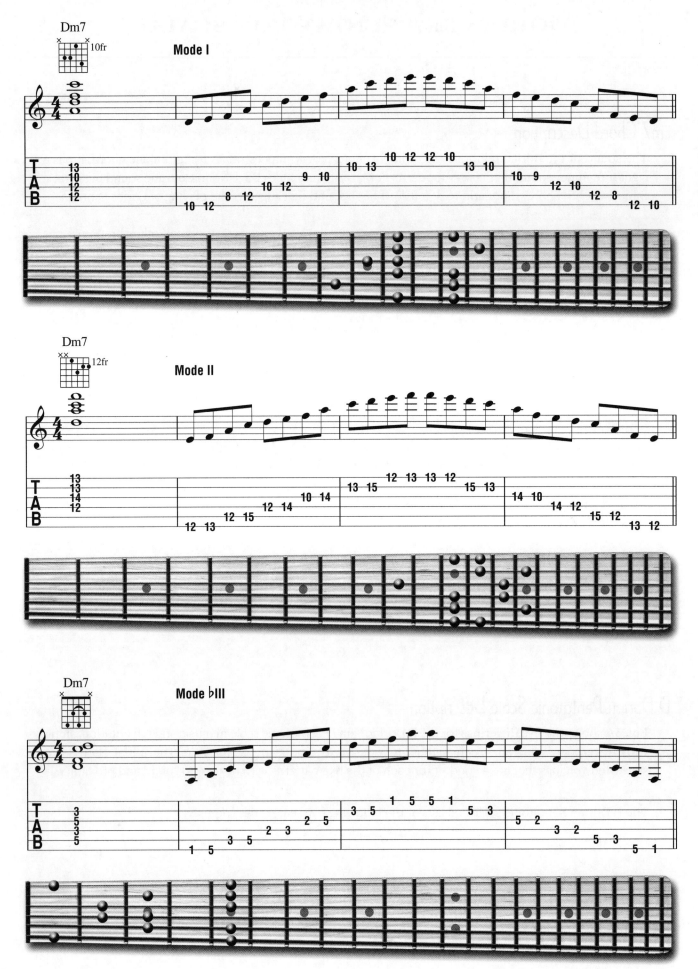

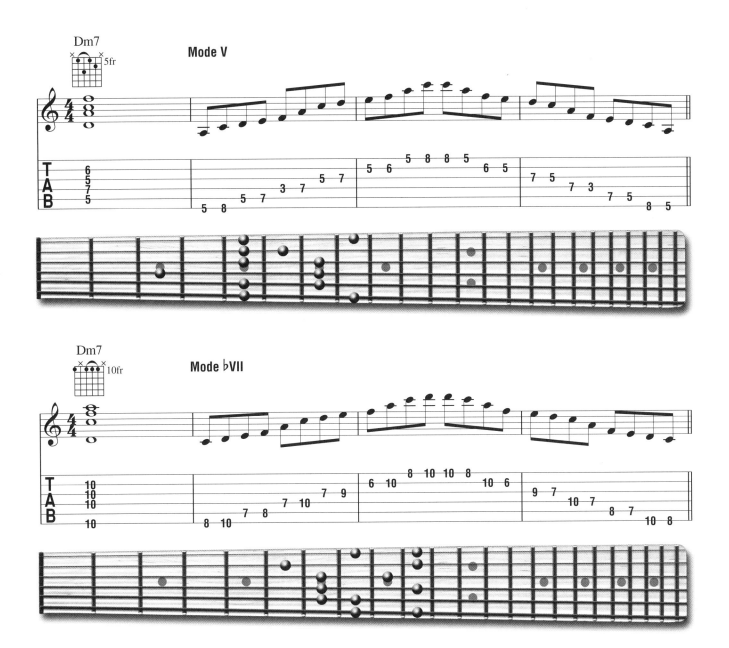

Soloing with the Dorian pentatonic scale imbues a very jazzy minor 9th sound that is quite different from the regular minor pentatonic scale or the seven-note Dorian mode.

The three scales are compared below:

Dorian Pentatonic Scale:	D	E	F		A		C
Minor Pentatonic Scale:	D		F	G	A		C
Dorian Mode:	D	E	F	G	A	B	C

The common suggestion for pentatonic soloing over the iim7 chord is to use the minor pentatonic scale (1–$\flat$3–4–5–$\flat$7). This pattern can work, as will be discussed in a later chapter. However, the subtle change of the one note (E instead of G) makes a big difference in:

- The sound of the scale (it sounds more "jazzy" than rock).

- The versatility of the scale with respect to playing different Dorian minor seventh chords in a measure or song and always sounding "right." (Try to play different combinations of iim7 chords and their relative scales to see how nicely they sound together.)

- Clearly distinguishing a modal-center contrast to any other modal minor or non-modal chords in a chord sequence (i.e., it sounds good with any chord sequence).

The E note (9th) in the Dorian pentatonic scale is much stronger than the G note (4th) in the regular minor pentatonic scale relative to the sound of the chord. This becomes even more evident when the iim7 chord is used in conjunction with the V7 chord. The Dorian (iim7) pentatonic scale creates a much better voice-leading transition to the V7 dominant seventh chord and should be used for all iim7 chords.

Fig. 3B presents four four-bar solos that use the D Dorian pentatonic scale. Note that the fourth example includes chromatic note ideas. Develop your own four-bar solos using the D Dorian pentatonic scale. Remember, the goal is to try to create phrases that are *melodic*.

Fig. 3B
Improvising with the Dorian Pentatonic Scale

*Chromatic notes

CHAPTER 4
PHRYGIAN (iiim7) PENTATONIC SCALE

iiim7 Chord Description

The Phrygian minor seventh (iiim7) chord is very important in jazz as a basic component of the iiim7–vim7–iim7–V7 chord progression. This chord progression is important as a stand-alone chord progression or as a turnaround chord sequence in jazz, Latin, and popular music. Mastering the iiim7 chord and the iiim7–vim7–iim7–V7 progression is absolutely critical and essential for soloing effectively over jazz songs.

The Phrygian scale is built on the 3rd degree of the major scale. In the key of C, for example, the Phrygian scale is:

E–F–G–A–B–C–D

The iiim7 chord is built on the following degrees of the Phrygian scale:

1–♭3–5–♭7

In the key of C, the notes for the Phrygian Em7 are:

E–G–B–D

Almost any iiim7 chord voicing or inversion that you use will sound good.

The only other related minor chord is the 11th (e.g., Em11 in the key of C). It can be substituted freely, subject to desired bass leading and chord voicing movements. The minor 9th, minor 6th, and m(maj7) chords do not work in the Phrygian tonality. For example, the following is a standard turnaround in C:

As shown below, each of the minor chords are different with respect to the modes from which they are derived.

Em7 = Phrygian mode (E–F–G–A–B–C–D)

Am7 = Aeolian mode (A–B–C–D–E–F–G)

Dm7 = Dorian mode (D–E–F–G–A–B–C)

While they all contain the same notes, the notes represent different intervals in the chords. For example, Dm9, Dm6, or Dm11 will work as substitutes for Dm7 since the color tones (9th, 6th, and 11th) are all in the Dorian mode. For Am7, only the Am9 and Am11 work. An Am6 could not be used as a substitute since the 6th (F♯) is not included in the Aeolian mode (key of C major). The same idea holds for the Em7 chord in this sequence. An Em9 or Em6 could not be used as substitute chords since the 9th (F♯) and 6th (C♯) notes do not occur in the Phrygian mode.

The iiim7 chord is notated in several different ways. For example, below are several ways that a iiim7 chord might appear (sometimes the "7" is incorrectly omitted):

Em7   E-7   Emin7   Emi7   E-   Em   Emin   Emi

E Phrygian Pentatonic Scale Description

Fig. 4A shows the five fingerings for the E Phrygian (iiim7) pentatonic scale in music and tab notation, along with a fretboard diagram. Each pattern follows the two-notes-per-string rule. The initial chords are suggested voicings that are a good fit for each of the five patterns with respect to sound and proximity.

The E Phrygian pentatonic scale consists of the following five scale tones (notes):

$$1-\flat3-4-5-\flat7 \ (\text{E G A B D})$$

Fig. 4A
E Phrygian Pentatonic Scale

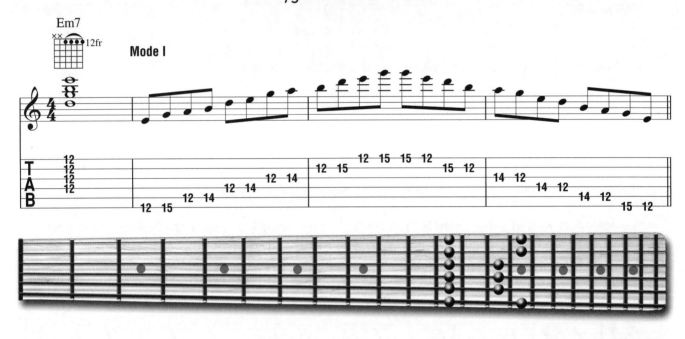

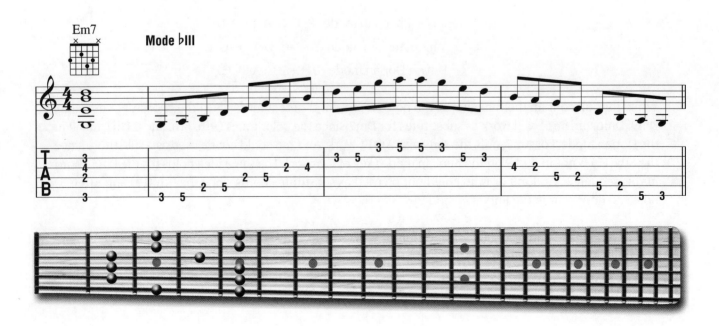

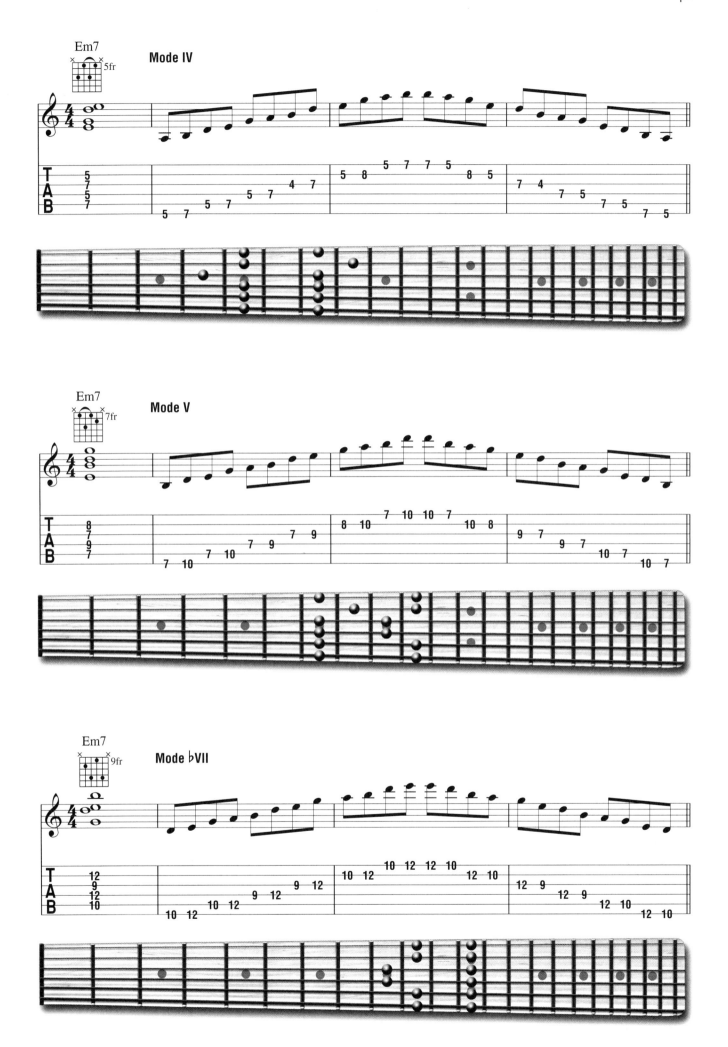

Soloing on the iiim7 is the easiest of all the scales described in this book because it is exactly the same scale as the regular minor pentatonic scale discussed in Chapter 1. The only real challenge is to learn all five positions, if you don't already know them.

The sound of the Phrygian (iiim7) pentatonic scale in this system is different from the normal Phrygian sound in the major scale. As shown earlier, the regular Phrygian scale (1–♭2–♭3–4–5–♭6–♭7) in the key of C is spelled E–F–G–A–B–C–D. While the Em7 chord (E–G–B–D) is clearly included, the ♭2 (F) gives this mode a very different feel from the other two minor modes (Dorian iim7 and Aeolian vim7) in the Ionian major scale. The Phrygian sound is usually described as a "Spanish" sound.

However, in jazz, the iiim7 chord usually functions as a substitute for the Imaj7 chord. In the key of C, for example, the Em7 acts as a substitute for the Cmaj7 chord. The root, ♭3rd, 5th, and ♭7th notes of the iiim7 chord work well as the 3rd, 5th, 7th, and 9th of the Imaj7 chord. That leaves one note to add for a iiim7 pentatonic scale. The choices are the ♭2, 4, or ♭6 of the Phrygian scale.

The ♭2 of a iiim7 chord is easily eliminated since a ♭9 in a iiim7 is too dissonant. In a Imaj7 chord, this note would be a 4th, which would be too neutral-sounding. The ♭6 of the Phrygian scale is the same as the root of the Imaj7 chord. On the other hand, the 4th of the Phrygian scale works as the 6th of the Imaj7 chord. Since the sound of the Phrygian 4th is a great color tone as a 6th for a Imaj7 chord, it is used instead of the bland neutral sound of the ♭6 of the Phrygian scale.

The relationship between the notes of the minor seventh Phrygian pentatonic scale and the Imaj7 chord in the key of C is shown below:

Em7 Phrygian pentatonic scale:	E	G	A	B	D
Cmaj7 chord:	3rd	5th	6th	7th	9th

Fig. 4B presents four four-bar solos that use the E Phrygian pentatonic scale. Note that the fourth example includes chromatic-note ideas. Develop your own four-bar solos using the E Phrygian pentatonic scale.

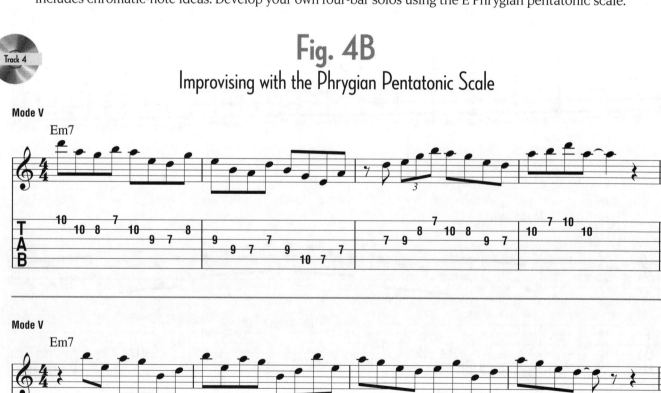

Track 4

Fig. 4B
Improvising with the Phrygian Pentatonic Scale

Mode V

Em7

Mode V

Em7

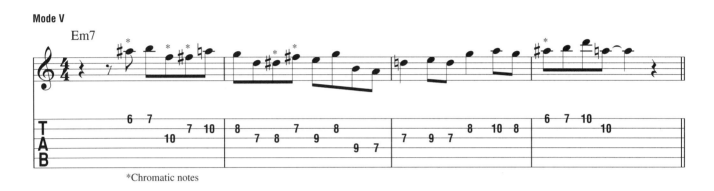

*Chromatic notes

Summary

The Phrygian (iiim7) pentatonic scale is the exact same scale as the standard minor pentatonic scale discussed in Chapter 1. However, in this section of the book, the Phrygian pentatonic scale will only be used to define the iiim7 chord, which functions as a substitute Imaj7 chord. For example, in the key of C, Em7 is functionally equivalent to Cmaj7.

CHAPTER 5
LYDIAN (IVmaj7) PENTATONIC SCALE

IVmaj7 Chord Description

In its basic form, the sound of the IVmaj7 chord is exactly the same as the sound of the Imaj7 chord. However, the IVmaj7 chord is built on the Lydian scale, which is the 4th degree of the major scale. In the key of C, for example, the Lydian scale is:

F–G–A–B–C–D–E

As with the Imaj7 chord discussed in Chapter 2, the IVmaj7 chord is built on the following note intervals:

1–3–5–7

In the key of C, the IVmaj7 chord is Fmaj7 and is built on the following notes:

F	A	C	E
root	3rd	5th	7th

Almost any IVmaj7 chord voicing or inversion that you use will sound good.

Other related major chords are 6ths and 9ths (e.g., F6, Fmaj9, and F6/9). They can be substituted freely, subject to desired bass leading and chord voicing movements. The IVmaj7#4 is also closely related and will be discussed further in Chapter 22.

Below are several ways that a IVmaj7 chord might appear:

Fmaj7   FM7   Fma7   FΔ7

F Lydian Pentatonic Scale Description

Fig. 5A shows the five fingerings for the F Lydian (IVmaj7) pentatonic scale in music and tab notation, along with a fretboard diagram. Each pattern follows the two-notes-per-string rule. The initial chords are suggested voicings that are a good fit for each of the five patterns with respect to sound and proximity.

Fig. 5A
F Lydian Pentatonic Scale

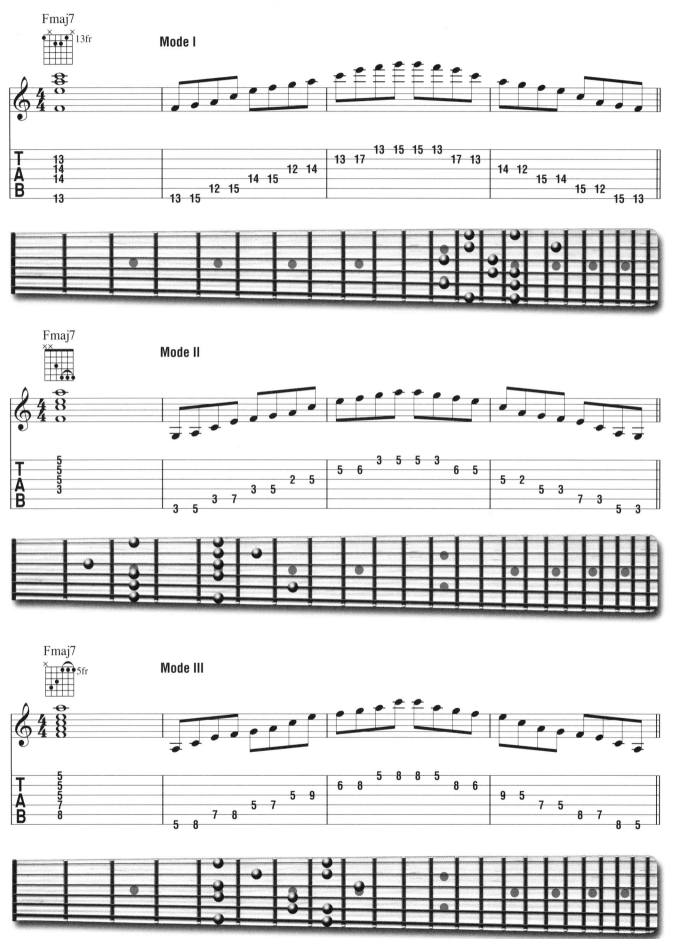

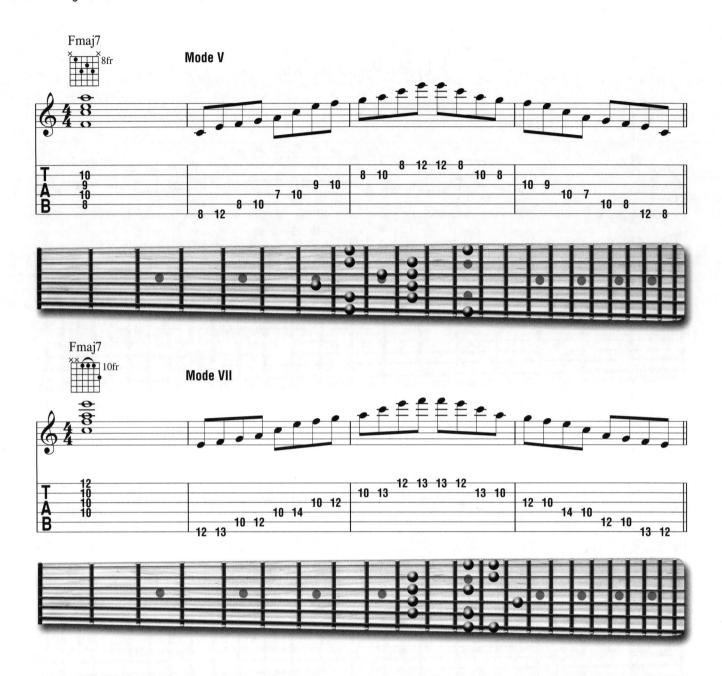

Fmaj7   Mode V

Fmaj7   Mode VII

The good news is that the fingerings are exactly the same as the fingerings for the C Ionian pentatonic scales presented in Chapter 2. The only difference will be position on the fretboard. The following chart maps the positions for both the F Lydian pentatonic scale and the C Ionian pentatonic scale in the key of C:

MODE	F Lydian Pentatonic Scale	C Ionian Pentatonic Scale
Mode V	Eighth position	Third position
Mode VII	Tenth position	Fifth position
Mode I	Twelfth position	Seventh position
Mode II	Third position	Tenth position
Mode III	Fifth position	Twelfth position

Therefore, like the C Ionian pentatonic scales, the F Lydian pentatonic scales consist of the same scale tones:

1–2–3–5–7

The corresponding notes for the F Lydian pentatonic scale are:

F–G–A–C–E

Soloing on the IVMaj7 chord involves the exact same finger patterns as the Imaj7 chord. However, a different "color" is still implied when used over a IVmaj7 chord in a progression.

For example, a basic, repetitive major-chord vamp is shown below:

In this case, you would use the C Ionian pentatonic scale over the first measure and the F Lydian pentatonic scale over the second measure.

For example, a comfortable soloing position for this progression is the fifth position on the fretboard (the index finger is positioned at the fifth fret). The diagram below shows which modes would be used for the progression at the fifth fret:

When playing **Fig. 5B** you will notice that, no matter what notes you play, there is a smooth transition from one chord to another and, more importantly, you can hear the chords changing based solely on what you are playing.

Fig. 5B
Diatonic maj7s

For now, no distinction is being made between a Imaj7 or IVmaj7 chord. They are both simply major seventh chords. The main advantage is that one set of fretboard shapes can be used for both types of major chords (Imaj7 and IVmaj7). The disadvantage is that the Lydian flavor of the IVmaj7 chord is lost. However, a pentatonic scale that emphasizes the Lydian nature of the IVmaj7 chord will be presented in a later chapter (Chapter 22). Also, substitute pentatonic scales will be presented, in Section 2, that will add the "Lydian flavor" to the IVmaj7 chord.

Fig. 5C presents four four-bar solos that use the F Lydian pentatonic scale. Develop your own four-bar solos using the F Lydian pentatonic scale.

Fig. 5C
Improvising with the Lydian Pentatonic Scale

Track 6

CHAPTER 6
MIXOLYDIAN (V7/I7) PENTATONIC SCALE

V7 Chord Description

The sound of the dominant seventh (V7 or I7) chord is very important in several ways. First, as a stand-alone chord, it has a characteristic bluesy sound that can be the basis for an entire song (e.g., "Land of 1000 Dances," "Shotgun," "Born on the Bayou"). Second, it implies movement to the tonic chord of a major or minor key. Third, it forms the basis of the 12-bar blues progression.

Even more importantly, like the minor seventh chord in Chapter 3, the dominant seventh chord is the other basic component of the iim7–V7 and iim7–V7–Imaj7 chord progressions that form the basis for much jazz, Latin, and popular music. Mastering the dominant seventh chord, the iim7–V7 progression, and the iim7–V7–Imaj7 progression is absolutely essential for soloing effectively over jazz songs and chord progressions.

The Mixolydian mode is built on the 5th degree of the major scale. In the key of C, the mixolydian scale is:

$$G–A–B–C–D–E–F$$

The V7 chord is built on the following degrees of the Mixolydian scale:

$$1–3–5–{}^\flat 7$$

In the key of C, the notes are: $\qquad$ G–B–D–F

Almost any dominant chord voicing or inversion that you use will sound good.

Other related dominant chords are 9ths, 13ths and 11ths (e.g., G9, G11, and G13). They can be substituted freely, subject to desired bass leading and chord voicing movements. Notice that chords built from the Mixolydian mode *do not* have altered 5ths or 9ths. Altered tones for a dominant seventh chord will be covered by different scales in subsequent chapters.

G Mixolydian Pentatonic Scale Description

Fig. 6A shows the five fingerings for the G Mixolydian pentatonic scale in music and tab notation, along with a fretboard diagram. Each pattern follows the two-notes-per-string rule. The initial chords are suggested voicings that are a good fit for each of the five patterns with respect to sound and proximity.

The G Mixolydian pentatonic scale consists of the following five scale tones (notes):

$$1–2–3–5–{}^\flat 7 \ (G–A–B–D–F)$$

Fig. 6A
G Mixolydian Pentatonic Scale

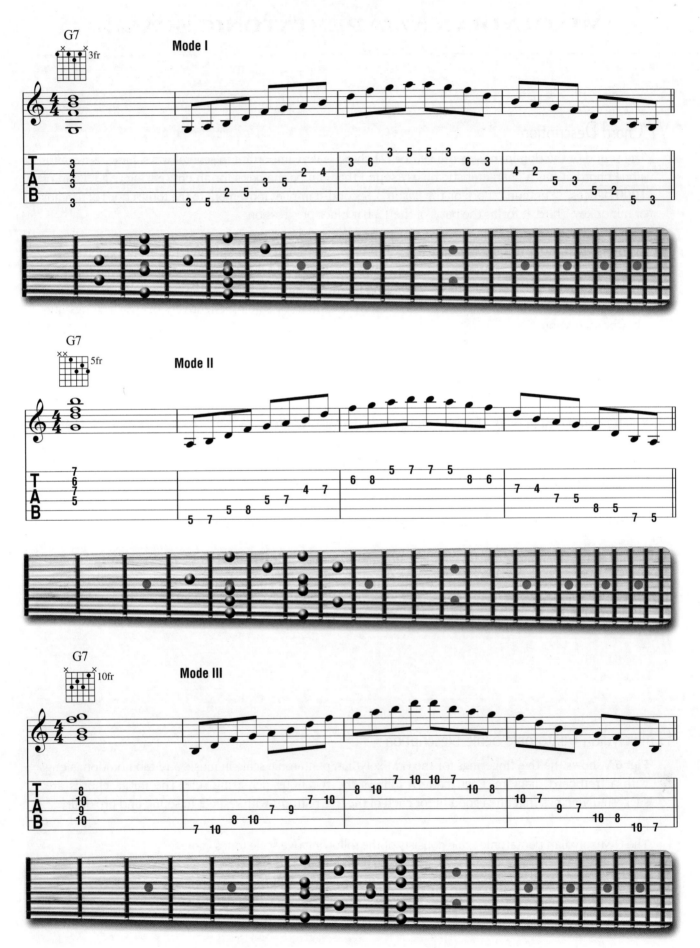

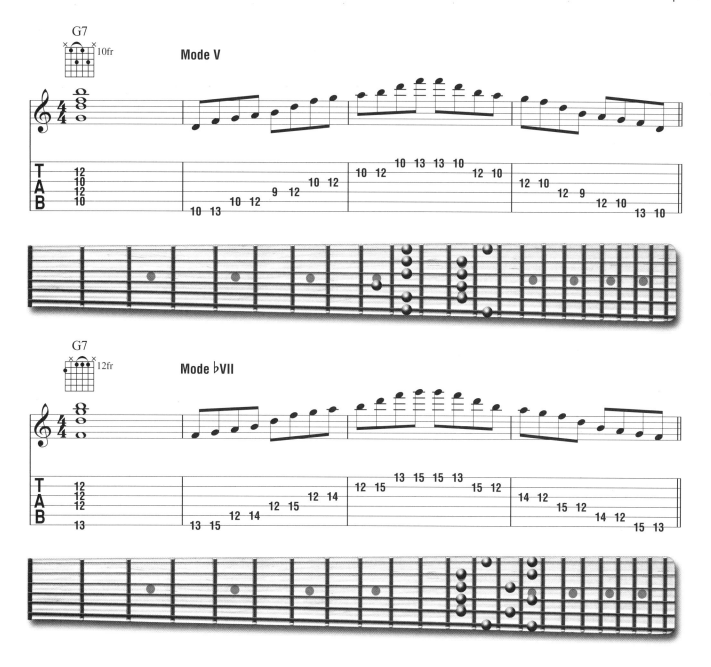

Fig. 6B presents four four-bar solos that use the G Mixolydian pentatonic scale. Note that the second and fourth examples include chromatic-note ideas to add interest to the melodic lines. Develop your own four-bar solos using the G Mixolydian pentatonic scale.

Fig 6B
Improvising with the Mixolydian Pentatonic Scale

Track 7

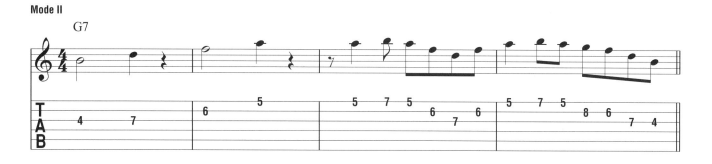

Mode I

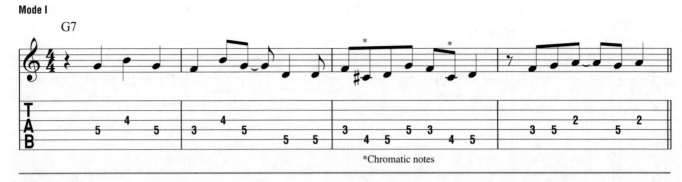

*Chromatic notes

Mode III

Mode I

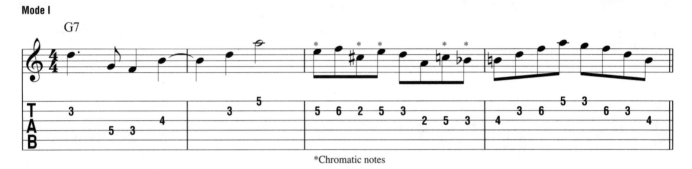

*Chromatic notes

The Mixolydian pentatonic scale is useful in several ways. First, in a static dominant seventh chord vamp, the scale implies a great jazz-blues feel. Second, the Mixolydian pentatonic scale can be mixed freely with any other scales that you may already be using. For example, the G Mixolydian pentatonic scale can be mixed with:

- G minor pentatonic scale (G–B♭–C–D–F)
- G minor blues scale (G–B♭–C–D♭–D–F)
- G major pentatonic scale (G–A–B–D–E)
- G major blues scale (G–A–B♭–B–D–E)
- G Mixolydian scale (G–A–B–C–D–E–F)
- G bebop scale (G–A–B–C–D–E–F–F♯)

Examples of using the G Mixolydian pentatonic scale with the aforementioned scales are shown in **Fig. 6C**.

Fig. 6C
Using the Mixolydian Pentatonic Scale: Static Dominant Chord

G Mixolydian - Mode III

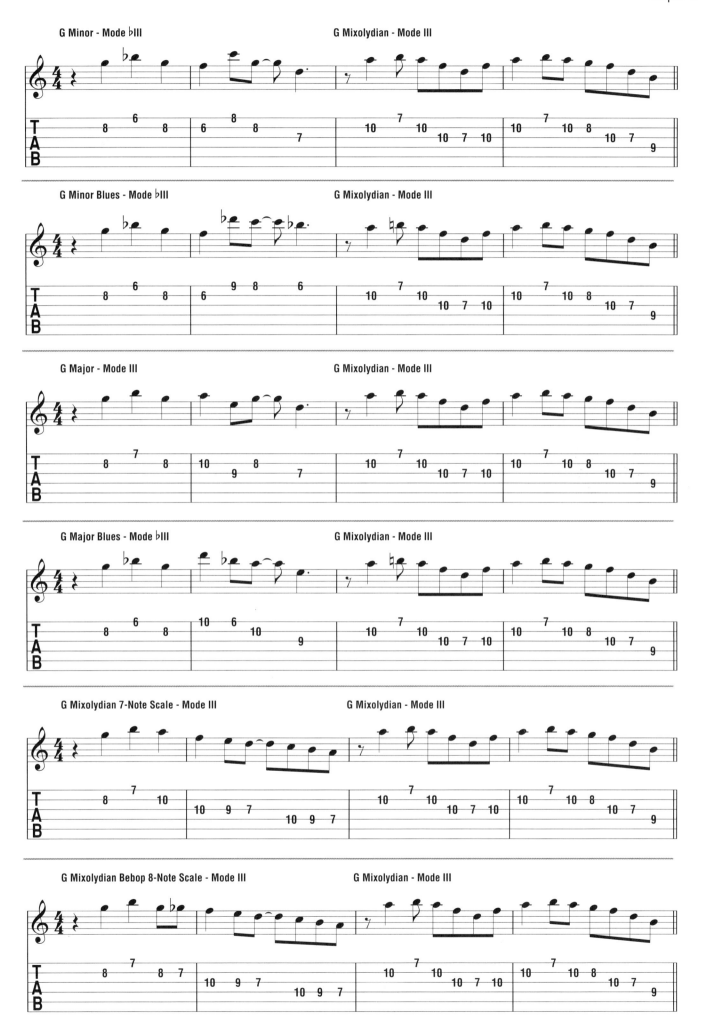

Practice the G Mixolydian pentatonic scale by resolving it to the tonic major chord of the key. For example, in the key of C, practice moving your solo lines from G7 to Cmaj7. This V7–Imaj7 movement is very important to hear and to play over. A really good way to practice V7–Imaj7 movement is to play freely over the Mixolydian pentatonic scale, but make sure that you end up on the 3rd or major 7th of the Imaj7 chord. In the key of C, with the G7 chord going to the Cmaj7, you would always end up on either the E (3rd of C) or the B (major 7th of C). The 5th (G) is another common choice for resolution over the Imaj7 chord. Examples are shown in **Fig. 6D**.

Fig. 6D
Using the Mixolydian Pentatonic Scale: ii–V Progression

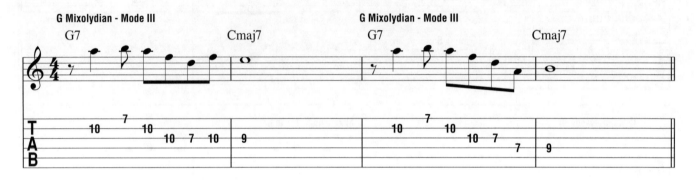

Further, the Mixolydian pentatonic scale needs to be practiced in conjunction with its related iim7 chord (e.g., Dm7 in the key of C). As mentioned earlier, the iim7–V7 progression is the basis for all of jazz. **Fig. 6E** shows two example exercises. The ii–V and ii–V–I progressions are covered in more depth in Chapters 26 and 27.

Fig. 6E
Using the Mixolydian Pentatonic Scale: ii–V–I Progression

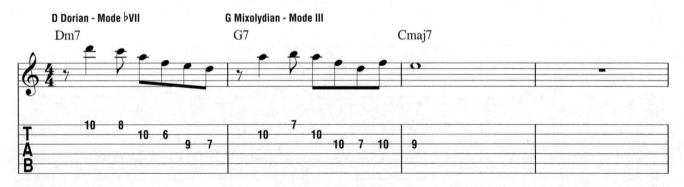

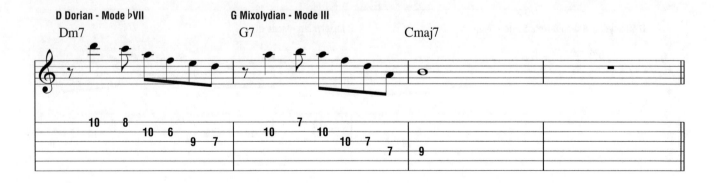

CHAPTER 7
AEOLIAN (vim7) PENTATONIC SCALE

vim7 Chord Description

The sound of the Aeolian minor seventh (vim7) chord has a signature tonic-minor sound. Also, the Aeolian minor seventh chord works well with the Imaj7 as a destination chord in a progression and can even serve as a substitution for the Imaj7 chord.

The Aeolian scale is built on the 6th degree of the major scale. In the key of C, the Aeolian scale is:

A–B–C–D–E–F–G

The vim7 chord is built on the following degrees of the Aeolian scale:

$1-\flat3-5-\flat7$

In the key of C, the notes are: A–C–E–G

Almost any vim7 chord voicing that you use will sound good.

Other related minor chords are 9ths and 11ths (e.g., Am9 and Am11). They can be substituted freely, subject to desired bass leading and chord voicing movements.

Below are several ways that a vim7 chord might appear (sometimes the "7" is incorrectly omitted):

| Am7 | A–7 | Amin7 | Ami7 | A– | Am | Amin | Ami |

A Aeolian Pentatonic Scale Description

Fig. 7A shows the five fingerings for the A Aeolian pentatonic scale in music and tab notation, along with a fretboard diagram. Each pattern follows the two-notes-per-string rule. The initial chords are suggested voicings that are a good fit for each of the five patterns with respect to sound and proximity.

The A Aeolian pentatonic scale consists of the following five scale tones (notes):

$1-2-\flat3-5-\flat7$ (A–B–C–E–G)

Fig. 7A
A Aeolian Pentatonic Scale

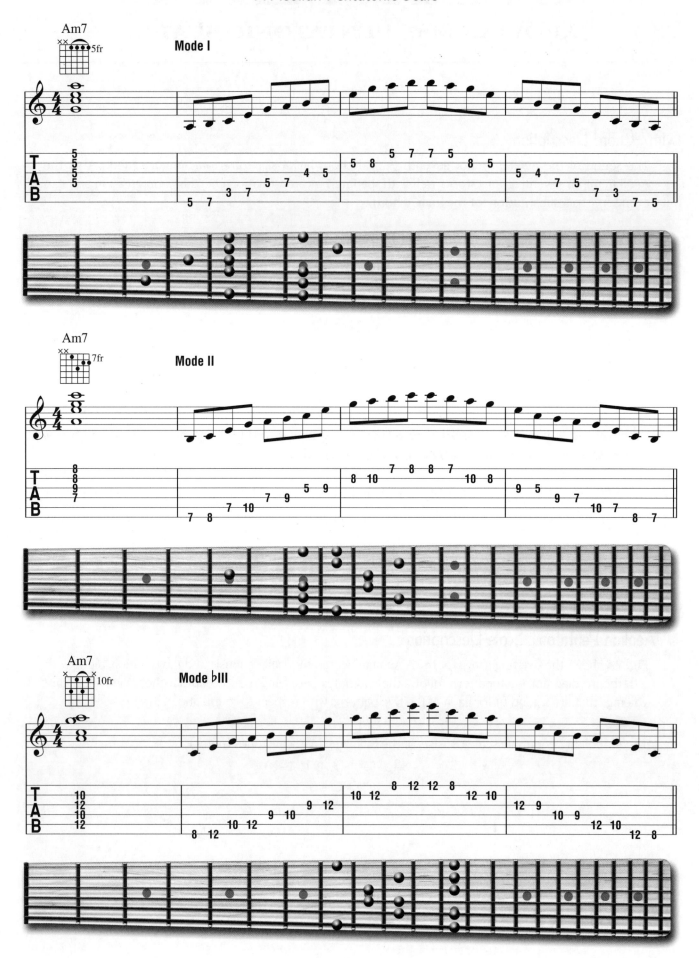

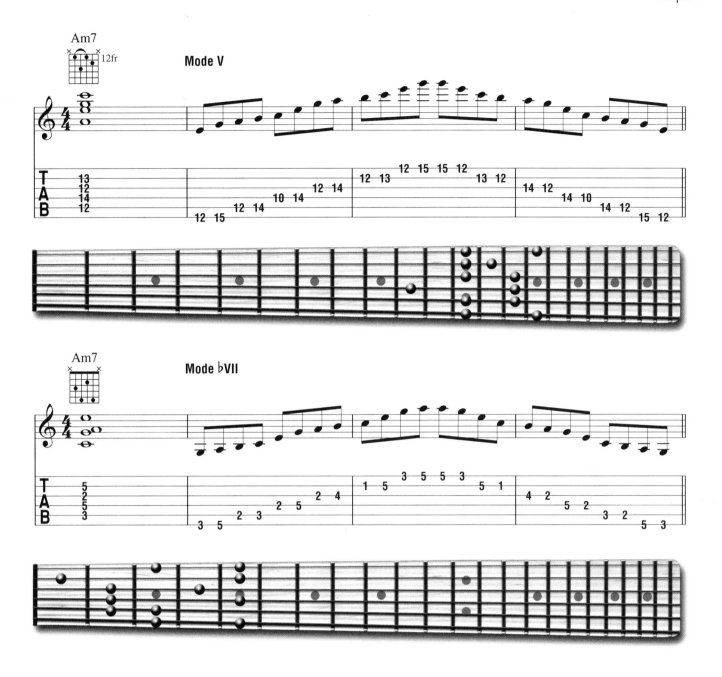

The good news is that the fingerings are exactly the same as the fingerings for the D Dorian (iim7) pentatonic scale that is presented in Chapter 3. The only difference will be position on the fretboard. The following chart maps the positions for both the A Aeolian and D Dorian pentatonic scales in the key of C:

MODE	A Aeolian Pentatonic Scale	D Dorian Pentatonic Scale
Mode I	Fifth position	Tenth position
Mode II	Seventh position	Twelfth position
Mode ♭III	Eighth position	First position
Mode V	Twelfth position	Fifth position
Mode ♭VII	Second position	Seventh position

Like the D Dorian pentatonic scales, the A Aeolian pentatonic scales consist of the following five scale tones (notes):

$$1-2-\flat3-5-\flat7$$

For the A Aeolian pentatonic scale, the corresponding notes are:

$$A-B-C-E-G$$

Fig. 7B presents four four-bar solos that use the A Aeolian pentatonic scale. To highlight the relationship between the Aeolian and Dorian pentatonic scales, Fig. 7C presents the same solo examples that were shown for the Dorian pentatonic scale in Fig. 3C. The only difference is that the solos have been transposed to the A Aeolian pentatonic scale. Note that the transposition process requires you to use different mode patterns. This is an important point. You should practice playing solo ideas using different mode patterns. Even though you are using the same notes, they sound different when played on different string sets or when transposed either up or down an octave.

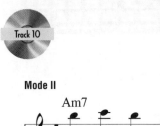

Fig. 7B
Improvising with the Aeolian Pentatonic Scale

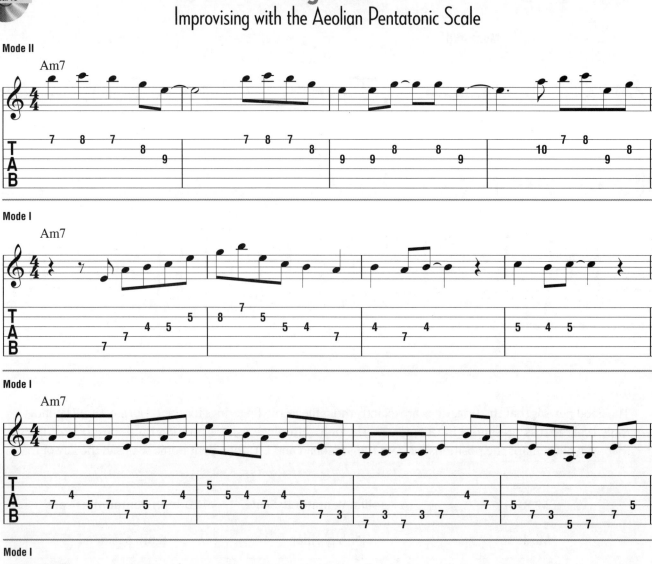

*Chromatic notes

Once again, soloing over the vim7 chord with the Aeolian pentatonic scale involves the exact same finger patterns as for the iim7 chord with the Dorian pentatonic scale. For example, a basic, repetitive minor-chord vamp is shown below:

In this case, the Am7 is functioning as a vim7 chord while the Dm7 is functioning as a iim7 chord in the key of C major. The soloing approach is to use the A Aeolian pentatonic scale over the first measure and the D Dorian pentatonic scale over the second measure. Once again, both scales use the exact same five pentatonic fretboard patterns—just in different locations on the fretboard.

For example, a comfortable soloing position for this progression is the fifth position on the fretboard. The example below shows which modes would be used for each chord:

Notice that no matter what notes you play, there is a smooth transition from one chord to the next and, more importantly, you can hear the chords changing based solely on what you are playing.

Several other approaches can be used to solo over a minor-tonality diatonic vamp like the previous example. **Fig. 7C** presents variations of the first example in Fig. 7B.

Fig. 7C
Aeolian Pentatonic Scale and Other Options

Track 10 (cont.)

The following variations are shown:

- A Aeolian pentatonic scale over both chords (same as first example in Fig. 7B)
- A Aeolian pentatonic scale over the Am7 and D Dorian pentatonic scale over the Dm7
- A minor pentatonic scale (A–C–D–E–G; Chapter 1) starting at the root of the vim7 chord for both chords
- A minor pentatonic scale starting at the root of the vim7 (Am7) chord and D minor pentatonic scale (D–F–G–A–C) starting at the root of the iim7 (Dm7) chord
- A minor blues scale (A–C–D–E♭–E–G) starting at the root of the vim7 chord for both chords
- A Aeolian mode (A–B–C–D–E–F–G) for both chords

Effective melodies can be created using any of the aforementioned approaches exclusively or in combinations. However, the exclusive use of the Aeolian minor seventh pentatonic scales for all vim7 chords and the Dorian minor seventh pentatonic scales for all iim7 (second example in Fig. 7B) chords is recommended as the starting point for developing improvisations.

Once again, even though the mode names are different, the five fretboard patterns are the same for both Aeolian (vim7) and Dorian (iim7) minor chords—they just start in different positions.

Another way to think of this relationship is that there is no difference in notes, patterns, or positions between the A Aeolian pentatonic scale in the key of C and the A Dorian pentatonic scale in the key of G. Both would use the exact same notes, fretboard patterns, and positions:

KEY	C	G
Pentatonic Scale	A Aeolian	A Dorian
Notes	A B C E G	A B C E G
Mode I position	Fifth	Fifth
Mode II position	Seventh	Seventh
Mode ♭III position	Eighth	Eighth
Mode V position	Twelfth	Twelfth
Mode ♭VII position	Third	Third

Summary

The patterns used for the Aeolian pentatonic scale are the same as those learned for the Dorian pentatonic scale in Chapter 3. Consequently, these patterns are extremely useful and flexible for dealing with progressions that include either, or both, of these types of minor chords.

CHAPTER 8
LOCRIAN (viim7♭5, iim7♭5) PENTATONIC SCALE

viim7♭5 Chord Description

The minor seventh flat five chord is also known as a half-diminished chord. It is used in this book in two unique and important ways. First, as a viim7♭5 chord, it is used as a substitute for a V7 chord in a major key. Second, as a iim7♭5 chord, it is used for the iim7♭5–V7 ("two-five") chord sequence in a minor key.

The viim7♭5 chord as a substitute for a V7 chord in a major key: In the major scale, the 7th degree is the Locrian mode (see Appendix A). In the key of C, the Locrian scale is:

B	C	D	E	F	G	A
1	♭2	♭3	4	♭5	♭6	♭7

The viim7♭5 chord is built on the following degrees of the Locrian mode:

1–♭3–♭5–♭7

In the key of C, this chord is a Bm7♭5 containing the following notes:

B–D–F–A

In the key of C major, the Bm7♭5 chord is used as a substitute for a G7, resulting in a rootless G9 chord, as shown below:

CHORD	B	D	F	A
Bm7♭5	root	♭3rd	5th	♭7th
G9	3rd	5th	♭7th	9th

This substitution will be discussed further in Chapter 16.

The iim7♭5 chord as a part of the iim7♭5–V7 (two-five) chord sequence in a harmonic minor key: In the harmonic minor scale, the 2nd degree is the Locrian 6 mode (see Appendix A). In the key of A harmonic minor, the notes of the Locrian 6 mode are:

B	C	D	E	F	G♯	A
1	♭2	♭3	4	♭5	6	♭7

Note that this harmonic minor B Locrian 6 mode is slightly different than the previous major B Locrian mode (B–C–D–E–F–G–A). The difference is in the 6th step of the scale. In the major B Locrian mode, the 6th step is a G. In the harmonic minor B Locrian 6 mode, the 6th step is a G♯. For purposes of this book, this difference does not matter since the 6th degree of either scale will not be used in any way.

The iim7♭5 chord is built on the following degrees of the Locrian 6 scale:

1–♭3–♭5–♭7

In the key of A harmonic minor, this chord is Bm7♭5 which contains the following notes:

B–D–F–A

Notice that this chord is identical to the one built from the C major scale. However, in a harmonic minor key, the minor seventh flat five chord does not function as a substitute dominant chord; it functions as a basic component of the iim7♭5–V7 chord progression for jazz, Latin, and popular music in minor keys. Mastering the iim7♭5–V7 progression (the minor-key version of the ii–V progression in major keys) is very important and essential for soloing effectively over many jazz songs and chord progressions. In this context, the minor seventh flat five chord is functioning as a iim7♭5 in a harmonic minor key rather than a viim7♭5 chord in a major key. The iim7♭5–V7 progression is discussed in more detail in Chapter 26.

Any viim7♭5 chord voicing or inversion that you use will sound good. However, the most common voicings contain the root or ♭5th in the bass.

Below are several ways that a viim7♭5 chord might appear:

Bm7♭5　　　　Bmin7♭5　　　　Bmi7–5　　　　B–7♭5　　　　Bø

Another related viim7♭5 chord is the viim11♭5 (e.g., Bm11♭5), which can be substituted freely, subject to desired bass leading and chord voicing movements.

B Locrian (viim7♭5, iim7♭5) Scale Description

Fig. 8A shows the five fingerings for the B Locrian pentatonic scale in music and tab notation, along with a fretboard diagram. Each pattern follows the two-notes-per-string rule. The initial chords are suggested voicings that are a good fit for each of the five patterns with respect to sound and proximity.

The B Locrian pentatonic scale consists of the following five tones (notes):

1–♭3–4–♭5–♭7　(B–D–E–F–A)

Fig. 8A
B Locrian Pentatonic Scale

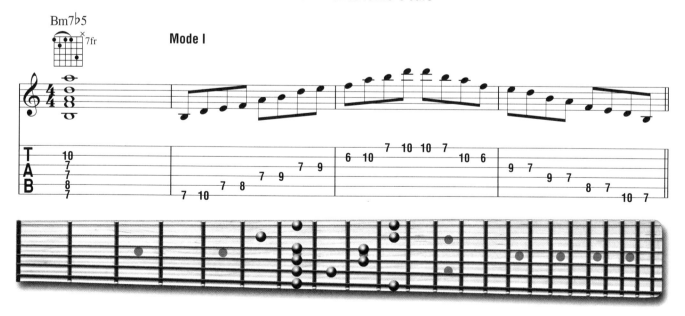

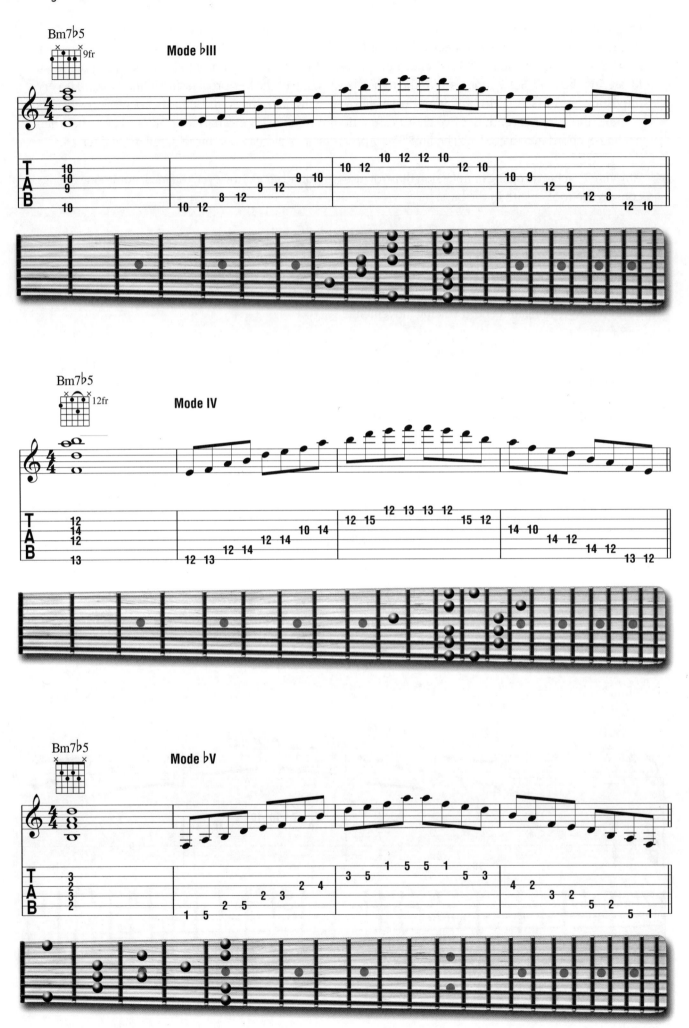

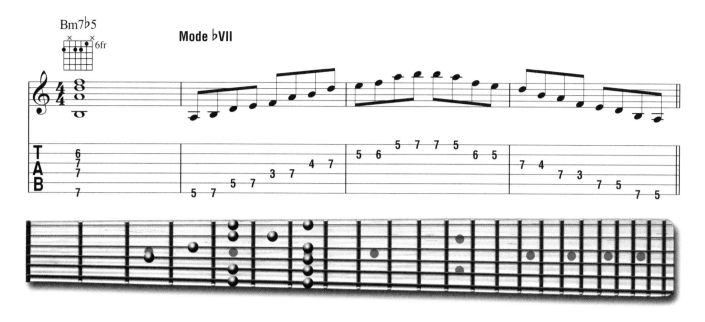

Bm7♭5

Mode ♭VII

This pentatonic scale will work for both types of the aforementioned minor seventh flat five chords. The five notes in the Locrian pentatonic scale are common to both the major Locrian mode and harmonic-minor Locrian 6 mode. Therefore, the Locrian pentatonic scale covers a minor seventh flat five chord from either the major scale (viim7♭5) or the harmonic minor scale (iim7♭5).

It is very important to note that this scale is very similar to the standard minor pentatonic scale, except for one note. The fourth step is a ♭5th instead of a perfect 5th. Consequently, the scale will be easy to learn by making small modifications to the minor pentatonic scales that you already know.

On a static minor seven flat five chord vamp, the Locrian pentatonic scale implies a great jazz minor tonality feel that results from the flatted fifth note in this scale. Also, as with all of the modal pentatonic scales in this book, there are no "wrong" or "bad" notes to worry about.

Fig. 8B shows four four-bar solos that use the B Locrian pentatonic scale.

Fig. 8B
Improvising with the Locrian Pentatonic Scale

Mode I

Bm7♭5

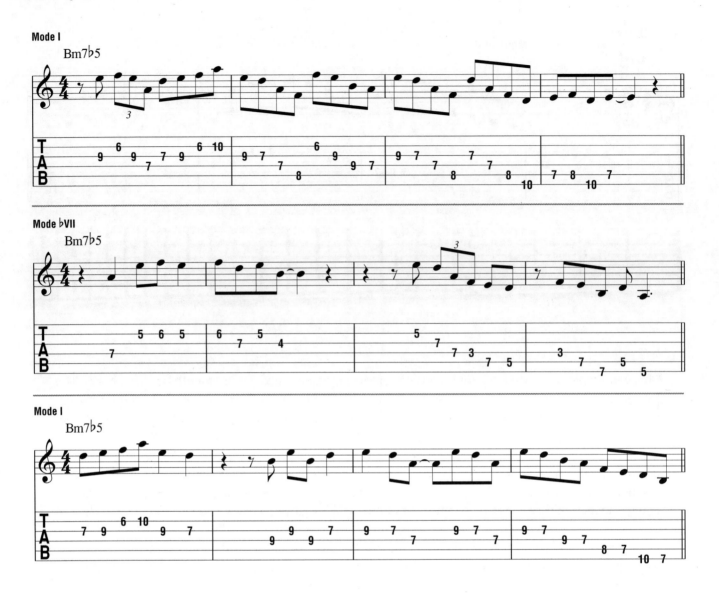

The Locrian pentatonic scale is an extremely important scale. In addition to the uses described in this chapter, it will be utilized as the blues pentatonic scale in Chapter 11 and as an important component of a minor ii–V–I chord progression in Chapter 26.

CHAPTER 9
MIXOLYDIAN ♭9 (7♭9) PENTATONIC SCALE

7♭9 Chord Description

The sound of the dominant seventh ♭9 chord is very important in jazz. It's an important component of the iim7♭5–V7♭9 and iim7♭5–V7♭9–i chord progressions that form the basis of minor progressions in jazz. Mastering the dominant seventh ♭9 chord, the iim7♭5–V7♭9 progression, and the iim7♭5–V7♭9–i progression is absolutely essential for soloing effectively over jazz songs and chord progressions in minor keys (e.g., "Summertime") or major keys that move temporarily to a minor key (e.g., "Autumn Leaves"). These important progressions are discussed in more detail in Chapter 26.

The dominant seventh ♭9 (V7♭9) chord is built on mode 5 of the harmonic minor scale (see Appendix A). Names for mode 5 of the harmonic minor scale include:

- Mixolydian ♭9 scale (used in this chapter)
- Mixolydian ♭9(♭13) scale
- Phrygian Dominant scale

To keep things close to the key of C, let's look at the key of Am, which is the relative minor of C major. In the key of Am, the harmonic minor scale is:

A–B–C–D–E–F–G♯

Therefore, the Mixolydian ♭9 scale uses the note of the A harmonic minor scale starting on the note E, as shown below:

E–F–G♯–A–B–C–D

The V7♭9 chord is built on the following scale degrees of the Mixolydian ♭9 scale:

1–3–5–♭7–♭9

In the key of Am, the notes for the V7♭9 (E7♭9) chord are:

E	G♯	B	D	F
Root	3rd	5th	7th	♭9th

Inversions with the root or 5th in the bass sound the best.

Any other altered dominant chord can be substituted freely, subject to desired bass leading and chord voicing movements.

E Mixolydian ♭9 Pentatonic Scale Description

Fig. 9A shows the five fingerings for the E Mixolydian ♭9 pentatonic scale (which would be played over any E7♭9 chord) in music and tab notation, along with a fretboard diagram. Each pattern follows the two-notes-per-string rule. The initial chords are suggested voicings that are a good fit for each of the five patterns with respect to sound and proximity.

The E Mixolydian ♭9 pentatonic scale consists of the following five scale tones (notes):

1–♭2–3–5–♭7 (E–F–G♯–B–D)

Fig. 9A
E Mixolydian ♭9 Pentatonic Scale

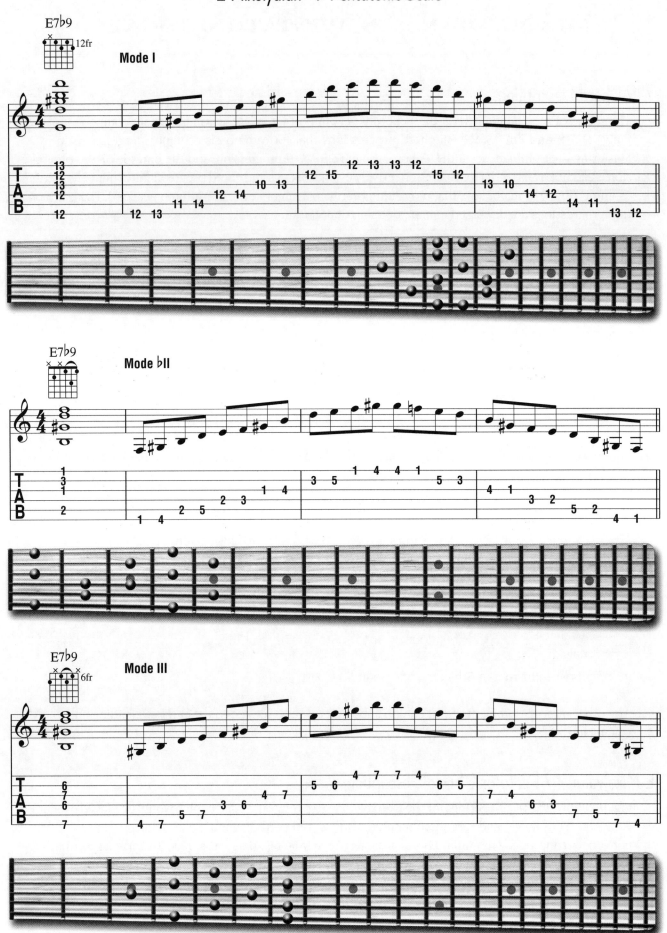

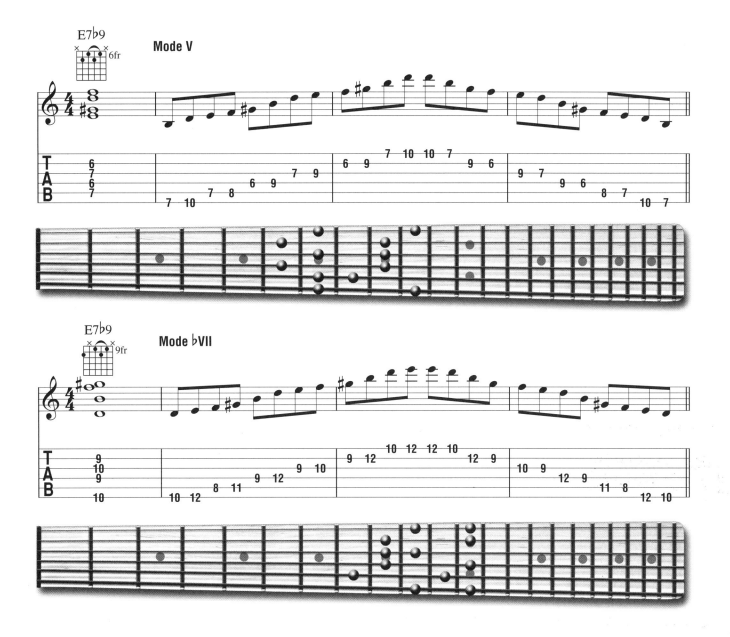

Mode V

Mode ♭VII

The Mixolydian ♭9 pentatonic scale sounds good on a V7♭9 moving to either major and minor chords.

For example, **Fig. 9B** demonstrates how these E7♭9 pentatonic shapes can be transposed to G over a G7♭9 chord resolving to Cmaj7 or Cm7. The first and second examples demonstrate a G Mixolydian ♭9 pentatonic scale (G7♭9) moving to the C Ionian pentatonic scale (Cmaj7). The third and fourth examples demonstrate a G Mixolydian ♭9 pentatonic scale (G7♭9) moving to the C Aeolian pentatonic scale (Cm7).

Fig. 9B
Improvising with the Mixolydian ♭9 Pentatonic Scale

Track 12

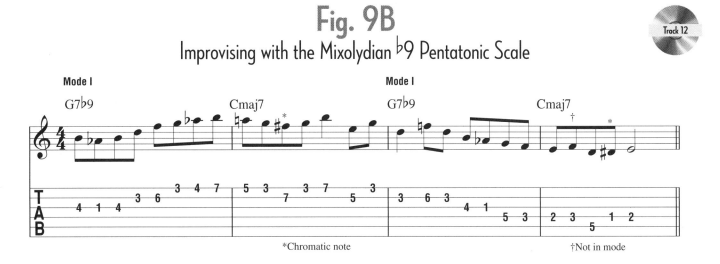

*Chromatic note   †Not in mode

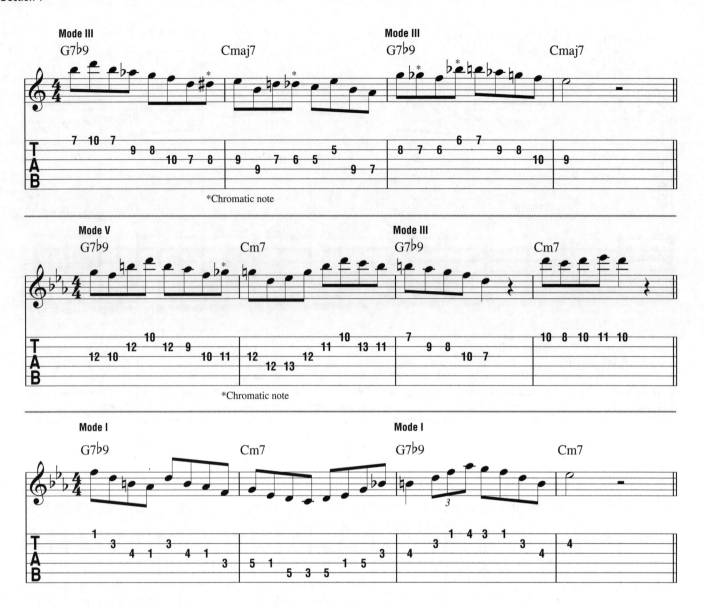

*Chromatic note

It is important to note that the Mixolydian pentatonic scale from Chapter 6 will not work when resolving to a minor chord. The reason is that the natural 9th note in the Mixolydian pentatonic scale does not fit when moving to a minor tonality. However, the Mixolydian ♭9 pentatonic scale has a flatted 9th note (♭9th) that creates a perfect resolution to a minor chord. For resolution to a major tonic chord (e.g., Cmaj7), either the Mixolydian pentatonic scale (for a G7 chord) or the Mixolydian ♭9 pentatonic scale (for a G7♭9 chord) will work fine.

Fig. 9C demonstrates soloing with the Mixolydian ♭9 pentatonic scale in the context of a tune. The first eight bars are the melody, while the last eight bars illustrate an example solo.

Track 12 (cont.)

Fig. 9C
"No One To"

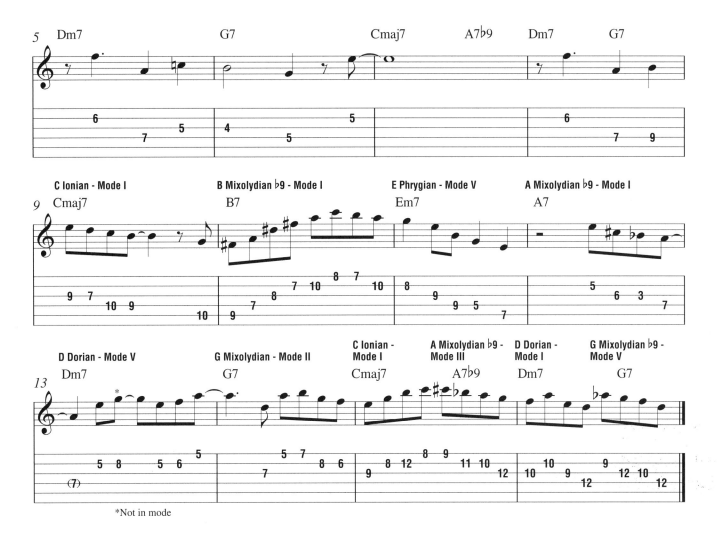

*Not in mode

Notice that the solo demonstrates the flexibility of the Mixolydian ♭9 pentatonic scale by using it over three different types of dominant seventh chords in the key of C.

- In Bar 10, the B Mixolydian ♭9 pentatonic scale is used for a dominant VII7 (B7) chord that moves to a iiim7 (Em7) chord.
- In Bar 12, the A Mixolydian ♭9 pentatonic scale is used for a dominant VI7 (A7) chord that moves to a iim7 (Dm7) chord.
- In Bar 16, the G Mixolydian ♭9 pentatonic scale is used for a dominant V7 (G7) chord that moves back to the beginning of a chorus that starts with a Imaj7 (Cmaj7) tonic major chord.

Summary

The Mixolydian ♭9 pentatonic scale is an extremely powerful tool for jazz improvisation. First, in a minor key, it's perfectly suited for the "two-five-one" (iim7♭5–V7♭9–i) progression. Second, the Mixolydian ♭9 pentatonic scale also provides an excellent transition to a major (or dominant) chord that is a 4th interval above.

CHAPTER 10
LYDIAN DOMINANT (7♭5) PENTATONIC SCALE

7♭5 Chord Description

The Lydian Dominant chord is useful in chord melody soloing and in jazz comping. This chapter will demonstrate how it can be used as a:

- II7♭5 substitute for a II7 chord
- V7♭5 substitute for a V7 chord
- ♭II7 substitute for a V7 chord

The notes and steps for a D7♭5 chord, for example, are:

D	F♯	A♭	C
Root	3rd	♭5th	♭7th

Any other altered dominant chord (e.g., D7♭9, D7♭9♭5, D7♭9♯5, D7♯9♭5, D7♯9♯5, D7♯9♭13, or D13♭9) can be substituted freely for the D7♭5, subject to desired bass leading and chord voicing movements.

The Lydian Dominant (7♭5) chord is built from Mode IV of the melodic (jazz) minor scale (see Appendix A). An example of a D7♭5 chord and how it relates to the A melodic minor scale is shown below.

A Melodic Minor	A	B	C	D	E	F♯	G♯
A Melodic Minor Mode IV	D	E	F♯	G♯	A	B	C
D7♭5	D		F♯	G♯/A♭			C
Intervals	Root		3rd	♭5th			♭7th

What makes this chord so powerful is that the scale (melodic minor) that it is built from has important color tones, including the 9th and 13th. Additionally, the "Lydian" quality of having both a natural 5th and a ♭5th (♯11), makes it very useful for creating jazz melodies.

The other powerful characteristic of the 7♭5 chord is that it is interchangeable with the 7♭5 chord a flatted 5th interval (six frets) above or below. For example, a D7♭5 chord contains the exact same notes as an A♭7♭5 chord.

D7♭5	D	F♯	G♯/A♭	C
	Root	3rd	♭5th	♭7th
A♭7♭5	D	F♯/G♭	A♭/G♯	C
	♭5th	♭7th	Root	3rd

This relationship is called a *tritone substitution* and is a fundamental concept in jazz soloing and chord substitutions. A tritone substitution is a dominant seventh chord whose root is a tritone (three whole steps, or six frets) up or down from the original dominant seventh chord. The chords are interchangeable. As will be shown later, this opens up some advanced chord substitution and soloing possibilities.

D Lydian Dominant Pentatonic Scale Description

Fig. 10A shows the five fingerings for the D Lydian Dominant pentatonic scale in music and tab notation, along with a fretboard diagram. Each pattern follows the two-notes-per-string rule. The initial chords are suggested voicings that are a good fit for each of the five patterns with respect to sound and proximity.

The D Lydian Dominant pentatonic scale consists of the following five scale tones (notes):

$$9-{\sharp}4-5-13-{\flat}7 \ (E-G{\sharp}-A-B-C)$$

It is important to note that the Lydian Dominant pentatonic scale does not contain the root or 3rd of its related chord. However, the root is not necessary since it is assumed that the root will be covered by the bass. Also, the lack of a 3rd gives the scale a level of ambiguity that also suggests a possible minor tonic a 4th (five frets) below.

Fig. 10A
D Lydian Dominant Pentatonic Scale

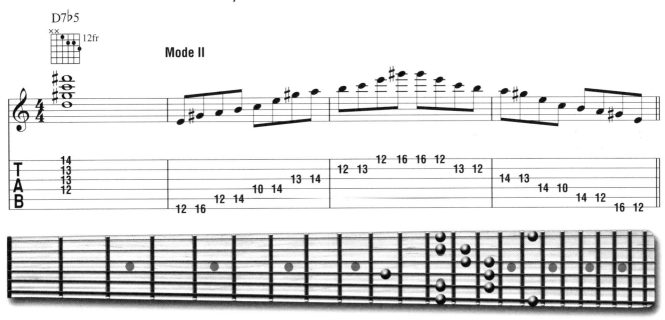

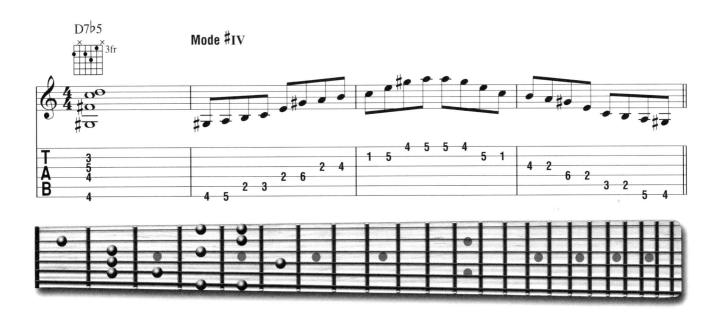

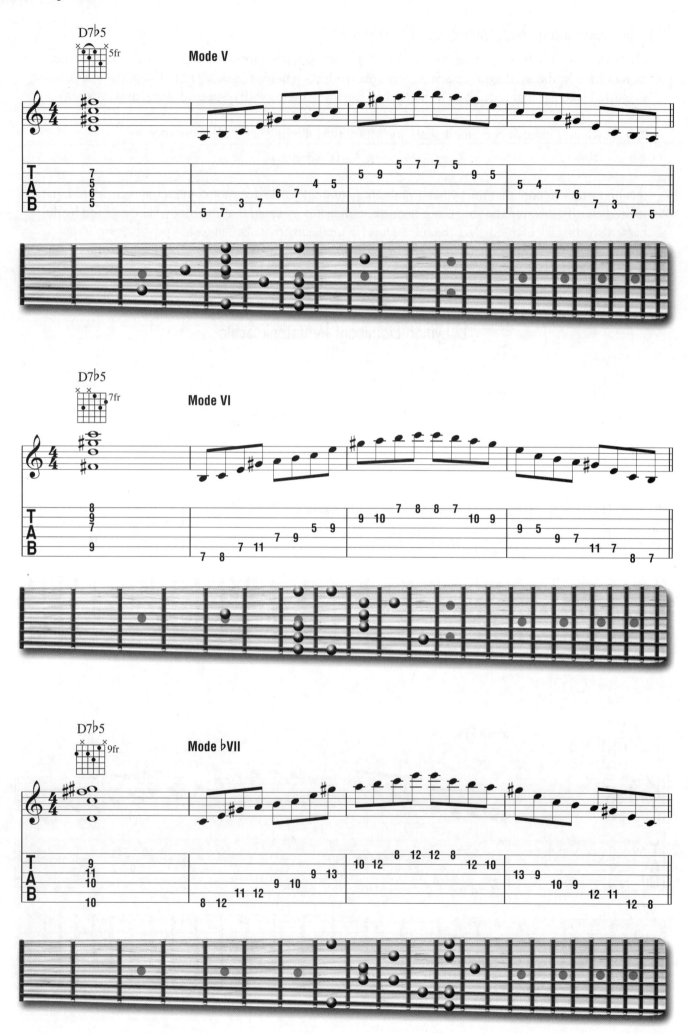

The primary use of the Lydian Dominant pentatonic scale is to cover dominant seven flat five chords (7♭5). It can also be used as a substitute for the Mixolydian pentatonic scale in two different ways: 1) as a tritone substitution scale, or 2) as a direct substitution scale.

Using a D7♭5 chord as an example, the D Lydian Dominant pentatonic scale consists of the following five scale tones (notes):

D7 Lydian Dominant Pentatonic Scale	E	*G♯	A	B	C
Chord Tones	9th	♯4th	5th	13th	♭7th

*Note that a ♭5th is enharmonic with a ♯4th, and the two are used interchangeably in this respect.

Most advanced jazz methods suggest using Mode IV of the melodic minor scale for soloing over a Lydian Dominant (7♭5) chord. However, the Lydian Dominant pentatonic scale described in this chapter is the recommended choice.

The two scales are compared below with respect to a D7♭5 chord:

A Melodic Minor, Mode IV	E	F♯	G♯	A	B	C	D
D7 Lydian Dominant Pentatonic Scale	E		G♯	A	B	C	
Chord Tones	9th	3rd	♯4th	5th	13th	♭7th	Root

Lydian Dominant Pentatonic and the Tritone Substitution

The Lydian Dominant pentatonic scale can be used to cover chords that are used as a ♭5th (tritone) substitutions for a dominant seventh chord. For example, below is a standard ii–V–I chord progression:

The G7 is a V7 dominant chord moving to a Cmaj7 (Imaj7) chord in this standard chord progression. A common chord substitution in jazz is the 7♭5 chord a ♭5th interval away (tritone substitution) from the dominant seventh chord. In this case, the chord **D♭7♭5 (♭II7)** is the tritone substitution for the G7 chord. Therefore, the **D♭ Lydian Dominant** pentatonic scale would be used if you wanted to imply the sound of the ♭5th chord substitution (D♭7♭5 or G7alt chord). This is a great-sounding substitution. The D♭ Lydian Dominant pentatonic scale (E♭–G–A♭–B♭–B) adds upper extension color tones to the sound of the V7 (G7) chord such as the ♭13th/♯5th (E♭), ♭9th (A♭), and ♯9th (B♭). In fact, this is an excellent scale to use when a G dominant chord is designated as a G7alt chord. This designation specifies a dominant chord with altered (sharped or flatted) 5ths and/or 9ths.

Fig. 10B presents four four-bar solos that demostrate two uses of the D♭ Lydian Dominant pentatonic scale in a standard ii–V–I progression. In the first three examples, the D♭7♭5 chord is being used as a triton-substitution chord for the G7 chord. This creates a standard ii–♭II7–I chord progression. Therefore, the D♭ Lydian Dominant pentatonic scale is used instead of the G dominant pentatonic scale.

In the fourth example, the G Lydian Dominant pentatonic scale is used to cover the V7 chord in the progression. This direct substitution gives you the sound of a G7♭5 chord substitution for the G7 chord.

Fig. 10B
Improvising with the Lydian Dominant Pentatonic Scale

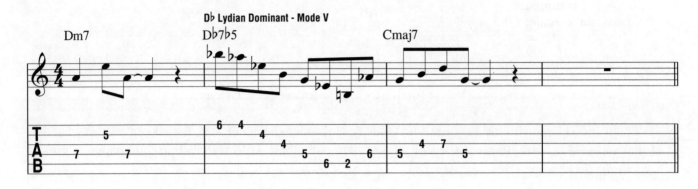

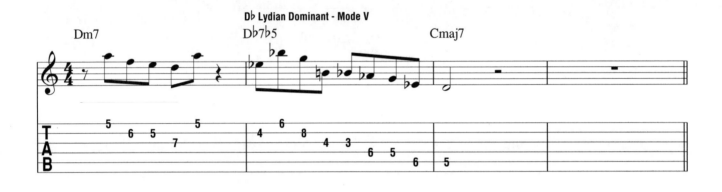

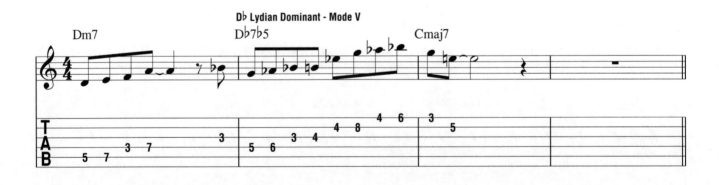

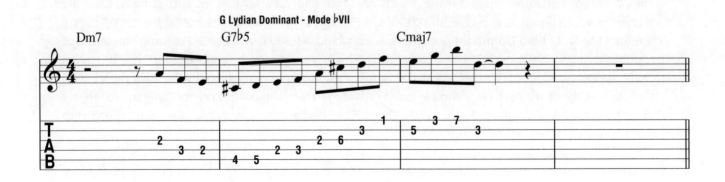

A standard jazz turnaround progression in the key of C is:

However, using tritone substitutions for the dominant chords (A7 and G7) results in the following progression:

The E♭7 and D♭7 Lydian Dominant pentatonic scales, respectively, are excellent choices for covering the dominant chords in either of the aforementioned progressions.

Lydian Dominant Pentatonic and the II7 dominant chord

The Lydian Dominant pentatonic scale is also recommended for covering a II7 dominant chord. For example, the D7 Lydian Dominant pentatonic scale should be used to cover the D7♭5 in the progression below:

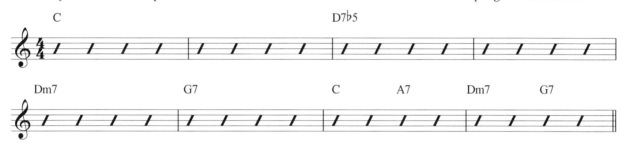

This example uses the Lydian Dominant pentatonic scale to cover the IIV7♭5 and the turnaround (measures 7–8) of the chord progression in **Fig. 10C**.

Fig. 10C
Lydian Dominant Pentatonic Scale Chord Progression

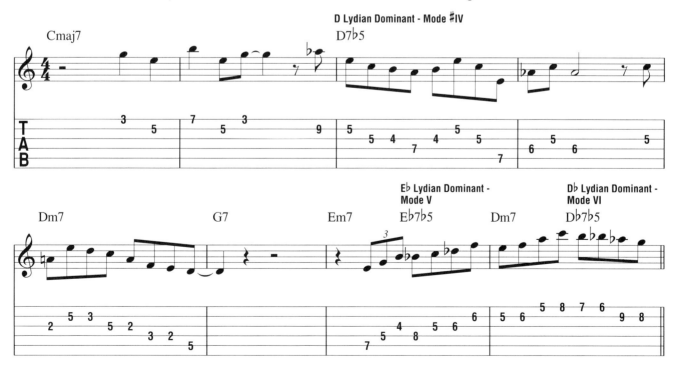

Fig. 10C focuses on the use of the Lydian Dominant pentatonic scale for a II7 dominant chord. Using the D7 Lydian Dominant pentatonic scale for the D7 chord gives the impression of an Am9(maj7) or D7♭5 chord. This sound conveys a strong sense of the A melodic minor scale from which both the Am9(maj7) and D7♭5 chords can be built. In a sense, you have an automatic, built-in ii–V progression in the notes that you use for soloing over this chord.

Many songs exist in which the Lydian Dominant pentatonic scale is used for a II7 dominant chord that occurs between a Imaj7 chord and a iim7 chord. Examples include "Take the A Train," "Girl from Ipanema," and "Desifinado." These songs all start with a Imaj7 chord that moves to a II7 (dominant) chord. Many jazz methods suggest using a Mixolydian scale over the II7 chord. However, this does not really sound "correct." If you are going to use a seven-note scale, the Lydian Dominant scale (Mixolydian scale with a ♯4th instead of a ♮4th) is a better choice because of the ♯4 leading tone. Further, the Lydian Dominant pentatonic scale is more "guitar friendly" because it requires fewer notes and can easily be played in two-note-per-string patterns. Also, as shown in Fig. 10D, the Lydian Dominant pentatonic scale provides an excellent transition to the iim7 chord that follows.

Summary

The Lydian Dominant pentatonic scale is extremely useful for improvising on chord changes in jazz. It is particularly useful for soloing over the II7 dominant chord and the tritone substitutions of a ♭III7 chord for a VI7 chord and a ♭II7 chord for a V7 chord.

CHAPTER 11
MINOR/MAJOR BLUES PENTATONIC SCALE

The basic minor/major pentatonic scale was presented in Chapter 1. Two versions were discussed: the minor pentatonic scale and its related major pentatonic scale. These two scales use identical patterns, with the major pentatonic scale a minor 3rd (three half steps) lower. These scales are the cornerstones of improvisation in rock, blues, pop, and Latin. They are also used extensively in jazz, funk, and swing.

As noted in Chapter 1, the addition of a ♭5th note to these scales results in the six-note minor blues and major blues scales. This greatly increases the melodic resources available for improvising. Therefore, it is extremely important to have the blues scale available as one of your improvisational tools. The six-note minor/major blues scale is perfectly appropriate to use in conjunction with our pentatonic approach to improvisation.

However, this chapter introduces the concept of a *pentatonic blues* scale! Fortunately, you already know it because it was covered in an earlier chapter, under a different name.

With the blues pentatonic scale at your disposal, virtually all soloing can be done using pentatonic scales exclusively.

A Minor/C Major Blues Pentatonic Scale Description

Fig. 11A shows the five fingerings for the A minor/C major blues pentatonic scale in music and tab notation, along with a fretboard diagram. Each pattern follows the two-notes-per-string rule.

Fig. 11A
A Minor/C Major Pentatonic Blues Scales

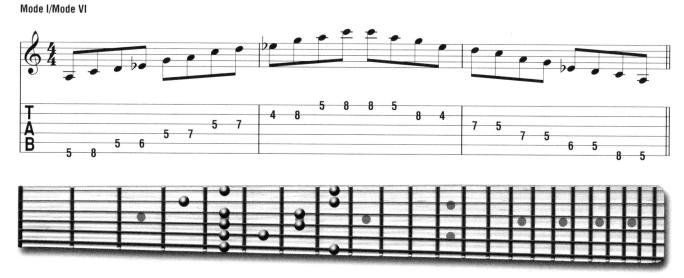

Mode ♭III/Mode I

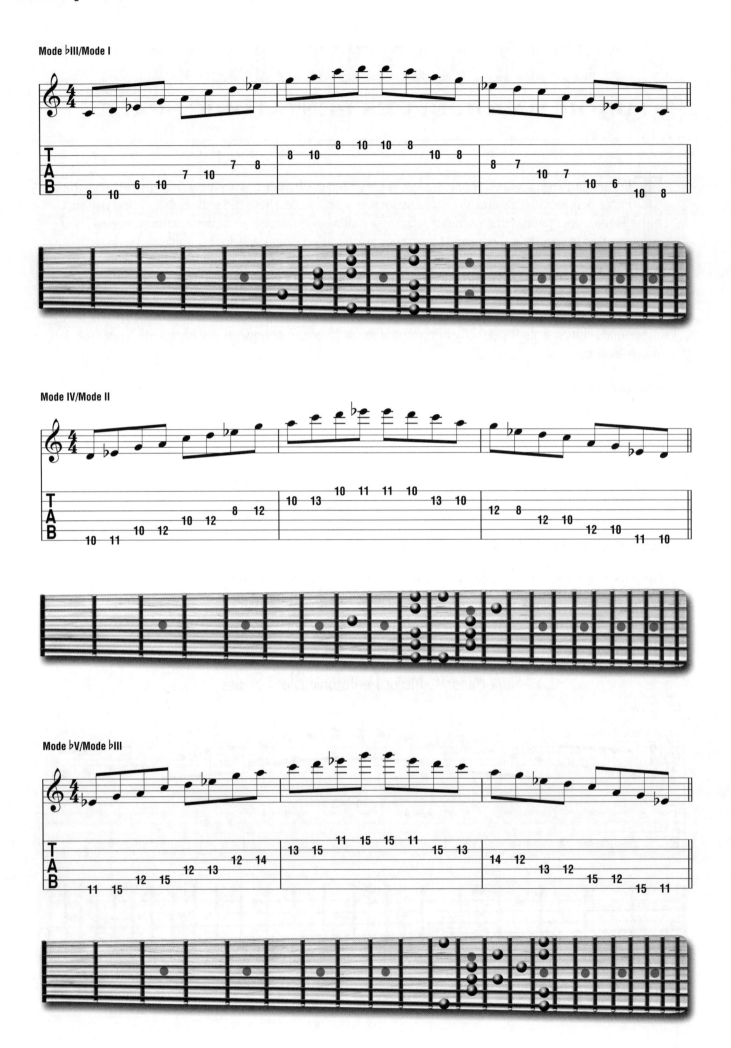

Mode IV/Mode II

Mode ♭V/Mode ♭III

Mode ♭VII/Mode V

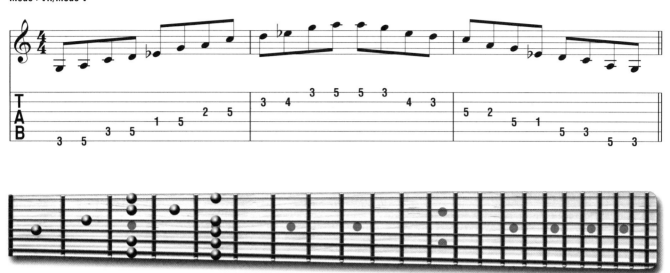

This scale should seem familiar to you. It is identical to the B Locrian pentatonic scale that was covered in Chapter 8. The only difference is that the A minor/C major blues pentatonic scale is transposed down one step.

Important: The minor/major blues pentatonic scale is identical to the minor seventh flat five pentatonic scale, as shown below:

A minor/C major blues pentatonic scale = A Locrian pentatonic scale
B♭ minor/D♭ major blues pentatonic scale = B♭ Locrian pentatonic scale
B minor/D major blues pentatonic scale = B Locrian pentatonic scale
C minor/E♭ major blues pentatonic scale = C Locrian pentatonic scale
C♯ minor/E major blues pentatonic scale = C♯ Locrian pentatonic scale

Etc., etc., etc...

Not only is this scale extremely powerful with regard to developing solos and improvising, it is the closest of all the pentatonic scales in this book to the fingering patterns of the basic minor/major pentatonic scale covered in Chapter 1. This makes it very easy to use.

The A minor blues pentatonic scale and the C major blues pentatonic scale consist of the same five notes. However, each note plays a different "color tone" role in the two relative scales. For example, the note E♭ is the ♭5th in the A minor blues pentatonic scale, but it's the ♭3rd in the C major blues pentatonic scale.

SCALE	A	C	D	E♭	G
A Minor	root	♭3rd	4th	♭5th	♭7th
C Major	6th	root	2nd/9th	♭3rd	5th

Each pattern follows the two-notes-per-string rule. No initial chords are suggested since these "blues" scales can represent many different chord types in a progression, blues or otherwise.

The fingerings are exactly the same for both scales. The only difference is position on the fretboard. The following chart maps the positions for both scales:

SCALE	A Minor Blues	C Major Blues
Fifth position	Mode I	Mode VI
Eighth position	Mode ♭III	Mode I
Tenth position	Mode IV	Mode II
Twelfth position	Mode ♭V	Mode ♭III
Third position	Mode ♭VII	Mode V

Once again, even though the mode names are different, the five fretboard patterns are the same for both minor blues pentatonic scale and its relative major blues pentatonic scale. For example, there is no difference between the A minor blues pentatonic scale and the relative C major blues pentatonic scale. Both use the exact same fretboard patterns and positions.

These scales can be used in many ways:

- As substitute scales for major, minor, and dominant chords
- As substitute scales for several chords in a progression
- As exclusive scales for entire tunes

The following examples are shown in the context of blues changes, rhythm changes, modal tunes, and standards.

The Blues

This simplified blues progression in the key of C, used in Chapter 1, is a good progression to demonstrate the use of both scales in a solo:

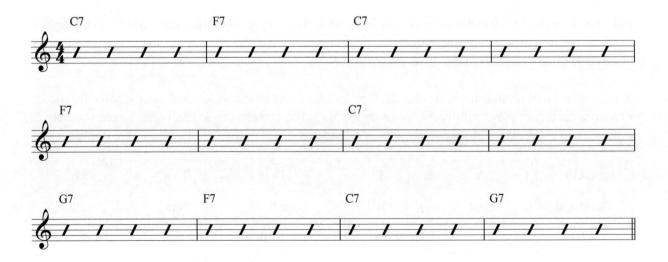

A good way to build facility for playing over blues changes is to start with four basic options.

Option 1: Use the C minor pentatonic scale as the basis for the entire progression [**Fig. 11B**].

Fig. 11B
C Minor Pentatonic Scale: 12-Bar Blues

Track 14

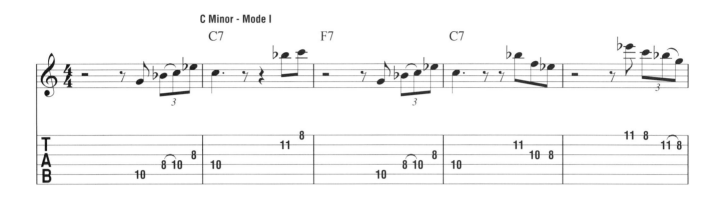

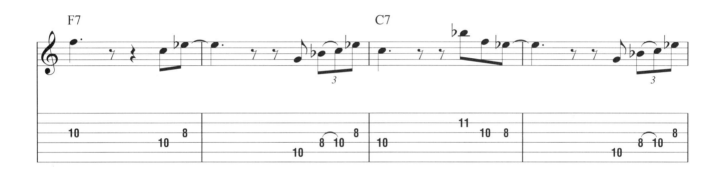

As noted in Chapter 1, the C minor pentatonic scale can be used for the entire progression, ignoring the chord changes. However, this approach is extremely limited. For one thing, there is no ♭5th "blue note," which is very important if you are playing the blues.

Option 2: Use the C minor blues pentatonic scale as the basis for the entire progression [**Fig. 11C**].

Track 14 (cont.)

Fig 11C
C Minor Blues Pentatonic Scale: 12-Bar Blues

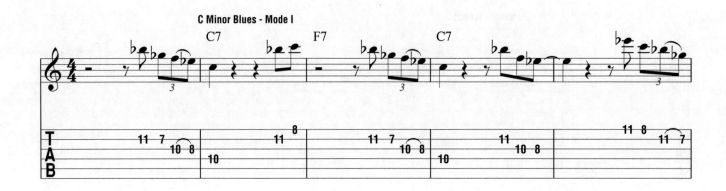

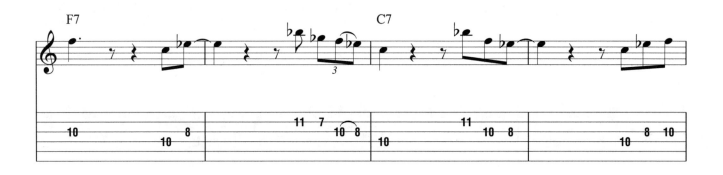

This option is a little better than using the C minor pentatonic scale for the entire progression. At least now you have the ♭5th "blue note" with which to work. However, the C minor blues pentatonic scale is still missing some important notes, particularly with respect to the C7 and F7 chords, whose 3rds are not found within this scale.

Option 3: Use both blues pentatonic scales as the basis for the entire progression [**Fig. 11D**].

Fig. 11D
C Major and Minor Blues: 12-Bar Blues

Track 14 (cont.)

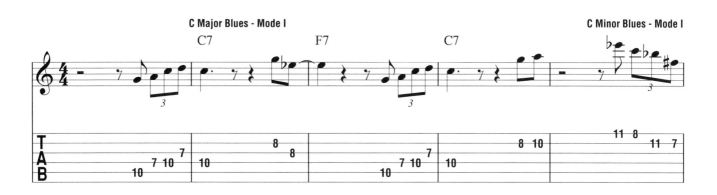

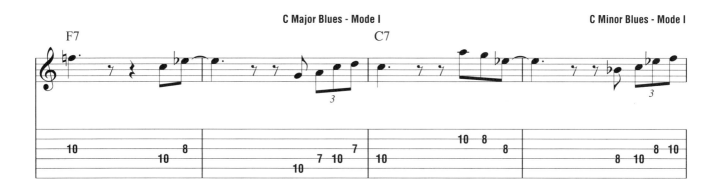

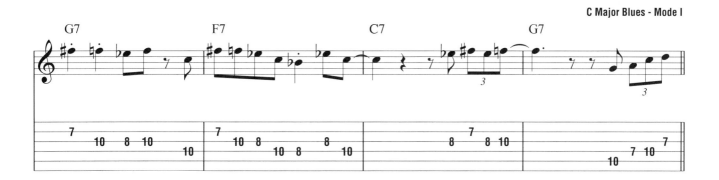

Use the C major blues pentatonic scale (or A minor blues pentatonic scale) for the C7 chord, and the C minor blues pentatonic scale for the other chords. Now you will get a much wider range of melodic movement while still using the same scale patterns.

Option 4: Use combinations of both blues pentatonic scales and both major/minor pentatonic scales [**Fig. 11E**].

Track 14 (cont.)

Fig 11E
All Four C Pentatonics: 12-Bar Blues

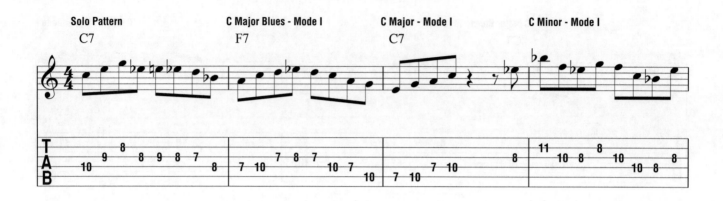

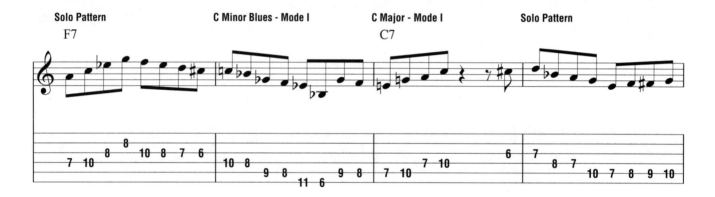

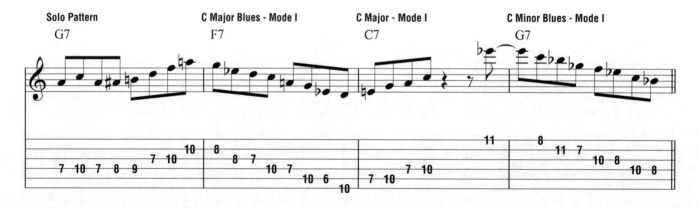

Now you have four scales at your disposal that only use two different sets of fingering patterns. This greatly increases the amount of harmonic richness that you can add to your solos. Fig. 11E is a pentatonic example of using these scale combinations, as summarized in the chart shown below. Solo patterns with chromatic notes are used in measures 1, 5, 8, and 9 to add additional harmonic interest to the example solo. To reemphasize the fact that each scale has two names, both are included in the chart. However, I recommend that you think in terms of the overall key. Since this blues progression is in the key of C, think of these scales in terms of the C tonal center.

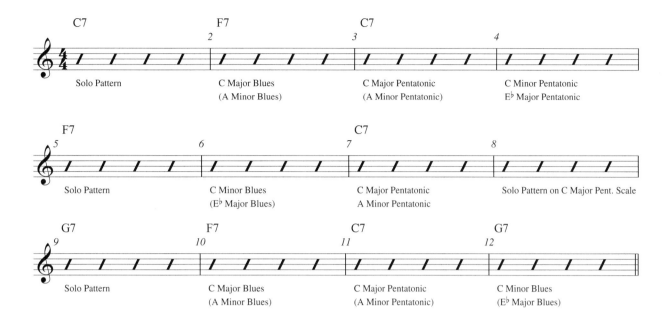

Notice that all four versions of the C pentatonic scales from Chapters 1 and 11 are used:

C major pentatonic scale: measures 3, 7, 11

C major blues pentatonic scale: measures 2, 10

C minor pentatonic scale: measure 4

C minor blues pentatonic scale: measures 6, 12

The important thing to note is that this is not the only combination of patterns that could be used. You can mix up the patterns in many other ways. You can also simplify your choices by using only one or two patterns for the entire song. Remember, the entire progression can be played using only one or two of the pentatonic scales. Or you can make your solos more complex by changing patterns every two beats or by adding your own solo patterns. You could also play only one scale the first half of the progression, and then change scales every four (or two) beats in the second half of the progression. The options are virtually limitless.

To gain further facility with the previous exercise, try to play the scales listed in only one position on the fretboard. For example, try to play the entire blues progression in fifth position. Next, try to play the exercise at the eighth position. Then, try the tenth position, and then the third, and finally the twelfth position. Now try different combinations of different positions.

Now try different tempos—slow, medium, fast, and faster.

Now try different keys, especially "jazz" keys like B♭, F, G, E♭, and D♭.

Once again, the options are virtually limitless.

Now transpose the solo in Fig. 11E to more complex chord variations like the ones in the B♭ blues progression of **Fig. 11F**.

Track 14 (cont.)

Fig. 11F
All Four B♭ Pentatonics: 12-Bar Jazz Changes

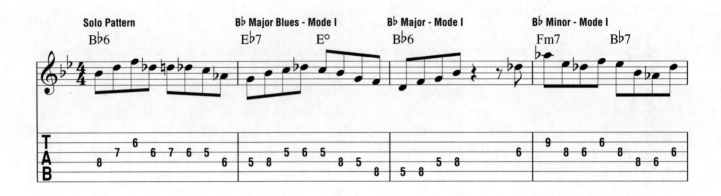

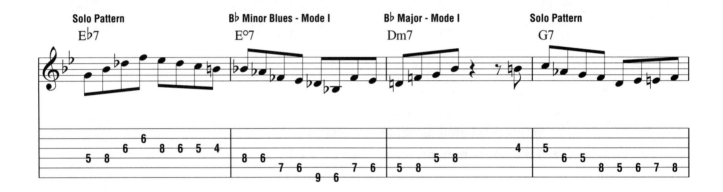

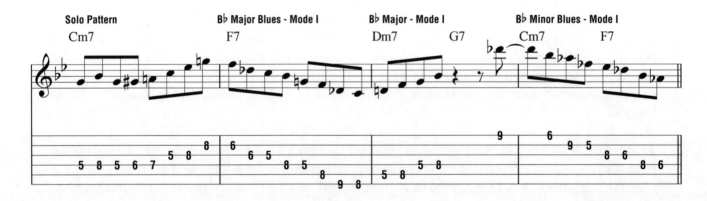

While more harmonic complexity has been added to the changes, it is still basically a 12-bar blues progression. Therefore, the blues pentatonic scales will still work in the same way as for a simple blues progression.

Rhythm Changes

"Rhythm Changes" refers to a standard chord progression that is based on the song "I've Got Rhythm," composed by George Gershwin. Many jazz tunes, especially bebop, are based on this progression. Being able to solo over these changes is an absolute requirement for playing jazz. Unfortunately, in addition to fast-changing chords, these progressions are usually played at fast-to-ridiculously-fast speeds. The song follows a standard AABA format, which means two verses are followed by a bridge and a third verse. Then the tune just keeps repeating.

Example chord changes for the first verse are shown below:

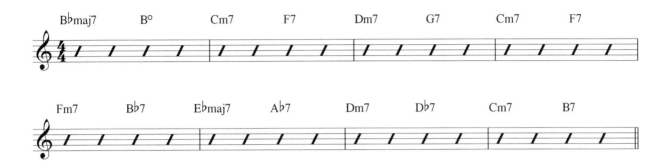

Notice that a chord change occurs every two beats. Also, depending on how you look at it, there are at least two, and perhaps three, key centers in the first eight bars. Unless you develop monster chops and/or the changes are played extremely slowly, there is no hope of playing a different scale for every chord. Even if you could do it, it would not sound "correct," since the "vibe" of the song would be missing. It would probably sound more like some kind of scale exercise. The fast tempo at which these changes are played make even simple arpeggios tough to execute.

When I was first learning guitar, I would hear players like Joe Pass, Wes Montgomery, Barney Kessel, George Benson, Pat Martino, and others effortlessly play over "rhythm changes" at virtually any fast tempo. Even though the tempos were blistering in speed, the solos were cohesive, melodic, and grooving. I was kind of able to get the sound I was hearing as long as I was playing over a one- or two-chord vamp. But when there was a lot of chord movement like "rhythm changes," I could not get that sound. I was convinced that there was some "magic" jazz scale that allowed the great jazz guitarists to disregard the changes and just focus on melodies. No matter how many scale books I researched or bought, I could not find this scale.

I finally learned that, unfortunately, there is no secret. It is all about extremely talented and gifted musicians who can hear melodies over any chord progression and, in turn, execute them on their guitar at any tempo. There is no "magic jazz scale."

However, there *is* a way for mere mortals like you and I to at least play credible solos over fast chord changes.

Instead of trying to "play the changes" (play a different scale over each chord), you can use the same approach that was described earlier for playing the blues—use various combinations of the major pentatonic scale and the major blues pentatonic scale for the entire progression. The following steps will guide you through the process of gaining this facility. To begin with, play these exercises in third position. Later, expand the exercises to all five positions on the fretboard.

Step 1: Use the B♭ major (G minor) pentatonic scale for the entire progression [**Fig. 11G**].

Track 15

Fig. 11G
Rhythm Changes: B♭ Major Pentatonic Scale

The B♭ major pentatonic scale (from Chapter 1) can be used for the entire progression, ignoring the chord changes. This approach actually works pretty well. For one thing, this is the pentatonic scale with which you are most familiar. Also, it is the scale that you can most likely play the fastest. In fact, the faster the tempo, the better this scale sounds over fast-changing chords in a common key. Your ear doesn't distinguish the individual chord changes as much—just the overall key of B♭. Even when the key briefly changes to E♭ in measures 5–6, the B♭ major pentatonic scale will still sound good.

Step 2: Add arpeggios and chromatics to the B♭ major (G minor) pentatonic scale for the entire progression [**Fig. 11H**].

Track 15 (cont.)

Fig. 11H
Rhythm Changes: B♭ Major Pentatonic Scale with Arpeggios and Chromatics

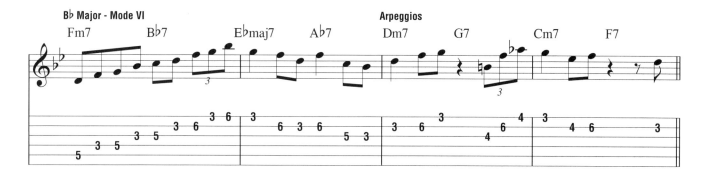

These two simple techniques add additional melodic options for the major pentatonic scale.

Step 3: Use both major pentatonic and major blues pentatonic scales in the progression **[Fig. 111]**.

Fig. 111
Rhythm Changes: B♭ Major/ B♭ Major Blues Pentatonic Scales

Track 15 (cont.)

Now you get the "best of both worlds" with respect to scale options. Since both scales sound good at any measure, you can "mix and match" them in countless variations. No matter what variations you use, all will sound good. Also, notice examples in which arpeggios (measures 3, 7, and 8) and chromatics (measure 4) are used to spice things up.

Once you get these sounds in your head, you are free to use either scale in any combination that feels right for you. For additional "flash," be sure to play these scales in different positions on the fretboard.

The B♭ minor pentatonic scale and B♭ minor blues pentatonic scale also work perfectly in conjunction with the B♭ major pentatonic scale and the B♭ major blues pentatonic scale described in this chapter.

You can also use the C minor pentatonic scale in measure 5 and the C minor blues pentatonic scale in measure 6. Now your have six pentatonic options [**Fig. 11J**]. The possibilities are truly limitless.

Fig. 11J
Rhythm Changes: Using All Six Major/Minor Pentatonic Scales

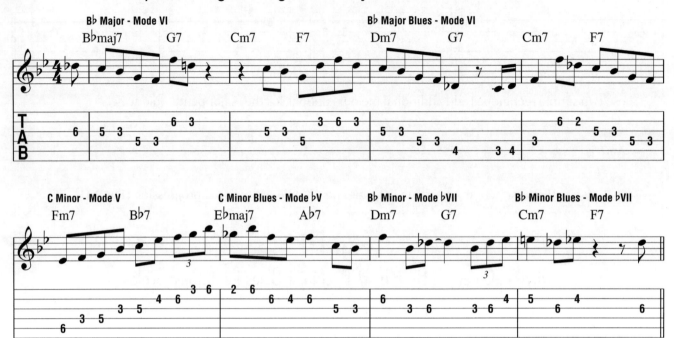

As will be described in Section 5, many more pentatonic options are available to include in your "rhythm changes" solos. For example, you can play pentatonic chord scales over selected chords for additional harmonic richness [**Fig. 11K**].

Fig. 11K
Rhythm Changes: Using Chord Mode Pentatonic Scales

In summary, the B♭ major blues pentatonic scale is an excellent vehicle for developing facility over B♭ "rhythm changes." But there are many options for applying a number of pentatonic scales.

Modal Tunes

In modal tunes, the pentatonic blues scales work great for adding variety to your solos. **Fig. 11L** provides four four-bar phrases that use the A minor pentatonic scale from Chapter 1 exclusively. All of these phrases can be used over a static Am7 chord vamp or in a modal tune that focuses on an Am7 chord. **Fig. 11M** illustrates four four-bar phrases that use the A minor blues pentatonic scale. Notice that the $\flat$5th in this scale ($E\flat$) results in a much more "bluesy" sound.

Fig. 11L

A Minor Pentatonic Scale Patterns

A Minor - Mode I

A Minor - Mode I

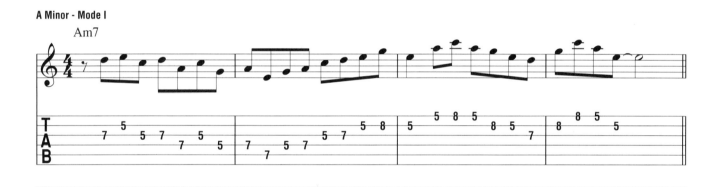

A Minor - Mode I

A Minor - Mode I

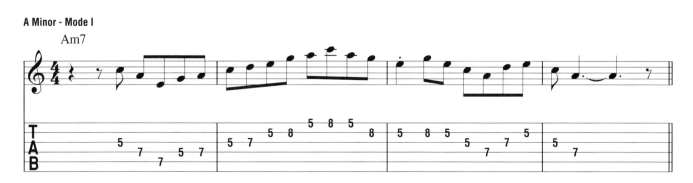

Fig. 11M
A Minor Blues Pentatonic Scale Patterns

You can also use the A major blues pentatonic scale over a static Am7 chord vamp or modal tune since this scale uses a minor 3rd interval instead of a major 3rd (C rather than C♯). **Fig. 11N** provides two four-bar phrases that are over the same static Am7 chord that was used in Fig. 11L–M.

Fig. 11N
A Major Blues Pentatonic Scale Patterns

Track 16 (cont.)

A Major Blues - Mode ♭III

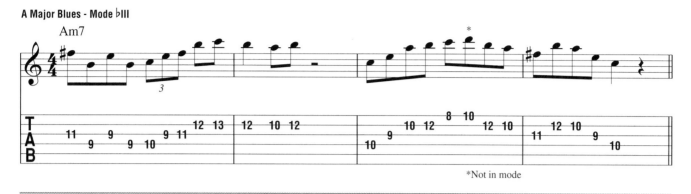

*Not in mode

A Major Blues - Mode I

Also, don't forget the A Aeolian pentatonic scale from Chapter 7. Now you have four pentatonic scales to use over a static minor seventh chord vamp or modal tune.

Finally, in addition to using the A minor pentatonic scale, A minor blues pentatonic scale, and A major blues pentatonic scale over the Am7 chord-vamp examples, these three scales will also work fine over a static A7 dominant chord vamp or modal tune.

In summary, the two blues pentatonic scales shown in this chapter are very useful in static chord vamps or modal tunes.

Standards

Being able to play credible solos over standards is the goal of every guitarist who aspires to play jazz. As promised, facility with the pentatonic scales in this book will enable you to play better than you ever imagined. Now you are able to cover virtually any chord progression by using pentatonic scales that are easy to play and assimilate into your own style of playing. However, no matter how well you can navigate the chords in standard songs by using the pentatonic chord scales in this book, other scales that you know, arpeggios, or sequences, something will be missing from your solos—the *blues*.

Jazz is based on the blues. Your solos *must* contain elements of the blues to remove the "sterility" that can characterize the solos of even highly proficient players. Remember, while technique is impressive, it does not replace "feeling" or "soulfulness" in a solo. In fact, the greatest jazz guitarists are not necessarily the greatest technicians or the "fastest" players. This is certainly true of the great blues guitar players who can get more feeling out of one note than others can get out of a hundred notes.

You need the blues in all of your solos!

The first step is to go back and listen to all of the great blues guitar players of in the past. Listen to B.B. King, Freddie King, Albert King, Albert Collins, and any of your other favorites, past or present. Listen to the "feeling" in their solos. This is what you want to capture.

Next, listen to the great jazz players known for the "bluesy" nature of their solos. Listen to early Kenny Burrell. Listen to anything by Grant Green. Listen to Tiny Grimes (very underrated but truly great). Listen to anything by Barney Kessel. Listen to early George Benson. Listen to Charlie Christian. A common element in all of these fantastic jazz guitar players is their extensive use of the blues in their playing. All of these great guitarists recorded blues and/or blues-based songs, and the blues element is obvious. Also, listen to their recordings of jazz standards. You will be able to hear, in their playing, their incorporation of the blues over the more complex chord changes of standards.

Make it your objective to contain elements of the blues in your improvisations. This will give your solos "life."

So, how do you do it?

A great way to start is to begin incorporating the blues pentatonic scales into your solos in specific places of standard tunes. There are segments in virtually all standard tunes where the blues pentatonic scales will work exceptionally well.

Rule #1: In standards, you can use the pentatonic blues scale over tonic (and/or temporary tonic) major and/or minor chords in the progression.

For example, below is a standard jazz progression in the key of G.

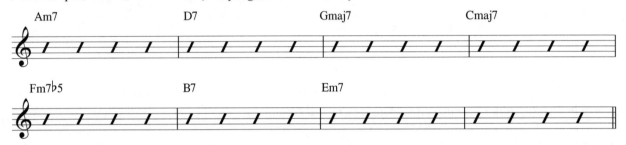

The chord scales presented in Section 1 of this book will work great over these changes, as shown in the following example [**Fig. 110**].

Fig 110
Pentatonic Chord Scales

Once again, you are exclusively using pentatonic scales in the familiar two-notes-per-string format. Your solos automatically have harmonic richness, and you can pretty much play as fast as you desire. Even though your solo will sound good by using only these pentatonic chord scales, the blues element is missing.

Now try to solo over the first four measures of the progression again, this time incorporating the G major blues pentatonic scale over the Gmaj7 and Cmaj7 chords. **Fig. 11P** shows an example of how this may be accomplished.

Fig. 11P
Pentatonic Chord Scales: G Major Blues Pentatonic Scale on Gmaj7 and Cmaj7

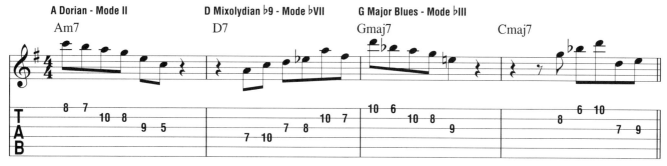

Notice how nicely the G blues pentatonic scale works over these chord changes in a standard tune.

To truly get the blues sound in your head, try the following exercises:

First, go through the first opening measures again, using the chord scales as shown in **Fig. 11Q**.

Fig. 11Q
Pentatonic Chord Scales

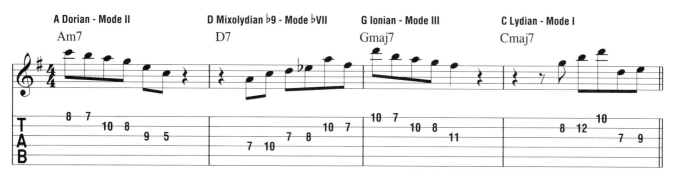

Second, use the pentatonic blues scale only for the Cmaj7 chord [**Fig. 11R**].

Fig. 11R
Pentatonic Chord Scales: G Major Blues on Cmaj7

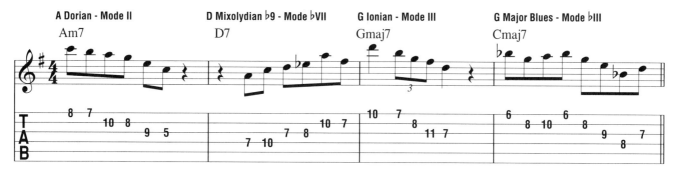

Third, use the pentatonic blues scale only for the Gmaj7 chord [**Fig. 11S**].

Track 17 (cont.)

Fig. 11S
Pentatonic Chord Scales: G Major Blues on Gmaj7

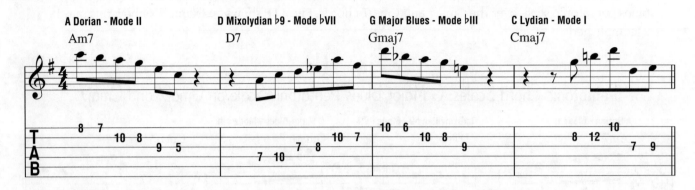

Fourth, use the G major blues scale for both chords [**Fig. 11T**].

Track 17 (cont.)

Fig. 11T
Pentatonic Chord Scales: G Major Blues on Gmaj7 and Cmaj7

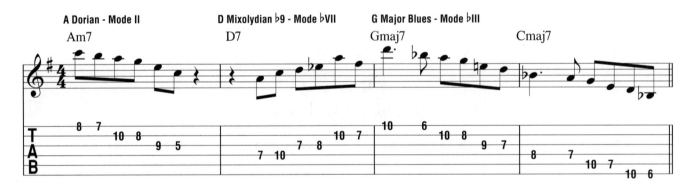

Fifth, repeat the previous four steps for the two measures of Em7 in the progression. **Fig. 11U–V** show the various combinations of the E minor blues pentatonic scale and E Aeolian pentatonic scale for the two measures of the Em7 chord.

Track 17 (cont.)

Fig. 11U
Pentatonic Chord Scales: E Aeolian Pentatonic Scale

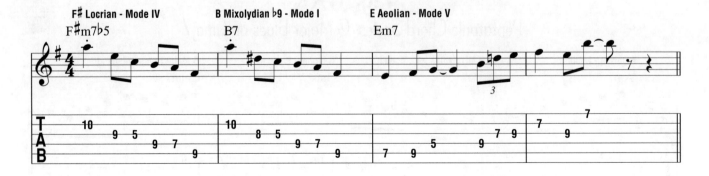

Fig. 11V

Pentatonic Chord Scales: E Aeolian and E Minor Blues Pentatonic Scales

Track 17 (cont.)

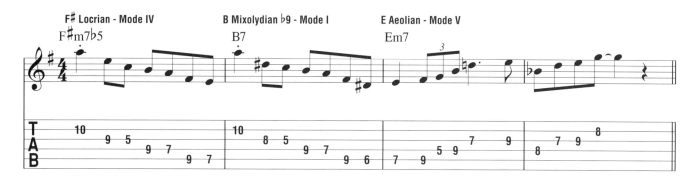

Fig. 11W

Pentatonic Chord Scales: E Minor Blues and E Aeolian Pentatonic Scales

Track 17 (cont.)

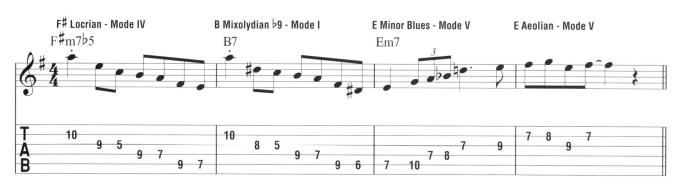

Fig. 11X

Pentatonic Chord Scales: E Minor Blues Pentatonic Scale for Em7

Track 17 (cont.)

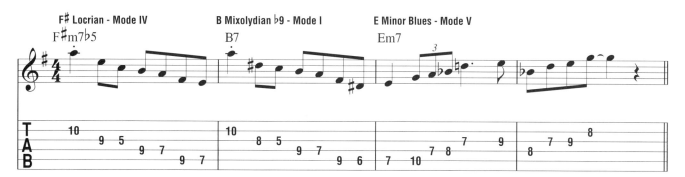

In just these small segments of a classic chord progression you can get a lot of variety with respect to the different combinations of the pentatonic blues scale that are available.

Rule #2: In standard tunes, you can use the pentatonic blues scale over turnarounds in: 1) verses, 2) the bridge, 3) intros, 4) outros, 5) connecting verses, and even 6) entire tunes.

Turnarounds are fundamental components of jazz, blues, rock, and pop tunes. A turnaround is a common chord progression that can be used in several ways, including:

- An introduction or introduction vamp
- A component of the verse or bridge
- An outro vamp
- A connection between the first and second verses
- An entire song

Sometimes turnarounds are oversimplified in music and are shown below (see Appendix B for more on the Roman numeral system):

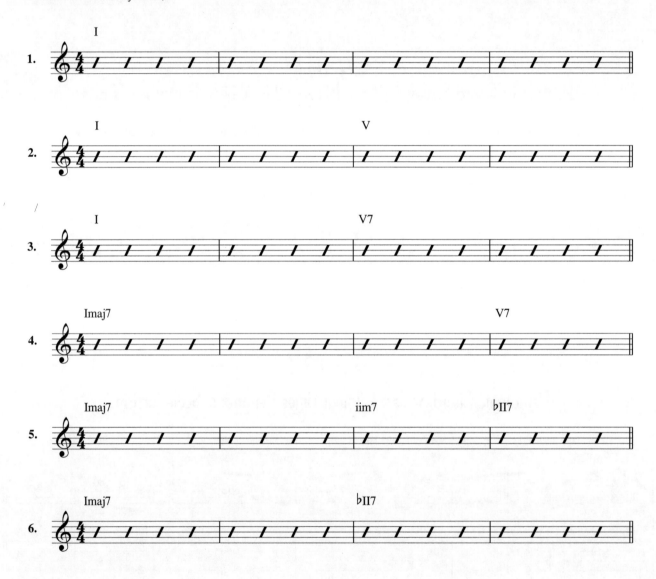

However, the progression above can easily be converted to the standard turnaround that is built around the following four chords:

Many variations on this pattern exist, ranging from simple substitutions to complex reharmonizations. Some examples are shown below:

Imaj7	VI7	iim7	V7
Imaj7	VI7	II7	V7
Imaj7	#i°7	iim7	V7
Imaj7	♭III7	iim7	V7
Imaj7	vim7	iim7♭5	V7
Imaj7	♭III7	iim7	♭II7
Imaj7	♭IIImaj7	♭VImaj7	♭IImaj7

| Imaj7 | IVmaj7 | Imaj7 | V7 |

iiim7	vim7	iim7	V7
iiim7	VI7	iim7	V7
iiim7	♭III7	iim7	V7
iiim7	♭III7	iim7	♭II7
iiim7	♭iii°7	iim7	V7
iiim7	♭iiim7	iim7	V7

| ♭VII7 | ♭III7 | ♭VI7 | ♭II7 |

Etc., etc., etc...

Each chord in a turnaround usually lasts either two or four beats. However, many other chords can be inserted to add harmonic movement to the turnaround. For example, below is a turnaround in the key of C:

Although eight chords comprise the progression, it is basically still a I–vi–ii–V progression with passing chords.

My younger brother, Dean Lemos, taught me this really cool turnaround. I am throwing it in as a bonus:

The whole point of all of this is that the turnaround progression is an ideal place to use the major blues scale, and even the minor blues scale. This method really sounds good when contrasted with the chord-scale approach.

Rule #2A. Turnarounds in the verses. Below are eight measures of a common turnaround chord progression:

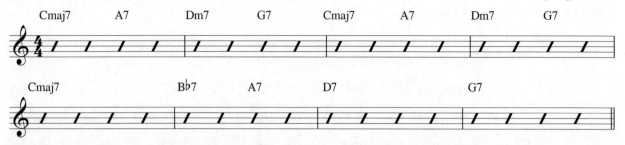

Notice that the first four measures consist of two turnaround progressions, with each chord receiving two beats; meanwhile, the second four measures consist of one turnaround, with each chord receiving four beats (except for measure 2).

To get the feel for how to use blues scales, try the following approaches:

1. Familiarize yourself with the melody in **Fig. 11Y**.

Track 18

Fig. 11Y
"Sylvia Melody"

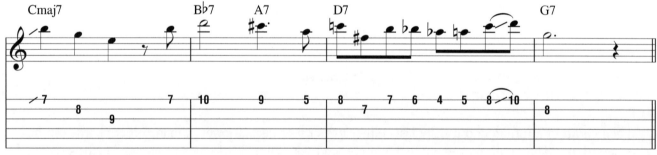

2. Play the melody on all of the chords, except the G7. For the G7, use the C major blues pentatonic scale. Notice how nicely it flows into the Cmaj7 chord [**Fig. 11Z**].

Track 18 (cont.)

Fig. 11Z
Melody with C Major Blues Pentatonic Scale Fills

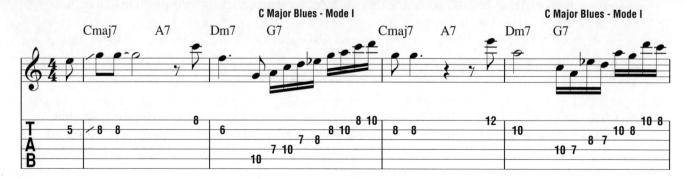

3. Play the solo by using pentatonic chord scales on all of the chords, except the G7. For the G7, use the C major blues pentatonic scale. Notice how "bluesy" this sounds as it flows nicely into the Cmaj7 chord [**Fig. 11AA**].

Fig. 11AA

Chord Scales and C Major Blues Pentatonic Solo

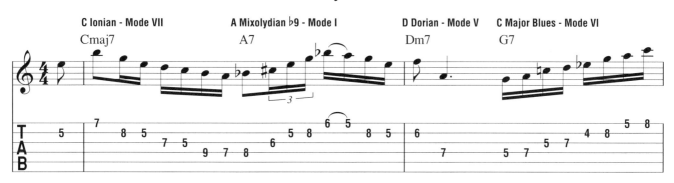

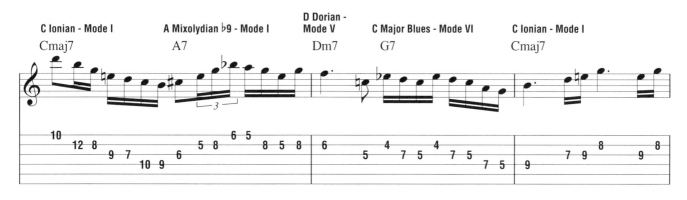

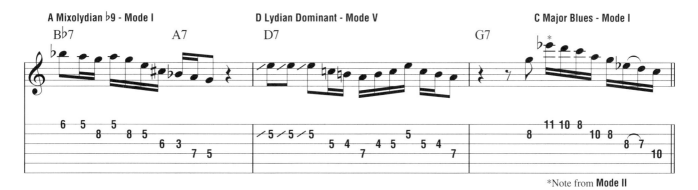

*Note from **Mode II**

4. Use pentatonic chord scales on all of the chords, except the G7. For the G7 chords, alternate between the C major blues pentatonic scale and the C minor blues pentatonic scale [**Fig. 11BB**].

Fig. 11BB
Chord Scales and C Minor/Major Blues Pentatonic Solo

Now you are ready to experiment with using the C major blues pentatonic scale in other places in the progression. The C major blues pentatonic scale will also work very well on the Cmaj7 chords. If you use melodic blues lines mixed with chord scales, the blues scales can work at any point in the progression.

Rule #2B. Turnarounds in the bridge. Below is a chord progression commonly found in the last two measures of the bridge (key of E♭) in many standard tunes.

Once again, start by using chord scales for each chord. **Fig. 11CC** shows three three-bar examples of chord pentatonic scale solos over the aforementioned progression. The next step is to add a blues element to this chord progression. **Fig. 11DD** illustrates two variations on the last example in Fig. 11DD. The second example in Fig. 11EE adds the E♭ major blues pentatonic scale to the last measure. The third example uses only one chord pentatonic scale (C Mixolydian ♭9 pentatonic scale). The other four chords are covered by the E♭ major, E♭ major blues, E♭ minor, and E♭ minor blues pentatonic scales.

Fig. 11CC

Bridge Turnaround: Chord Pentatonics Solos

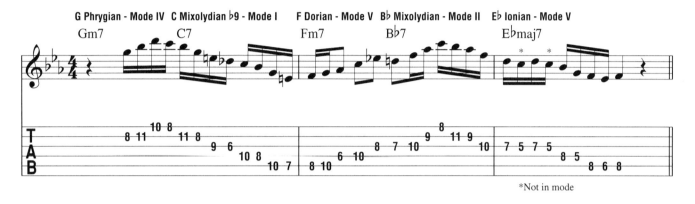

*Not in mode

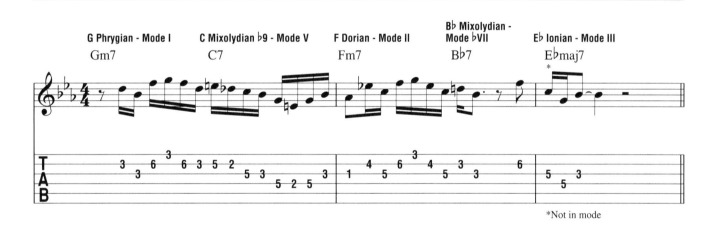

*Not in mode

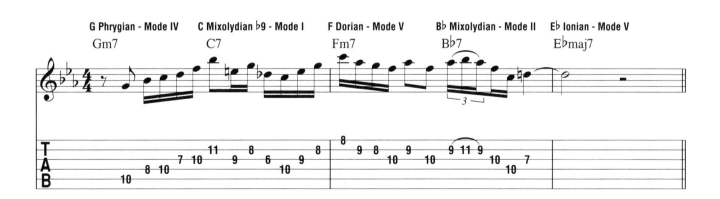

Fig. 11DD

Bridge Turnaround: Major, Major Blues, Minor, and Minor Blues Pentatonic Solos

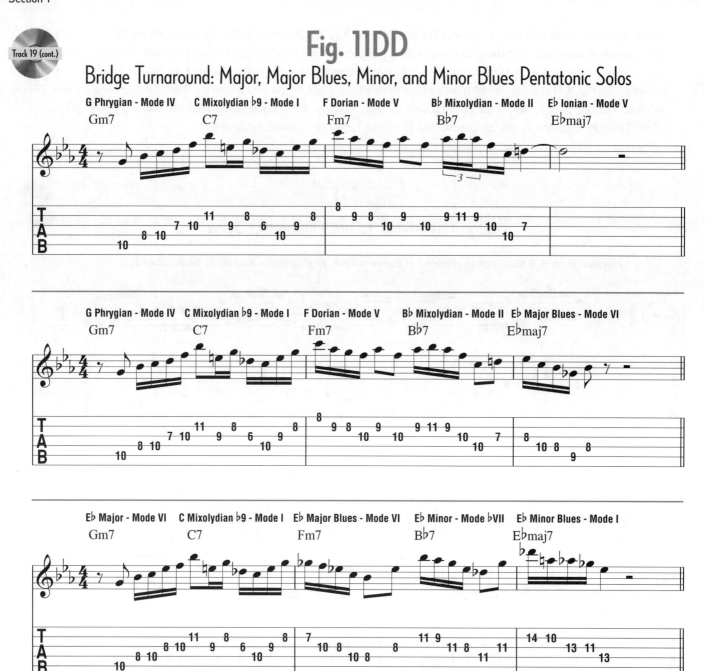

As you can see, there is a wealth of pentatonic scale options available for this standard chord progression. Most importantly, many blues-scale ideas can be combined with chord pentatonic scales in a virtually infinite number of combinations and variations. In fact, the entire progression can be covered using only one of the following pentatonic scales: E♭ major, E♭ major blues, E♭ minor, or E♭ minor blues.

Rule #2C. Turnarounds in intros. Using a turnaround for an intro to a song is pretty standard, perhaps even a cliché. However, it's a great way to set the mood and tempo of a song. It is also a great tool if you are playing with different musicians for the first time. The turnaround can even be a vamp to give the singer or soloist time to come in when they are ready. In any event, playing combinations of the major pentatonic scale and the major blues pentatonic scale will be highly effective. In these cases in particular, it is best to use the major blues pentatonic scale as "seasoning" in the solo. In other words, do not overuse this scale. It's most effective when used sparingly in conjunction with the major pentatonic scale and the pentatonic chord scales. Also, if used even more sparingly, the minor blues pentatonic scale can add considerable "flavor" to a song's intro solo. The minor blues pentatonic scale works particularly well if you "save it" for the end of the intro, to bring in the singer or soloist.

Rule #2D. Turnarounds in outros. Using a turnaround as an outro is also pretty standard. It makes it easier to flow out of the song, and also gives people time to watch for the ending of the song. When soloing through the outro, the same rules apply as for the intros.

Rule #2E. Turnarounds for connecting verses. Using a turnaround to connect verses of a song is very standard in jazz and popular music. These turnarounds are usually two measures in length but can sometimes be as long as four measures. In any event, practice these turnarounds in the same methodical way described in "turnarounds in the verses" (Section A).

Rule #2F. Turnarounds as entire tunes. Some tunes are built entirely, or mostly, on a turnaround chord progression. The turnaround is the primary chord progression for hundreds of doo-wop and dance songs of the fifties and sixties. More recently, songs like "If I Ain't Got You," by Alicia Keys, is basically a turnaround in G. A good example of a song that is based entirely on a turnaround progression is "Breezin'," by George Benson. The guitar playing on this song is masterful. George Benson uses a wide range of devices to maintain a guitar performance that is at once groovin', melodic, and bluesy. He also gives hints of his prodigious technique. This is a great song to learn and to practice pentatonic scales over, particularly the major pentatonic and major blues pentatonic scales.

Fig. 11EE is an example of a song that is based entirely on a turnaround progression in the key of D. The four measure melody is played in octaves first, and four solo variations that use pentatonic scales in different ways are included.

Fig. 11EE
"Believing"

Track 20

Believing: Melody

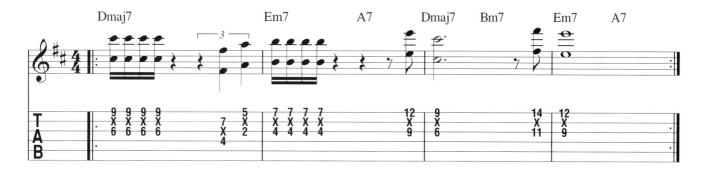

Believing: Solo Variation 1

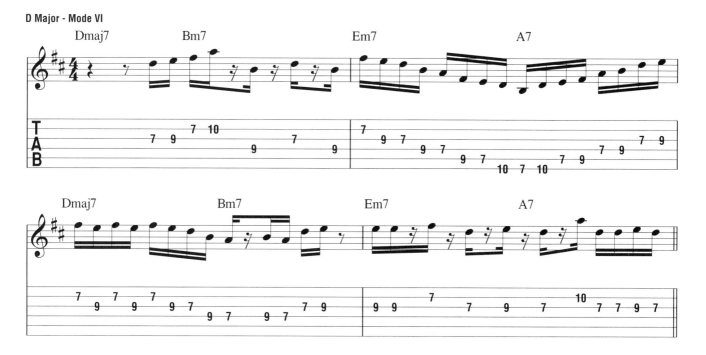

Believing: Solo Variation 2

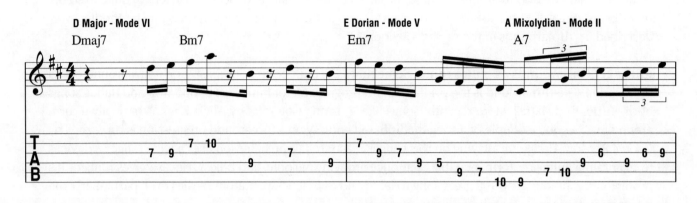

Believing: Solo Variation 3

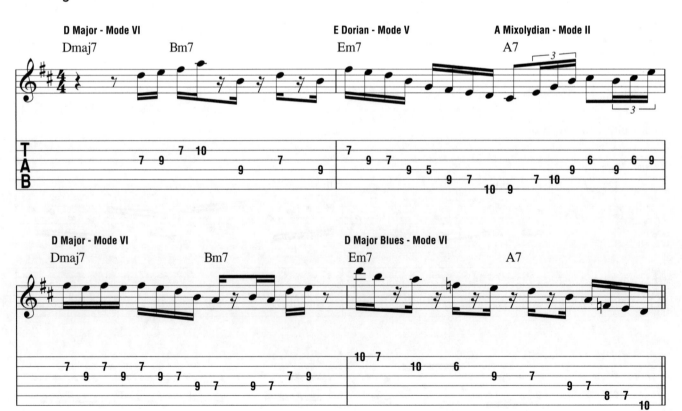

Believing: Solo Variation 4

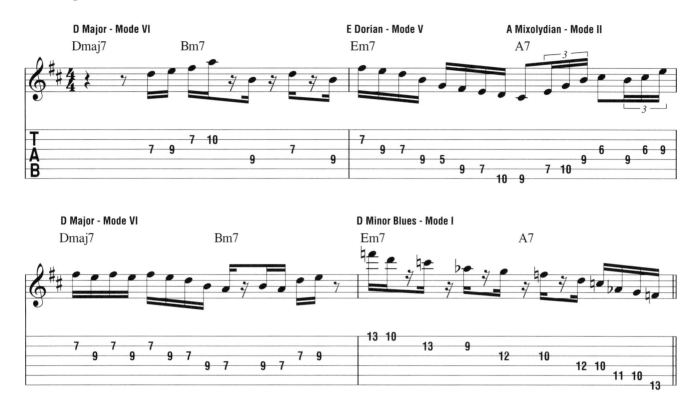

Solo variation 1 uses the D major pentatonic scale exclusively. Solo variation 2 uses chord pentatonic scales for the Em7 and A7 chords. Solo variation 3 adds the D major blues pentatonic scale for the last measure, and solo variation 4 uses the D minor blues pentatonic scale for the last measure. These last two variations demonstrate the flexibility of the blues pentatonic scales in turnaround chord progressions.

Rule #3: You can use the pentatonic blues scale for entire non-turnaround tunes.

As long as all of the chords are diatonic (they all belong to the same key), you can freely use the related major/minor pentatonic scale and major/minor blues pentatonic scale along with the pentatonic chord scales anywhere in the song. Most importantly, these sets of scales all complement each other.

Summary

A lot of material was covered in this chapter. However, in many ways it is the most important chapter since the major/minor blues pentatonic scale will bring "life" and "groove" to your solos. Also, these scales are easy to incorporate into your playing since they are so similar to the finger patterns of the major/minor pentatonic scales that you already know. Finally, as demonstrated in the examples, you can maximize the utility of these scales by mixing and matching them with the other pentatonic scales in this book—particularly the relative major/minor pentatonic scale.

SECTION 2

Substitute Scales

This section illustrates how you can use the scales in Section 1 to provide additional options for soloing over a variety of chords and chord progressions. No new scales will be presented. Instead, the scales in Section 1 will be used in a wider range of situations, increasing the utility of the scales tremendously and adding greater options for increasing the melodic richness of your solos.

CHAPTER 12
C IONIAN (Imaj7) PENTATONIC SCALE
SUBSTITUTIONS

The C Ionian pentatonic scale was covered in Chapter 2. This scale can be used to cover any chord that functions as a tonic major chord. Examples of tonic major chords in the key of C are:

C   Cmaj7   Cmaj9   C6/9   C6

The C Ionian pentatonic scale consists of the following five scale tones (notes):

1–2–3–5–7 (C–D–E–G–B)

This scale provides a very rich major 7th/9th sound. For additional "color" choices, four additional pentatonic scales can also be used on a Cmaj7 chord functioning as a tonic major chord. Therefore, you have five pentatonic scale choices for soloing over a Cmaj7 chord by using only scales that have been previously learned.

The five choices are listed below in order of consonance. For a Cmaj7 chord, the C Ionian pentatonic scale is the most consonant, while the B Phrygian pentatonic scale is the most dissonant.

Basic Scale	Chord	
C Ionian (Imaj7) Pentatonic Scale	Cmaj9	consonant
		↑
Substitute Scale		
E Phrygian (iiim7) Pentatonic Scale	Cmaj7/6	
A Aeolian (vim7) Pentatonic Scale	Cmaj7/6	↓
C Major (A Minor) Pentatonic Scale	C6	
B Minor Pentatonic Scale	Cmaj9♯4	dissonant

The intervals and notes for these scales, as they relate to a Cmaj7 chord, are shown below:

INTERVALS	Root	9th	3rd	♯4th	5th	6th	7th
Cmaj7 Chord	C		E		G		B
C Ionian (Imaj7) Pentatonic Scale	C	D	E		G		B
E Phrygian (iiim7) Pentatonic Scale		D	E		G	A	B
A Aeolian (vim7) Pentatonic Scale	C		E		G	A	B
C Major (A Minor) Pentatonic Scale	C	D	E		G	A	
B Minor Pentatonic Scale		D	E	F♯		A	B

Fig. 12A is a four-bar solo that uses the C Ionian pentatonic scale over a static Cmaj7 chord. **Fig. 12B** demonstrates four variations of this solo by using the substitute scales that are described in this chapter.

Track 21

Fig. 12A
Cmaj7 Solo: C Ionian Pentatonic Scale

C Ionian (Imaj7) Pentatonic Scale: This scale was presented in Chapter 2. It is the most consonant scale for a tonic Cmaj7 chord. It implies the sound of a Cmaj9 chord, which is a very consonant sound for a Cmaj7 chord.

Track 21 (cont.)

Fig. 12B
Cmaj7 Solo: Substitute Pentatonic Scale Variations

E Phrygian (iiim7) Pentatonic Scale: This scale is an excellent alternative to the C Ionian pentatonic scale. It was first presented in Chapter 4. Although it omits the root, the E Phrygian pentatonic scale includes the note A, which adds an important major 6th sound to the scale when used over a Cmaj7 chord, implying the sound of a Cmaj7/6. More importantly, it represents a specific chord substitution. Basically, you are substituting an Em7 for a Cmaj7 in a chord progression—a very standard chord substitution in jazz, particularly for turnarounds.

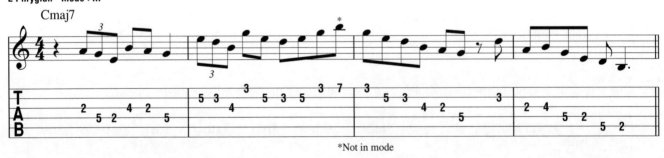

*Not in mode

A Aeolian (vim7) Pentatonic Scale: This scale, covered in Chapter 7, is very close in sound to the E Phrygian pentatonic scale when it is used over a Cmaj7 chord. It is useful if you wish to superimpose an Am9 sound over a Cmaj7 chord.

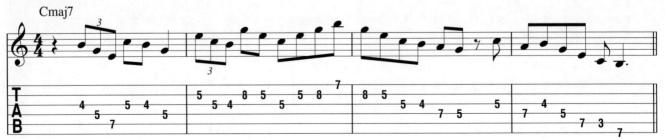

C Major (A Minor) Pentatonic Scale: This scale was presented in Chapter 1. Many jazz methods suggest the basic major pentatonic scale as the first-choice scale for soloing over a Imaj7 chord. For blues, country, or rock tunes, I would also suggest that the C major pentatonic scale be used over a tonic major or major-sixth chord. However, this scale does not include the very important major-7th tone that gives the tonic major its "jazzy" feeling. On the other hand, the C major pentatonic scale would be the first choice in a jazz tune if you consciously wanted to play the sound of a C6 chord, as opposed to a Cmaj7 chord.

C Major - Mode VI

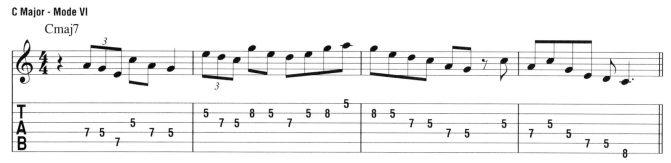

B Minor Pentatonic Scale: This scale was presented in Chapter 1. This scale is the only true dissonant scale in the group. Basically, you are playing a standard B minor pentatonic scale over a Cmaj7 chord. This scale is extremely rich in color tones, including the major 7th, 9th, 6th, and ♯4th. This scale is the only scale from Section 1 that gives a Lydian quality to a major seventh chord. The sound of the ♯4th over a major seventh chord is very important in jazz. However, it does take experience and taste to use it effectively.

B Minor - Mode I

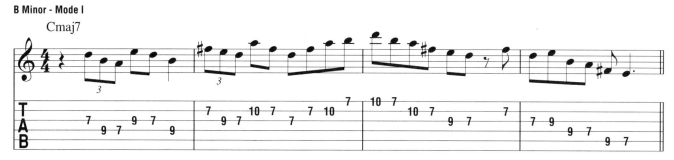

In addition to playing over a static vamp, as demonstrated in Fig. 12B, use the minor pentatonic scale on a major seventh (Imaj7) chord, one half step lower, in a ii–V–I progression to get this "outside" sound in your ears and under your fingers. **Fig. 12C** is an example solo over a Dm7–G7–Cmaj7 progression.

Track 21 (cont.)

Fig. 12C
Cmaj7 Solo: B Minor Pentatonic Scale

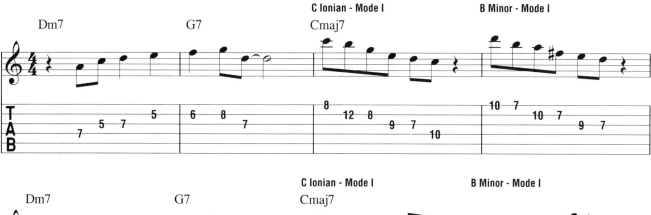

Use the D Dorian (iim7) pentatonic scale for the Dm7 chord and the G Mixolydian (V7) pentatonic scale for the G7 chord. For the Cmaj7 chord, Fig. 12C demonstrates using both the C Ionian pentatonic scale and the B minor pentatonic scale. Notice how nice the B minor pentatonic scale sounds in this context. Also notice how "bluesy" the F♯ note sounds as the last note in the example phrase.

Summary

A Cmaj7 tonic major chord can be covered with five of the scales presented in Section 1. All of the scales will sound correct, no matter which notes you play. All of the scales use patterns that have already been covered. It is simply a matter of deciding what specific "colors" you wish to use for your solo.

CHAPTER 13
D DORIAN (iim7) PENTATONIC SCALE
SUBSTITUTIONS

The D Dorian pentatonic scale was introduced in Chapter 3. This scale can be used to cover any chord that functions as a iim7 chord. Examples of iim7 chords in the key of C are:

Dm7   Dm9   Dm11

The D Dorian pentatonic scale consists of the following five scale tones (notes):

1–2–♭3–5–♭7 (D–E–F–A–C)

This scale provides a very rich minor seventh/ninth sound. For additional "color" choices, six additional pentatonic scales can also be used on a Dm7 chord that functions as a iim7 chord. Therefore, you have seven pentatonic scale choices for soloing over a Dm7 chord.

The seven choices are listed below in order of consonance. For a Dm7 chord, the D Dorian pentatonic scale is the most consonant, and the B Locrian pentatonic scale is the most dissonant.

Basic Scale	Chord	
D Dorian (iim7) Pentatonic Scale	Dm9	consonant
Substitute Scale		⬆
F Lydian (IVmaj7) Pentatonic Scale	Fmaj7	
D Minor Pentatonic Scale	Dm7	
A Minor Pentatonic Scale	Dm11	
A Aeolian (vim7) Pentatonic Scale	Dm6/7	⬇
E Minor Pentatonic Scale	Dm11	
B Locrian (viim7♭5) Pentatonic Scale	Dm6/9	dissonant

The intervals and notes for these scales, as they relate to a Dm7 chord, are shown below.

INTERVALS -	Root	9th	♭3rd	4th	5th	6th	♭7th
Dm7 Chord	D		F		A		C
D Dorian (iim7) Pentatonic Scale	D	E	F		A		C
F Lydian (IVmaj7) Pentatonic Scale		E	F	G	A		C
D Minor Pentatonic Scale	D		F	G	A		C
A Minor Pentatonic Scale	D	E		G	A		C
A Aeolian (vim7) Pentatonic Scale		E		G	A	B	C
E Minor Pentatonic Scale	D	E		G	A	B	
B Locrian (viim7♭5) Pentatonic Scale	D	E	F		A	B	

Fig. 13A is a four-bar solo that uses the D Dorian pentatonic scale over a static Dm7 chord. **Fig. 13B** contains six variations of this solo using the substitute scales described in this chapter (see below).

Track 22

Fig. 13A
Dm7 Solo: D Dorian Pentatonic Scale

D Dorian (iim7) Pentatonic Scale: This scale was first presented in Chapter 3. It is the most consonant scale for a Dm7 (iim7) chord. It implies the sound of a Dm9 chord, a very consonant sound for a Dm7 chord.

D Dorian - Mode I

Track 22 (cont.)

Fig. 13B
Dm7 Solo: Substitute Pentatonic Scale Variations

F Lydian (IVmaj7) Pentatonic Scale: This scale is an excellent alternative for the D Dorian pentatonic scale. It was presented in Chapter 5. Although it omits the root, it includes the note G, which adds an important 4th/11th sound to the scale when used over a Dm7 chord. This scale implies the sound of an Fmaj7, a great substitute chord for a Dm7.

F Lydian - Mode VII

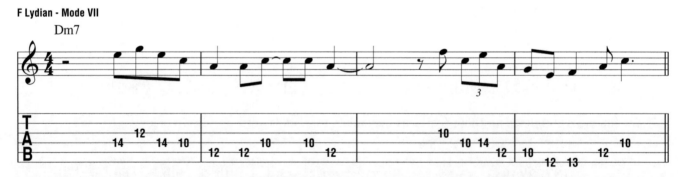

D Minor Pentatonic Scale: This is the standard minor pentatonic scale that was described in Chapter 1. The biggest advantage of this scale is its familiarity—you already know it. The disadvantage is its blandness; there is no strong color tone beyond the ♭7th note. Without a complementary 2nd/9th note, the 4th does not add character to this scale. In general, this scale will sound better over a sustained iim7 chord in a progression.

D Minor - Mode V

A Minor Pentatonic Scale: This scale was presented in Chapter 1. Many jazz methods suggest the basic minor pentatonic scale, five steps/frets lower, as a second-choice scale for soloing over a iim7 chord. The lack of the minor 3rd, combined with the upper extensions of a 9th and an 11th, give this scale a very open sound over a Dm7 chord.

A Minor - Mode I

A Aeolian (vim7) Pentatonic Scale: This scale was presented in Chapter 7. The A Aeolian pentatonic scale adds a 6th to the sound of a iim7 chord, giving it more of a iim6 sound. This is not necessarily bad; it's just that the 6th is a very "strong" tone and does not resolve to a V7 dominant chord as "smoothly" as a iim7 chord does. However, the combination of the 6th and 7th in this scale, when used over a iim7 chord, clearly defines the Dorian nature of the scale. This means that an A Aeolian pentatonic scale substitution is particularly useful when vamping on a modal iim7 chord sequence like the example in Fig. 13B.

A Aeolian - Mode I

E Minor Pentatonic Scale: This scale was presented in Chapter 1. Many jazz methods suggest the basic minor pentatonic scale, two steps/frets higher, as an "outside" scale for soloing over a iim7 chord. The lack of the minor 3rd, combined with the upper extensions of a 6th, 9th, and an 11th, give this scale a very "open" sound over a Dm7 chord.

E Minor - Mode V

B Locrian (viim7♭5) Pentatonic Scale: This scale is a little more "out" because it is missing the important 7th tone of a iim7 chord. Instead, it has a 6th and 9th tone. Therefore, you are, in effect, substituting the sound of a Dm6/9 chord for a Dm7 chord. Once again, this is fine if that is the sound you want to hear. As with the previous A Aeolian pentatonic scale substitution, this scale is particularly useful when vamping on a modal iim7 chord sequence like the example in Fig. 13B.

Summary

A Dm7 (iim7) chord can be covered with seven of the scales presented in Section 1. All of the scales will sound correct, no matter which notes you play. Plus, all of the scales use patterns that you have already learned—it is simply a matter of deciding what specific "colors" you wish to use for your solo.

CHAPTER 14
E PHRYGIAN (iiim7) PENTATONIC SCALE
SUBSTITUTIONS

The E Phrygian pentatonic scale was covered in Chapter 4. This scale can be used to cover any chord that functions as a Phrygian minor chord. Examples of Phrygian minor chords in the key of C are:

Em   Em7   Em11

The E Phrygian pentatonic scale consists of the following five scale tones (notes):

$1-\flat3-4-5-\flat7$ (E–G–A–B–D)

As stated in Chapter 4, this scale provides the basic minor pentatonic scale sound that guitarists learn first. For purposes of soloing, the iiim7 chord is assumed to be a substitute Imaj7 chord.

There are six choices for soloing over an Em7 Phrygian chord. These choices are listed below in order of consonance. For an Em7 chord, the E Phrygian pentatonic scale is the most consonant, while the B♭ Lydian Dominant pentatonic scale is the most dissonant (or, more accurately, a reharmonization).

Basic Scale	Chord	
E Phrygian (iiim7) Pentatonic Scale	Em7	consonant

Substitute Scale

C Ionian (Imaj7) Pentatonic Scale	Cmaj7
A Aeolian (vim7) Pentatonic Scale	Em($\flat$6)
A Minor Pentatonic Scale	Em7($\flat$6)

Reharmonized Scale

E Mixolydian $\flat$9 (V7$\flat$9) Pentatonic Scale	E7$\flat$9	
B♭ Lydian Dominant (7$\flat$5) Pentatonic Scale	B♭7$\flat$5	dissonant

The intervals and notes for these scales, as they relate to an Em7 chord, are shown below.

INTERVALS -	Root	♭2nd	♭3rd	4th	5th	♭6th	♭7th
Em7 Chord	E		G		B		D
E Phrygian (iiim7) Pentatonic Scale	E		G	A	B		D
C Ionian (Imaj7) Pentatonic Scale	E		G		B	C	D
A Aeolian (vim7) Pentatonic Scale	E		G	A	B	C	
A Minor Pentatonic Scale	E		G	A		C	D
E Mixolydian ♭9 (V7♭9) Pentatonic Scale	E	F	G#*		B		D
B♭ Lydian Dominant (7♭5) Pentatonic Scale	E	F	G, G#*			C	

*major 3rd

Fig. 14A shows a four-bar solo using the E Phrygian pentatonic scale over a static Em7 chord. **Fig. 14B** includes three variations of this solo using the substitute scales described in this chapter. **Fig. 14C–D** demonstrate the use of reharmonized scales—as opposed to substitute scales—for the Em7 (iiim7) chord.

Track 23

Fig. 14A
Em7 Solo: E Phrygian Pentatonic Scale

E Phrygian (iiim7) Pentatonic Scale: This scale was presented in Chapter 4. It is the most consonant scale for a Phrygian Em7 chord. It clearly outlines an Em7 chord, with an added extension of a 4th (A). It is important to note that this scale is also the E minor pentatonic scale (Chapter 1)—i.e., they are the same scale. However, in the context of a iiim7 chord, it is preferable to think of the scale as a modal Phrygian pentatonic scale.

E Phrygian - Mode V

Track 23 (cont.)

Fig. 14B
Em7 Solo: Substitute Pentatonic Scale Variations

C Ionian (Imaj7) Pentatonic Scale: This scale is an excellent alternative for the Em7 Phrygian pentatonic scale, which was presented in Chapter 2. Since an Em7 Phrygian (iiim7) chord is considered to be a substitution for a Cmaj7 Ionian (Imaj7) chord, the C Ionian pentatonic scale is a very close direct substitution.

C Ionian - Mode I

A Aeolian (vim7) Pentatonic Scale: When used over an Em7 Phrygian (iiim7) chord, this scale, covered in Chapter 7, is useful if you wish to have more of a "pure" minor sound. The lack of a ♭7th and the inclusion of a ♭6th give the scale a more "Phrygian" sound.

A Aeolian - Mode I

A Minor Pentatonic Scale: This scale was presented in Chapter 1. This substitution has the important intervals of the root, ♭3rd, ♭7th, and 4th/11th. In addition to using in a static Em7 vamp like Fig. 14C, the scale is a good choice to use in a iii–vi (e.g., Em7–Am7) or vi–iii (Am7–Em7) vamp.

Fig. 14C

Em7 Progression: E Mixolydian ♭9 Pentatonic Scale Reharmonization

E Mixolydian ♭9 (V7♭9) Pentatonic Scale: A noted earlier, this scale is not a true substitution; it is really a reharmonization (i.e., changing the original chord). In this case, you would be changing the basic quality of the chord—minor to dominant. However, this type of reharmonization is done very frequently in jazz with regard to a Phrygian (iiim7) chord.

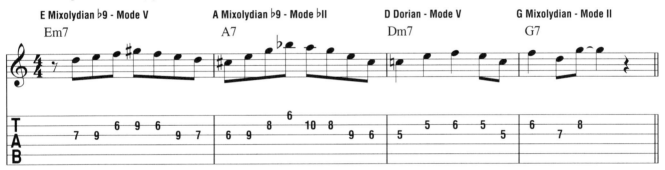

For example, review the standard turnaround chord progression below.

A very common jazz reharmonization of this progression is to replace the Em7 with an E7♭9. Now the progression would become:

The E7♭9 chord is perfectly covered with an E Mixolydian ♭9 pentatonic scale. In practice, you could even make this scale substitution while the rhythm section is playing an Em7. The ear "accepts" this superimposition because an Em7 chord is very close in sound to an E7♯9 chord, which, in turn, is a very close substitution for the E7♭9 chord. Fig. 14C shows an example of using the E Mixolydian ♭9 pentatonic scale over an Em7.

Fig. 14D

Track 23 (cont.)

Em7 Progression: B♭ Lydian Dominant Pentatonic Scale Reharmonization

B♭ Lydian Dominant (7♭5) Pentatonic Scale: This scale is also a reharmonization (i.e., changing the original chord). In this case, you are really creating a "flat five" reharmonization of the E7♭9, which is a reharmonization of the Em7. Once again, you are changing the basic quality of the original iiim7 chord—minor to dominant. As noted earlier, this type of reharmonization is done very frequently in jazz with regard to a Phrygian (iiim7) chord.

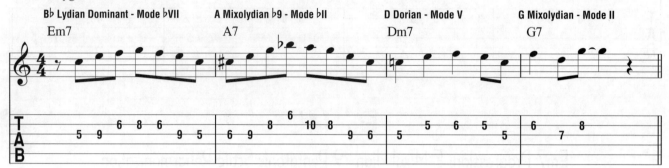

For example, review the chord progression below.

The jazz reharmonization of this progression, which was presented earlier, would be to replace the Em7 with an E7♭9. Now the progression would become:

Now, if we reharmonize the E7♭9 by a ♭5th ("flat five" substitution), we get the following progression:

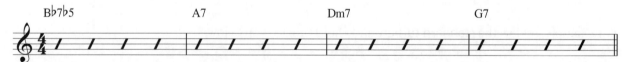

The B♭7♭5 chord is perfectly covered with a B♭ Lydian Dominant pentatonic scale. In practice, you could even make this scale substitution without changing the Em7. The ear accepts this superimposition because an Em7 chord is very close in sound to an E7♯9 chord, which, in turn, is a very close substitution for the B♭7♭5 chord.

Summary

An Em7 Phrygian minor chord can be covered with six of the scales presented in Section 1. All of the scales will sound correct, no matter which notes you play. All of the scales use patterns that have already been learned; thus, it is simply a matter of deciding what specific "colors" you wish to use for your solo.

CHAPTER 15
F LYDIAN (IVmaj7) PENTATONIC SCALE
SUBSTITUTIONS

The F Lydian pentatonic scale was covered in Chapter 5. This scale can be used to cover any chord that functions as a IVmaj7 chord. Examples of IVmaj7 chords in the key of C are:

Fmaj7   Fmaj9   Fmaj7♭5   Fmaj9♯11

The F Lydian pentatonic scale consists of the following five scale tones (notes):

1–2–3–5–7 (F–G–A–C–E)

This scale provides the exact same major 7th/9th sound as the Ionian pentatonic scale from Chapter 2. However, the Lydian pentatonic scale does not provide the ♭5th note that is the characteristic Lydian tone. If this sound is desired, it can be achieved by using a substitute scale, as illustrated in this chapter.

Six additional pentatonic scales can also be used over an Fmaj7 chord that functions as a IVmaj7 chord. Therefore, you have seven pentatonic scale choices for soloing over an Fmaj7 chord, using only scales that have been previously learned.

The seven choices are listed below in order of consonance. For an Fmaj7 chord, the F Lydian pentatonic scale is the most consonant, while the E minor pentatonic scale is the most dissonant.

Basic Scale	**Chord**	
F Lydian (IVmaj7) Pentatonic Scale	Fmaj9	consonant
Substitute Scale		
D Dorian (iim7) Pentatonic Scale	Fmaj7/6	
F Major Pentatonic Scale	F6, F6/9	
C Ionian (Imaj7) Pentatonic Scale	Fmaj9♯4	
A Minor Pentatonic Scale	Fmaj9/6	
A Aeolian (vim7) Pentatonic Scale	Fmaj9♯11	
E Minor Pentatonic Scale	Fmaj6/9♯11	dissonant

The intervals and notes for these scales, as they relate to an Fmaj7 chord, are shown below.

INTERVALS -	Root	9th	3rd	♯4th	5th	6th	7th
Fmaj7 Chord	F		A		C		E
F Lydian (IVmaj7) Pentatonic Scale	F	G	A		C		E
D Dorian (iim7) Pentatonic Scale	F		A		C	D	E
F Major Pentatonic Scale	F	G	A		C	D	
A Minor Pentatonic Scale		G	A		C	D	E
C Ionian (Imaj7) Pentatonic Scale		G		B	C	D	E
A Aeolian (vim7) Pentatonic Scale		G	A	B	C		E
E Minor Pentatonic Scale		G	A	B		D	E

Fig. 15A is a four-bar solo that uses the F Lydian pentatonic scale over a static Fmaj7 chord. **Fig. 15B** contains six variations of this solo using the substitute scales described in this chapter.

Fig. 15A
Fmaj7 Solo: F Lydian Pentatonic Scale

F Lydian (IVmaj7) Pentatonic Scale: This scale was presented in Chapter 5. It is the most consonant scale for an Fmaj7 (IVmaj7) chord. It implies the sound of an Fmaj9 chord, which is a very consonant sound for an Fmaj7 chord.

F Lydian - Mode III

Fig. 15B
Fmaj7 Solo: Substitute Pentatonic Scale Variations

D Dorian (iim7) Pentatonic Scale: This scale, first presented in Chapter 3, is an excellent alternative for the F Lydian pentatonic scale. As was noted in Chapter 3, most IVmaj7 chords notated in jazz are really subs for iim7 chords; consequently, the D Dorian pentatonic scale can be considered more of an alternate scale, rather than a substitute scale. The D Dorian pentatonic scale actually gives a stronger IV feeling because it uses a 6th instead of a 9th, which is used in the F Lydian pentatonic scale. Therefore, this scale is preferred for a IVmaj7/6 or IV6 chord.

D Dorian - Mode V

F Major Pentatonic Scale: This scale was presented in Chapter 1. The main value of this scale is its familiarity as the basic major pentatonic scale. Also, many jazz methods suggest the F major pentatonic scale as a first choice for soloing over an Fmaj7 chord. However, while it contains the rich 6th and 9th tones of an F chord, it lacks the important major 7th tone.

F Major - Mode III

A Minor Pentatonic Scale: This scale was presented in Chapter 1. The lack of the F root in this scale, combined with the upper extensions of a major 7th, 6th, and 9th, give this scale a very open sound over a Fmaj7 chord.

A Minor - Mode VI

C Ionian (Imaj7) Pentatonic Scale: This scale has two very important advantages as a substitute scale for an Fmaj7 chord. First, you don't have to distinguish between a Imaj7 and a IVmaj7—just use the Ionian (Imaj7) pentatonic scale over any major seventh chord. Second, the C Ionian pentatonic scale includes the ♯4th tone, which gives a IVmaj7 chord its correct Lydian quality. While this scale lacks the root and 3rd of a IVmaj7 chord, it is rich with chord extensions (♯4th, 6th, 7th, and 9th). These extensions give the scale a very open sound over a IVmaj7 chord.

C Ionian - Mode VI

A Aeolian (vim7) Pentatonic Scale: Originally presented in Chapter 7, this scale is very rich in higher extensions over a IVmaj7 chord, including the ♯4th, major 7th, and 9th. Consequently, it implies the sound of an Fmaj9♯11 chord.

A Aeolian - Mode I

E Minor Pentatonic Scale: This scale was presented in Chapter 1 and is rich in upper extensions, including a major 7th, 6th, 9th, and ♯11th.

E Minor - Mode IV

Summary

An Fmaj7 (IVmaj7) Lydian chord can be covered with seven of the scales presented in Section 1. All of the scales will sound correct, no matter which notes you play. Moreover, all of the scales use patterns that have already been learned; thus, it is simply a matter of deciding what specific "colors" you wish to use for your solo.

CHAPTER 16

G MIXOLYDIAN (V7/I7) PENTATONIC SCALE
SUBSTITUTIONS

The G Mixolydian (V7/I7) pentatonic scale was presented in Chapter 6. This scale can be used to cover any chord that functions as a Mixolydian dominant chord. Examples of Mixolydian dominant chords in the key of C are:

G7   G9   G13

The G Mixolydian (V7/I7) pentatonic scale consists of the following five scale tones (notes):

$1-2-3-5-{}^\flat7$ (G–A–B–D–F)

The dominant seventh chord is unique in that it can be altered in many more ways than other chords. For example, the 5th and 9th can be flatted and/or sharped in various combinations, depending on voice-leading intentions. Also, the dominant seventh chord can often be reharmonized into one a $\flat$5th interval higher or lower. This gives you additional options for soloing over a dominant seventh chord.

As shown below, there are nine pentatonic scale choices for soloing over a G7 Mixolydian chord. These scale choices, along with their implied chord sound, are categorized below in terms of being substitute scales or scales based on a reharmonization of the dominant seventh chord. Within each category, multiple scale options are listed in order of consonance.

Basic Scale	Chord	
G Mixolydian (V7/I7) Pentatonic Scale	G7, G9	consonant
Substitute Scale: Unaltered 5th		
B Locrian (viim7$\flat$5) Pentatonic Scale	G13	
G Major (E Minor) Pentatonic Scale	G6/9	
G Mixolydian $\flat$9 (V7$\flat$9) Pentatonic Scale	G7$\flat$9	dissonant
Substitute Scale: Altered 5th ($\sharp$4th/$\sharp$11th)		
G Lydian Dominant (II7$\flat$5) Pentatonic Scale	G7$\flat$5, G13$\sharp$11	dissonant
Reharmonized Scale: Altered 5th		
D$\flat$ Lydian Dominant ($\flat$II7$\flat$5) Pentatonic Scale	D$\flat$7$\flat$5, D$\flat$9$\sharp$11	dissonant
F Locrian (viim7$\flat$5) Pentatonic Scale	D$\flat$13	
D$\flat$ Mixolydian $\flat$9 (V7$\flat$9) Pentatonic Scale	D$\flat$7$\flat$9	more dissonant
Reharmonized Scale: Unaltered 5th		
D Locrian (viim7$\flat$5) Pentatonic Scale	Fm, Dm7$\flat$5, Fm6, Fm7	dissonant

The intervals and notes for these scales, as they relate to a G7 chord, are shown below.

INTERVALS -	Root	♭9	2/9	#9	3	4	♭5/#11	5	#5	6/13	♭7
G7 Chord	G				B			D			F
G Mixolydian (V7/I7) Pentatonic Scale	G		A		B			D			F
B Locrian (viim7♭5) Pentatonic Scale			A		B			D		E	F
G Major (E Minor) Pentatonic Scale	G		A		B			D		E	
G Mixolydian ♭9 (V7♭9) Pentatonic Scale	G	A♭			B			D			F
G Lydian Dominant (II7♭5) Pentatonic Scale			A				C#	D		E	F
D♭ Lydian Dominant (♭II7♭5) Pentatonic Scale	G	A♭		B♭	B				D#		
F Locrian (viim7♭5) Pentatonic Scale		A♭		B♭	B				D#		F
D♭ Mixolydian ♭9 (V7♭9) Pentatonic Scale		A♭			B		D♭	D			F
D Locrian (viim7♭5) Pentatonic Scale	G	A♭				C		D			F

Fig. 16A is a four-bar solo that uses the G Mixolydian pentatonic scale over a static G7 chord. **Fig. 16B** presents nine variations of the first three measures of the G7 phrase from Fig. 16A, resolving to a tonic Cmaj7 chord. These scales are described below.

Track 25

Fig. 16A
G7 Solo: G Mixolydian Pentatonic Scale

G Mixolydian (V7/I7) Pentatonic Scale: This scale was presented in Chapter 6. It is the most consonant scale for a Mixolydian dominant seventh chord and clearly outlines a G9 chord, a close extension of a G7 chord.

Track 25 (cont.)

Fig. 16B
G7 Progression: Substitute Pentatonic Scale Variations

B Locrian (viim7♭5) Pentatonic Scale: This scale was presented in Chapter 8. It represents an excellent—and preferred—scale substitution for the G Mixolydian (V7/I7) pentatonic scale. More importantly, it implies a "jazzier" G13 chord, making it an excellent companion to a preceding iim7 scale.

G Major (E Minor) Pentatonic Scale: This scale was presented in Chapter 1. Not at all dissonant, this scale lacks the dominant sound because of the absence of the 7th tone (in this case, F). However, it does have the upper extensions of a 9th and 13th, which imply a G13 chord.

G Mixolydian ♭9 (V7♭9) Pentatonic Scale: This scale was presented in Chapter 9 and is another excellent substitution for the G Mixolydian (V7/I7) pentatonic scale. As shown later in this chapter, this scale also makes a very smooth transition to a tonic minor (i minor) chord.

G7 Lydian Dominant (II7♭5) Pentatonic Scale: The Lydian Dominant (7♭5) pentatonic scale was discussed in Chapter 10. This scale is most useful over a dominant chord that functions as a II7 dominant chord in a progression.

In addition, the previous example demonstrates that, when used over a V7 dominant chord, the G7 Lydian Dominant pentatonic scale provides a nice, dissonant G13♯11 sound.

D♭ Lydian Dominant (♭II7♭5) Pentatonic Scale: Strictly speaking, this scale is not a substitution; instead, it is a reharmonization (i.e., changing the original chord). In this case, you would be performing a "flat five" reharmonization of the V7 chord (changing a V7 dominant chord to a ♭II7 dominant).

As described in Chapter 10, this type of reharmonization is done very frequently in jazz with regard to a Mixolydian (V7) or other dominant (e.g., III7, VI7, or VII7) chords. In fact, this reharmonized sound is very characteristic of solos by jazz guitarists such as Joe Pass and Wes Montgomery.

The previous example demonstrates how the D♭ Lydian Dominant pentatonic scale can be used as a flat five substitute scale when resolving to a Cmaj7 chord.

F Locrian (viim7♭5) Pentatonic Scale: This scale was presented in Chapter 8. As in the previous example, this scale is not a substitution, but rather a reharmonization of the original chord. In this case, you would be performing a flat five reharmonization of the V7 chord (changing a V7 dominant chord to a ♭II7 dominant). The basic difference between the F Locrian reharmonization and the previous D♭ Lydian Dominant (♭II7♭5) reharmonization is the "color" of the substitute ♭II7 chord. The D♭ Lydian Dominant (♭II7♭5) scale contains the sound of the ♭5th in the D♭7 chord, while the F Locrian pentatonic scale implies an unaltered (5th/9th) D♭13 chord.

D♭ Mixolydian ♭9 (V7♭9) Pentatonic Scale: This scale was presented in Chapter 9. As in the previous example, this scale is not a scale substitution; instead, it is a reharmonization (i.e., changing the original chord). In this case, you would be performing a fundamental flat five (tritone) reharmonization—G7 dominant chord reharmonized with a D♭7 dominant chord.

D Locrian (viim7♭5) Pentatonic Scale: This scale is also a reharmonization (i.e., changing the original chord). Here, the basic quality of the chord is changed from a dominant tonality to a minor tonality. This type of reharmonization is performed very frequently in jazz.

A very common jazz reharmonization is to replace a G7 (moving to a Cmaj7) with the sound of Fm, Fm6, Fm7, Fm9, or Dm7♭5. All of these chords are functionally equivalent (i.e., they have the same "sound" and serve the same function when moving to a Cmaj7 [Imaj7] chord).

In summary, a G7 Mixolydian dominant chord can be covered with nine variations of five of the pentatonic scales presented in Section 1.

These include:

1. The Basic Major Pentatonic Scale (Chapter 1)
    G Major Pentatonic Scale

2. The Mixolydian Pentatonic Scale (Chapter 6)
    G Mixolydian (V7/I7) Pentatonic Scale

3. The Locrian Pentatonic Scale (Chapter 8)
    B Locrian (viim7♭5) Pentatonic Scale
    F Locrian (viim7♭5) Pentatonic Scale
    D Locrian (viim7♭5) Pentatonic Scale

4. The Lydian Dominant Pentatonic Scale (Chapter 10)
    D♭ Lydian Dominant (7♭5) Pentatonic Scale
    G Lydian Dominant (7♭5) Pentatonic Scale

5. The Mixolydian ♭9 Pentatonic Scale (Chapter 9)
    G Mixolydian ♭9 (V7♭9) Pentatonic Scale
    D♭ Mixolydian ♭9 (V7♭9) Pentatonic Scale

No matter which notes you play, all of these scales will sound correct. Moreover, all of these scales use patterns that have already been learned, so it is simply a matter of deciding what specific "colors" you wish to use for your solo.

Although dominant chords most often resolve to minor or major chords, not all of the eight scales work for resolving to a minor chord. In general, a dominant seventh chord scale with a 9th, 13th, or ♭5th does not resolve correctly to a minor chord. Dominant seventh chord scales with a ♯5th and/or ♭9th work the best. For example, while all nine scales in this chapter will resolve nicely to a C major chord, only the following four G pentatonic chord scale substitutes/reharmonizations work best for resolving to a Cm chord.

- G Mixolydian ♭9 (V7♭9) Pentatonic Scale
- D♭ Lydian Dominant (♭II7♭5) Pentatonic Scale
- F Locrian (viim7♭5) Pentatonic Scale
- D Locrian (viim7♭5) Pentatonic Scale

Using the aforementioned pentatonic scales and resolving to a tonic Cm chord, **Fig. 16C** includes four variations of the first three measures of the G7 phrase in Fig. 16A.

Fig. 16C

G7–Cm Progression: Substitute Pentatonic Scale Variations

Summary

This chapter has presented a wealth of pentatonic scale alternatives for covering a dominant seventh chord.

CHAPTER 17
A AEOLIAN (vim7) PENTATONIC SCALE
SUBSTITUTIONS

The A Aeolian (vim7) pentatonic scale was presented in Chapter 7. This scale can be used to cover any chord that functions as an Aeolian minor chord. Examples of Aeolian minor chords in the key of C are:

| Am | Am7 | Am9 | Am11 |

The A Aeolian (vim7) pentatonic scale consists of the following five scale tones (notes):

$1-2-{\flat}3-5-{\flat}7$ (A–B–C–E–G)

This scale provides a very rich minor seventh/ninth sound. For additional "color" choices, five alternate pentatonic scales can be used over an Am7 chord functioning as a vim7 chord. Therefore, you have six pentatonic scale choices for soloing over an Am7 chord, using only scales that have been previously learned.

The six choices for soloing over an Am7 Aeolian chord are listed below in order of consonance. For an Am7 chord, the A Aeolian (vim7) pentatonic scale is the most consonant, while the E${\flat}$ Lydian Dominant (7${\flat}$5) pentatonic scale (a reharmonization) is the most dissonant.

Basic Scale	Chord	
A Aeolian (vim7) Pentatonic Scale	Am7	consonant
Substitute Scale		
A Minor Pentatonic Scale	Am7	
C Ionian (Imaj7) Pentatonic Scale	Am9	
E Minor Pentatonic Scale	Am11	
Reharmonized Scale		
A Mixolydian ${\flat}$9 (V7${\flat}$9) Pentatonic Scale	A7${\flat}$9	
E${\flat}$ Lydian Dominant (7${\flat}$5) Pentatonic Scale	E${\flat}$7${\flat}$5	dissonant

The intervals and notes for these scales, as they relate to an Am7 chord, are shown below.

INTERVALS -	Root	${\flat}$2nd	2nd	${\flat}$3rd	4th	5th	${\sharp}$5th	${\flat}$7th
Am7 Chord	A			C		E		G
A Aeolian (vim7) Pentatonic Scale	A		B	C		E		G
A Minor Pentatonic Scale	A			C	D	E		G
C Ionian (Imaj7) Pentatonic Scale			B	C	D	E		G
E Minor Pentatonic Scale	A		B		D	E		G
A Mixolydian ${\flat}$9 (V7${\flat}$9) Pentatonic Scale	A	B${\flat}$		C${\sharp}$*		E		G
E${\flat}$ Lydian Dominant (7${\flat}$5) Pentatonic Scale	A	B${\flat}$		C, C${\sharp}$*			F	

*major 3rd

Fig. 17A is a four-bar solo that uses the A Aeolian pentatonic scale over a static Am7 chord. Using the substitute scales described in this chapter, Fig. 17B presents three variations of this solo. Fig. 17C–D demonstrate the use of reharmonized scales—as opposed to substitute scales—for the Am7 (vim7) chord.

Track 26

Fig. 17A
Am7 Solo: A Aeolian Pentatonic Scale

A Aeolian (vim7) Pentatonic Scale: This scale was presented in Chapter 7. It is the most consonant scale for an Aeolian Am7 chord and implies the sound of an Am9 chord.

A Aeolian - Mode I

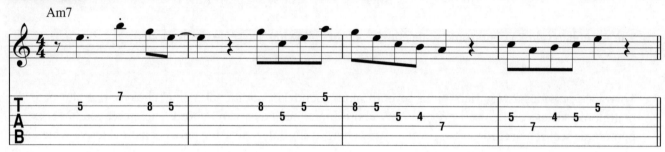

Track 26 (cont.)

Fig. 17B
Am7 Solo: Substitute Pentatonic Scale Variations

A Minor Pentatonic Scale: This is the standard minor pentatonic scale that was described in Chapter 1. The biggest advantage of this scale is its familiarity—you already know it. The disadvantage is its blandness. Beyond the ♭7th note, there is no strong color tone. Without a complementary 2nd/9th note, the 4th does not add character to this scale. In general, this scale will sound better over a vim7 chord of long duration in a progression. It is important to note that this scale can also be referred to as an A Phrygian (iiim7) pentatonic scale (i.e., they are the same scale). However, in the context of a vim7 chord, it is more logical to think of the scale as an A minor pentatonic scale.

A Minor - Mode I

C Ionian (Imaj7) Pentatonic Scale: This scale is an excellent substitute for the A Aeolian (vim7) pentatonic scale, which was presented in Chapter 2. Since an Am7 or Am9 can be used as a direct substitute for a Cmaj7 Ionian chord, the C Ionian pentatonic scale is a direct substitution for an A Aeolian pentatonic scale. The C Ionian pentatonic scale sounds very rich with the inclusion of the 9th and 11th upper extensions.

C Ionian - Mode VII

E Minor Pentatonic Scale: This scale was presented in Chapter 1. The absence of the minor 3rd of the vim7 chord, coupled with the higher extensions of a 9th and 11th, give this scale a very "open" sound over a vim7 chord.

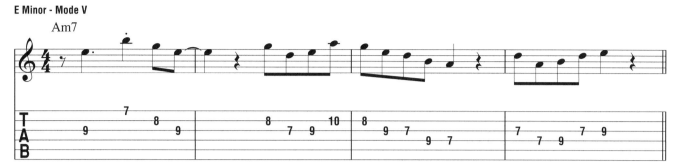

Fig. 17C

Am7 Progression: A Mixolydian ♭9 Pentatonic Scale Reharmonization

Track 26 (cont.)

A Mixolydian ♭9 (V7♭9) Pentatonic Scale: Strictly speaking, this scale is not a substitution; instead, it is a reharmonization (i.e., changing the original chord). In this case, the basic quality of the chord is changed from minor to dominant. With respect to an Aeolian (vim7) chord, this type of reharmonization is used frequently in jazz.

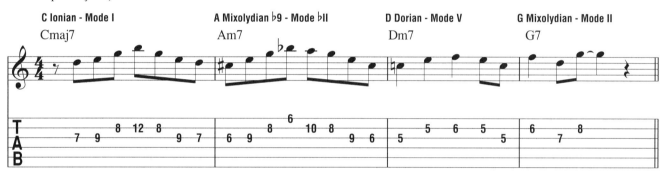

Review the chord progression below:

A very common jazz reharmonization of this progression replaces the Am7 with an A7♭9. Now the progression would become:

Here, the A Mixolydian ♭9 pentatonic scale is better suited for the A7♭9 chord. In practice, you could even make this scale substitution without changing the Am7. The ear accepts this superimposition because an Am7 chord is very close in sound to an A7♯9 chord, which, in turn, is a very close substitution for the A7♭9 chord. Fig. 17C is an example of using the A Mixolydian b9 pentatonic scale over an Am7 in the aforementioned progression.

Fig. 17D

Am7 Progression: E♭ Lydian Dominant Pentatonic Scale Reharmonization

Track 26 (cont.)

E♭ Lydian Dominant (7♭5) Pentatonic Scale: Technically, this scale is not a substitution, but rather a reharmonization (i.e., changing the original chord). Here, a "flat five" reharmonization is performed over the A7♭9 chord, which itself is a reharmonization of the Am7. Once again, the basic quality of the original vim7 chord is changed from minor to dominant. With respect to an Aeolian (vim7) chord, this type of reharmonization is done very frequently in jazz.

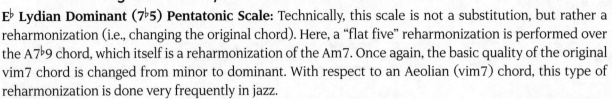

Review the chord progression below:

As presented earlier, the jazz reharmonization of this progression is to replace the Am7 with an A7♭9:

Now if we reharmonize the A7♭9 with a tritone substitution (i.e., flat five substitution), we get the following progression:

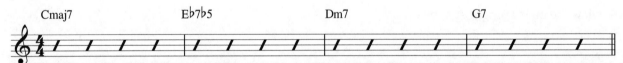

Consequently, the E♭7♭5 chord would be perfectly covered with an E♭ Lydian Dominant pentatonic scale. Fig. 17D illustrates an example of using the E♭ Lydian Dominant pentatonic scale over an Am7 chord in the Cmaj7–Am7–Dm7–G7 progression.

Summary

An Am7 Aeolian minor chord can be covered with six of the scales presented in Section 1. All of the scales will sound correct, no matter which notes you play. Further, all of the scales use patterns that have already been learned, so it is simply a matter of deciding what specific "colors" you wish to use for your solo.

CHAPTER 18

B LOCRIAN (viim7♭5, iim7♭5) PENTATONIC SCALE SUBSTITUTIONS

The B Locrian pentatonic scale was introduced in Chapter 8. This scale can be used to cover any chord that functions as a minor seventh flat five chord, including minor seventh flat five chords in the key of C (viim7♭5 = Bm7♭5) or Am (iim7♭5 = Bm7♭5).

The B Locrian pentatonic scale consists of the following five scale tones (notes):

$$1-♭3-4-♭5-♭7 \ \ (B-D-E-F-A)$$

The minor seventh flat five chord is primarily used as a iim7♭5 chord in the iim7♭5–V7–im chord progression in jazz, Latin, and popular music. For additional "color" choices, three other pentatonic scales can also be used as substitutes for a Bm7♭5 chord functioning as a iim7♭5 chord. Therefore, by using only scales that have been previously learned, you have four pentatonic scale choices for soloing over a Bm7♭5 chord.

The four choices are listed below in order of consonance. For a Bm7♭5 chord, the B Locrian pentatonic scale is the most consonant, although the D Dorian (iim7) pentatonic scale is very close. The F Lydian (IVmaj7) pentatonic scale is less consonant.

Basic Scale	Chord	
B Locrian (iim7♭5) Pentatonic Scale	Bm7♭5	consonant
Substitute Scale		
D Dorian (iim7) Pentatonic Scale	Dm9	
D Minor Pentatonic Scale	Dm7	
F Lydian (IVmaj7) Pentatonic Scale	Fmaj9	less consonant

The intervals and notes for these scales, as they relate to a Bm7♭5 chord, are shown below.

INTERVALS -	Root	♭9th	♭3rd	4th	♭5th	♭6th	♭7th
Bm7♭5 Chord	B		D		F		A
B Locrian (iim7♭5) Pentatonic Scale	B		D	E	F		A
D Dorian (iim7) Pentatonic Scale		C	D	E	F		A
D Minor Pentatonic Scale		C	D		F	G	A
F Lydian (IVmaj7) Pentatonic Scale		C		E	F	G	A

Fig. 18A is a four-bar solo using the B Locrian pentatonic scale over a static Bm7♭5 chord. Using the substitute scales described in this chapter, **Fig. 18B** includes three variations of this solo.

Track 27

Fig. 18A
Bm7♭5 Solo: B Locrian Pentatonic Scale

B Locrian (iim7♭5) Pentatonic Scale: This scale was presented in Chapter 8. It is the most consonant scale for a Bm7♭5 chord and implies the sound of a Bm11♭5 chord. It works perfectly for a Bm7♭5 chord that functions as either a iim7♭5 chord from the A harmonic-minor scale or a viim7♭5 chord from the C major scale.

B Locrian - Mode ♭VII

Bm7♭5

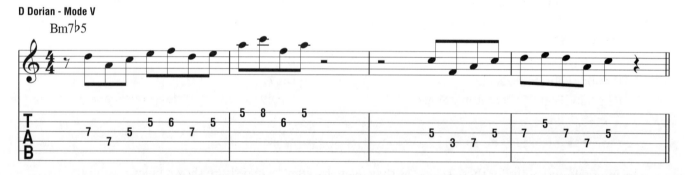

Track 27 (cont.)

Fig. 18B
Substitute Pentatonic Scale Variations

D Dorian (iim7) Pentatonic Scale: This scale was presented in Chapter 3. Like the B Locrian pentatonic scale, it is a very consonant scale for a Bm7♭5 chord. While it lacks the root of the Bm7♭5, it contains the ♭3rd, ♭7th, ♭5th, and 11th of the chord.

D Dorian - Mode V

Bm7♭5

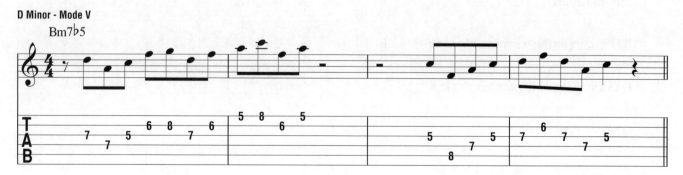

D Minor Pentatonic Scale: This scale was presented in Chapter 1. The major strength of this scale is its familiarity. Also, it flows nicely into either the V7♭9 chord or even straight to the tonic minor chord (in this case, the Am chord).

D Minor - Mode V

Bm7♭5

F Lydian (IVmaj7) Pentatonic Scale: This scale was presented in Chapter 5. While this scale provides a ♭7th and ♭5th of a minor seventh flat five chord, it is more ambiguous because it lacks the important ♭3rd tone and the root.

F Lydian - Mode III

Summary

A Bm7♭5 chord can be covered with four of the scales presented in Section 1. All of the scales will sound correct, no matter which notes you play. All of the scales use patterns that have already been learned, so it is simply a matter of deciding what specific "colors" you wish to use for your solo. Using the Locrian pentatonic scale in the context of major and minor II–V–I progressions will be covered in Chapter 26.

SECTION 3

Symmetrical Pentatonic Scales

This section introduces a pentatonic approach to improvising over chords that are built upon two symmetrical scales—the diminished scale and the whole tone scale. These scales are unique in that the intervals between notes in the scale are symmetrical. In the case of the diminished scale, all of the notes are either a whole step (two frets) or a half step (one fret) apart. In the case of the whole tone scale, the notes are all a whole step (two frets) apart. Chords built from these scales are very important in jazz, particularly with respect to passing chords and reharmonized chords.

The pentatonic approach described in this section will enable you to understand the role of diminished chords in jazz. Consequently, you will be able to use pentatonic scales that you have already learned in previous chapters to cover every situation that involves diminished chords.

The pentatonic approach described in this section for whole tone chords will enable you to greatly expand your options for playing over altered dominant chords.

CHAPTER 19
DIMINISHED PENTATONIC SCALE

Diminished chords provide useful "colors" to a chord progression and are also very useful as passing chords. However, soloing over diminished chords is a difficult challenge. Virtually all jazz theory books recommend using a diminished scale as the primary choice for improvising over a diminished chord. While this approach is "theoretically" correct, it is not useful in an actual playing situation for several reasons that will be discussed in this chapter. Instead, this chapter illustrates how using two different pentatonic scales, already covered in earlier chapters, are the most effective option for soloing over the three possible diminished chords (I°, #I°, and II°).

C°7 Chord Description

The diminished and diminished seventh chords are unique in that they do not have a true tonal center. The sound of the diminished chord is one of tension and ambiguity—it sounds as though it needs to resolve. Because of this tension and ambiguity, the diminished chord is very useful in chord-melody playing and as a passing chord while comping.

The notes of a C° chord are:

C	E♭	G♭
Root	♭3rd	♭5th

Adding a fourth note a minor 3rd above the diminished triad results in a diminished seventh chord.

The notes of a C°7 chord are:

C	E♭	G♭	A
Root	♭3rd	♭5th	♭♭7th

Each note in the chord is a minor 3rd (three frets) apart. Each of the notes in the chord can also be considered the root, as shown below. In effect, the chords are interchangeable since they are all built with the same notes.

$$C°7 \quad = \quad E♭°7 \quad = \quad G♭°7 \quad = \quad A°7$$

If you move up one half step from C°7, you get a second set of interchangeable diminished chords, as shown below.

$$D♭°7 \quad = \quad E°7 \quad = \quad G°7 \quad = \quad B♭°7$$

Moving up yet another half step gives you the third set of diminished chords:

$$D°7 \quad = \quad F°7 \quad = \quad A♭°7 \quad = \quad B°7$$

Therefore, there are really only three sets of diminished chords. If you move up an additional half step from D°7, you would get E♭°7—which is part of the first set of diminished chords. (Note: for purposes of this book, the terms "diminished" and "diminished seventh" are used interchangeably.)

Really, only three distinct diminished seventh chords exist, and they can be notated in any of the following ways:

Idim7	#Idim7	IIdim7
I°7	#I°7	II°7

The sets of equivalent diminished seventh chords are shown below.

I°7	=	♭III°7	=	♭V°7	=	VI°7
♯I°7	=	III°7	=	V°7	=	♭VII°7
II°7	=	IV°7	=	♭VI°7	=	VII°7

Here they are translated into chords:

C°7	=	E♭°7	=	G♭°7	=	A°7
C♯°7	=	E°7	=	G°7	=	B♭°7
D°7	=	F°7	=	A♭°7	=	B°7

Once again, notice that each set of related diminished chords contains the same notes that move up or down symmetrically by minor 3rds (three frets/half steps). These sets are important to understand because there is no real standard that is used when notating diminished chords in songs or fake books. This means that, for soloing purposes, you have to figure out if the diminished chord is functioning as a I°7, ♯I°7, or II°7 chord, independent of which inversion is notated in the music. For example, review the progression below.

C	B♭°7	Dm7	G7
C	G°7	Dm7	G7
C	E°7	Dm7	G7
C	C♯°7	Dm7	G7

All of these diminished chords will sound "right" since they are all built from the same notes. However, for soloing purposes, it is important to understand if the diminished chord is functioning as a I°7, ♯I°7, or II°7 chord. Put another way, only one of the above progressions is truly notated "correctly." This is covered in the next section of this chapter.

For a guitarist, there are basically four practical chord shapes for the diminished seventh chord. They are shown in **Fig. 19A** for a C°7 (root in the bass).

Fig. 19A

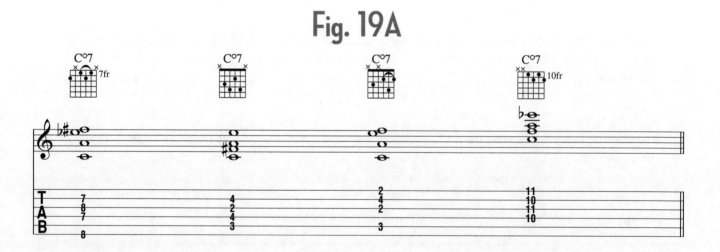

Descriptions of the Two Diminished Scales

Diminished chords are built from either of two eight-note diminished scales. Both scales contain eight notes and a symmetrical pattern of intervals between those notes.

- Diminished (whole step/half step): contains a whole step between the first and second notes
- Diminished (half step/whole step): contains a half step between the first and second notes

The two diminished scales are demonstrated below with a C°7 chord (chord tones are in bold type).

C Diminished Scale (whole step/half step)

C	D	**E♭**	F	**G♭**	A♭	**A**	B

- Non–chord tones are a half step below the next chord tone (half-step approach note for each chord tone)
- Chord choices: C°, C°7, Cm7♭5
- Also known as Auxiliary Diminished Scale (George Russell, 1959)

C Diminished Scale (half step/whole step)

C	D♭	**E♭**	E	**G♭**	G	**A**	B♭

- Non–chord tones are a whole step below the next chord tone
- Chord choices: C7♭9, C7♯9, C13♭9, C13♯9
- Also known as Auxiliary Diminished Blues Scale (George Russell, 1959)

There is a lot of theory and opinion in regard to soloing over a diminished chord. The most comprehensive study on the application of diminished scales is found in *The Lydian Chromatic Concept of Tonal Organization* by George Russell. This book is very deep and requires a lot of advanced study and practice to assimilate. It is recommended for advanced studies in improvisation. However, as you will see, this chapter takes a much simpler approach.

Below is a summary of standard options for soloing over a diminished chord.

- Ignore the diminished chord, particularly if its duration is one or two beats. It is probably only a passing chord, anyway.
- Ignore the diminished chord. It is probably a wrong chord. In song folios and fake books, the diminished chord is notorious for being notated incorrectly or being just plain wrong.
- Use three-note or four-note arpeggio patterns.
- Use one of the two diminished scales. The challenge is figuring out which one to use. One approach is to try both to hear which sounds better to you. Another approach is to figure out if the chord is a true diminished chord or a mislabeled V7♭9 chord. This will be discussed shortly.

Any of the aforementioned approaches will work. However, for a diminished/diminished seventh chord, this chapter offers a much more effective approach.

What Is "Wrong" with the Diminished Scale

When soloing over a diminished or diminished seventh chord, using the appropriate eight-note diminished scale is theoretically correct. However, with eight notes, this scale is very harmonically rich. For a diminished seventh chord that is functioning as a rootless dominant seventh ♭9 chord, the half step/whole step diminished scale built from the root of said dominant chord contains the ♭9, ♯9, ♭5, and 13th tones, in addition to the root, 3rd, 5th, and ♭7th. For example, if, in the key of C, you have a B°7 (B–D–F–A♭) functioning as a G7♭9 chord, the G half/whole diminished scale will contain the root (G), ♭9th (A♭), ♯9th (B♭), 3rd (B), ♯11th/♭5th (C♯), 5th (D), 13th (E), and ♭7th (F). This is a lot of harmonic complexity, especially if all that is desired is the sound of a dominant seventh ♭9 chord.

Also, if the diminished scale is "forced" over a diminished chord, it sounds "forced." Too much attention is brought to this scale, thus it will probably interfere with the melodic continuity of what is played before and after the diminished chord. What this means in a practical playing situation is that you must consciously avoid certain notes so that unwanted harmonic complexity is not introduced into your solo. Furthermore, most diminished chords only appear for two beats in a chord progression. Unless a diminished scale is simply played at a fast speed, you will need to make instant note choices of less than eight notes. Once again, you are faced with the challenge avoiding certain notes.

Pentatonic Scale Alternatives to the Diminished Scale

Instead of using a diminished scale, this chapter illustrates how all diminished chords can be handled with one of two pentatonic scales from Chapters 9 and 11: the major blues pentatonic scale (for I°7 chords) or the Mixolydian ♭9 pentatonic scale (for #I°7 or II°7 chords).

The Major Blues Pentatonic Scale

The major blues pentatonic scale (Chapter 11) should be used for I°7 (= ♭III°7 = ♭V°7 = VI°7) chords. It consists of the following five scale tones (notes):

$$1-2-♭3-5-6$$

To demonstrate how well the major blues pentatonic scale works for the I°7/♭III°7/♭V°7/ VI°7 chord, below is a standard jazz chord progression:

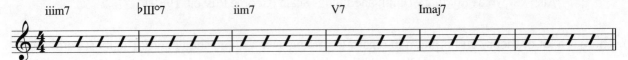

This chord progression appears in many standard, jazz, and bossa-nova songs. For example, below are the last six measures of the chord progression to "All the Things You Are" (key of A♭).

If one of the inversions of a diminished chord has the same root as the key of the progression (the tonic), it can be considered a I°7. In the previous case, the B°7 (♭III°7) chord is an inversion of an A♭°7 chord. Therefore, the A♭ major blues pentatonic scale (A♭–B♭–B–E♭–F) is the "correct" scale choice for the B°7 chord in this example.

Another example of this progression is the bridge to "Meditation":

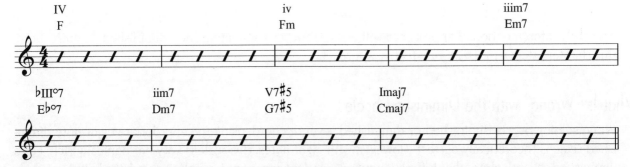

Notice that the E♭°7 chord is a ♭III°7 chord, which is equivalent to a I°7 (C°7) chord. Therefore, the C major blues pentatonic scale (C–D–E♭–G–A) is the correct scale choice.

A third example can be found in measures 9–16 of "Night and Day":

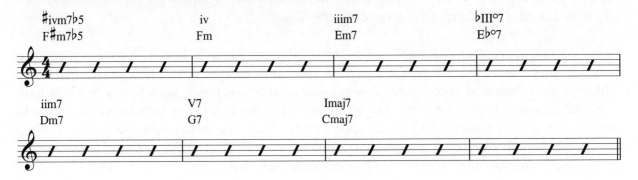

As in the previous example, the E♭°7 chord is a ♭III°7 chord, which is equivalent to a I°7 (C°7) chord and would be covered by the C major blues pentatonic scale.

Fig. 19B is an example solo over this chord progression in the key of A♭. Notice how well the A♭ major blues pentatonic scale works with the other pentatonic chord scales.

Fig. 19B
Major Blues Pentatonic Scale: For ♭III Diminished Seventh Chord

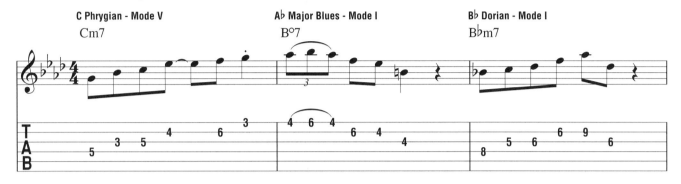

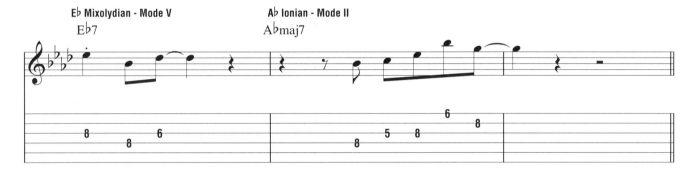

The Mixolydian ♭9 Pentatonic Scale

The Mixolydian ♭9 pentatonic scale (Chapter 9) should be used for chords functioning as ♯I°7 or II°7 chords. It consists of the following five scale tones (notes):

$$1 - ♭2 - 3 - 5 - ♭7$$

Most diminished chords notated in jazz, Latin, and pop music are mislabeled. They are really rootless V7♭9 chords that are moving to a Imaj7, iim7, IV, V7/I7, or vim7/VI7 chord. The Mixolydian ♭9 pentatonic scale should be used for these types of diminished chords. This is the situation for all ♯I°7 and II°7 chords, as shown below.

Diminished Chord Resolving to a Major Chord: If any note of the diminished seventh chord lies a half step below the major chord to which it resolves, it is actually a rootless 7♭9 chord a 4th (five steps) below the major chord. Therefore, the corresponding Mixolydian ♭9 pentatonic scale would be used.

For example, here is a common progression:

B°7 is an inversion of the D°7 chord. (B is a half step below C.) Therefore, the G Mixolydian ♭9 pentatonic scale (G–A♭–B–D–F) would be used because B°7 (D°7) is really functioning as a rootless G7♭9 chord [**Fig. 19C**].

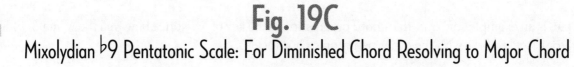

Fig. 19C
Mixolydian ♭9 Pentatonic Scale: For Diminished Chord Resolving to Major Chord

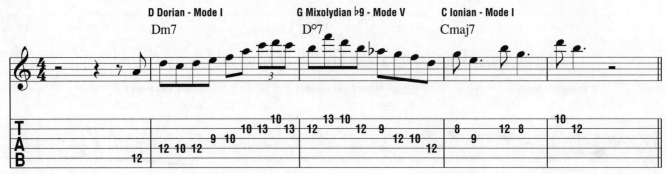

Diminished Chord Resolving to a Minor Chord: If any note of the diminished seventh chord lies one half step below the minor chord to which it resloves, it is actually a rootless 7♭9 chord a 4th (five steps) below the minor chord. Therefore, the corresponding Mixolydian ♭9 pentatonic scale would be used.

Below is a typical turnaround progression that includes a diminished chord moving to a iim7 chord.

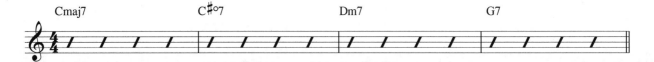

C♯ is a half step below D. Therefore, the A Mixolydian ♭9 pentatonic scale (A–B♭–C♯–E–G) would be used because C♯°7 is really functioning as a rootless A7♭9 chord [**Fig. 19D**].

Fig. 19D
Mixolydian ♭9 Pentatonic Scale: For Diminished Chord Resolving to Minor Chord

Diminished Chord Moving to a Dominant Chord: If any note of the diminished seventh chord is a half step above the following dominant chord, it is a rootless 7♭9 chord alteration of the dominant chord. Therefore, the corresponding Mixolydian ♭9 pentatonic scale would be used.

For example, here is a common progression:

A♭°7 is an inversion of the F°7 chord. (A♭ is a half step above G.) Therefore, the G Mixolydian ♭9 pentatonic scale (G–A♭–B–D–F) would be used because A♭°7 (F°7) is functioning as a rootless G7♭9 chord **[Fig. 19E]**.

Fig. 19E

Track 28 (cont.)

Mixolydian ♭9 Pentatonic Scale: For Diminished Chord Moving to Dominant Chord

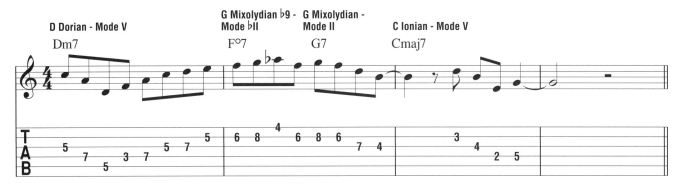

Diminished Chord Functioning as a ♭III°7 (♭V°7/VI°7/I°7): For the sake of "completeness," it should be noted that the Mixolydian ♭9 pentatonic scale, one half step below a ♭III°7 chord, can be used as an alternative to the tonic major blues pentatonic scale.

For example, in Fig. 19B, the A♭ major blues pentatonic scale was used to cover the B°7 chord, which is functioning as a ♭III°7 chord. As shown in **Fig. 19F**, the B♭ Mixolydian ♭9 pentatonic scale can also be used as an alternative scale choice. However, the major blues pentatonic scale is the preferred choice because it adds an important "bluesy" element to soloing over a chord progression that includes a ♭III°7 (♭V°7/VI°7/I°7) chord.

Fig. 19F

Track 28 (cont.)

Mixolydian ♭9 Pentatonic Scale: Alternate for Major Blues Pentatonic Scale

Sometimes No Pentatonic Scale Works

If it is difficult to figure out how a diminished chord is functioning in a chord progression, the best thing is to try the major blues pentatonic scale and the Mixolydian ♭9 pentatonic scale to see if one sounds "right." If a pentatonic scale that sounds "right" cannot be found, it is most probable that the diminished chord is incorrectly notated in the music. If there are melody notes over the diminished chord and they clash with the notes of the chord, this is a strong clue that the diminished chord is either incorrectly notated (i.e., missing a flat or a sharp) or does not belong in the music.

Lastly, you also have the option to "just forget about it." The diminished chord is probably only one or two beats in duration. Skipping it will generally not be a problem while soloing over the chord progression.

Summary

This chapter demonstrates how to improvise over diminished chords with two pentatonic scales—the major blues pentatonic scale and the Mixolydian ♭9 pentatonic scale. The major blues pentatonic scale is the recommended choice for all I°7 chords. The Mixolydian ♭9 pentatonic scale is the recommended choice for all ♯I°7 and II°7 chords.

CHAPTER 20
WHOLE TONE PENTATONIC SCALE

7♭5/9♭5 Chord Description

Dominant chords that are built from the whole tone scale are characterized by a ♭5th sound. For additional richness, a 9th can be added to these chords.

The whole tone scale is a six-note symmetrical scale that is unique in that each note in the scale is two frets apart.

For example, the G whole tone scale is shown below:

$$G-A-B-D♭-D♯-F$$

Two G dominant seventh chords that are built on the G whole tone scale are shown below:

$$G7♭5 \ (G-B-D♭-F)$$
$$G9♭5 \ (G-B-D♭-F-A)$$

An extremely important relationship exists between ♭5th chords and their ♭5th (tritone) inversions. For example, below are the notes for both the G7♭5 and the D♭7♭5.

G7♭5:	G	B	D♭	F
	Root	3rd	♭5th	♭7th

D♭7♭5:	D♭	F	G	B
	Root	3rd	♭5th	♭7th

Notice that both chords, G7♭5 and D♭7♭5, contain the same notes. This means that the chords are completely interchangeable. This relationship is called the tritone (♭5) substitution and is extremely important in jazz. Basically, a dominant ♭5 chord is interchangeable with a dominant ♭5 chord a ♭5th interval (six frets) apart. This concept can be generalized to include any dominant chord. The ♭5 substitution relationship allows the improviser to add a great deal of "jazzy" color to chord soloing, comping, and single-note soloing. However, chord voicings built upon the root or the ♭5th are the most practical.

Other related dominant chords are 9ths and ♯5ths (e.g., G9♭5, G9♯5, and G7♯5), as well as 9ths, ♭5ths, and ♯5ths from the related ♭5th dominant chord (e.g., D♭7♭5, D♭9♭5, D♭9♯5, and D♭7♯5). They can all be substituted freely, subject to desired bass leading and chord voicing movements.

G7/D♭9 Whole Tone Pentatonic Scale Description

The five-note whole tone pentatonic scale is based on the six-note whole tone scale. Furthermore, it is also based on the tritone relationship described earlier. In other words, each whole tone pentatonic scale is actually two whole tone pentatonic scales.

Fig. 20A shows the five fingerings for the G7/D♭9 whole tone pentatonic scale in music and tab notation, along with a fretboard diagram. Each pattern follows the two-notes-per-string rule. The initial chords are suggested voicings that are a good fit for each of the five patterns with respect to sound and proximity.

The scale consists of the following five scale tones (notes), which are common to both chords:

G7 (Mode I):	1	3	♭5	#5	♭7
	G	B	D♭	D#	F
D♭9 (Mode ♭V):	1	2	3	♭5	♭7
	D♭	D#	F	G	B

Fig. 20A
G7/D♭9 Whole Tone Pentatonic Scale

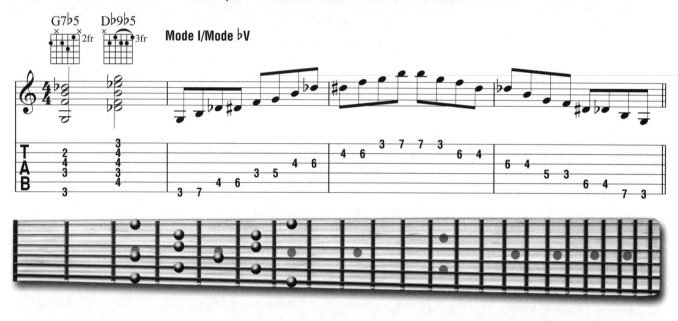

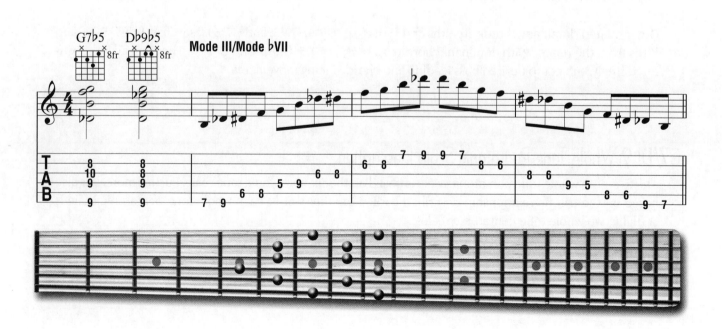

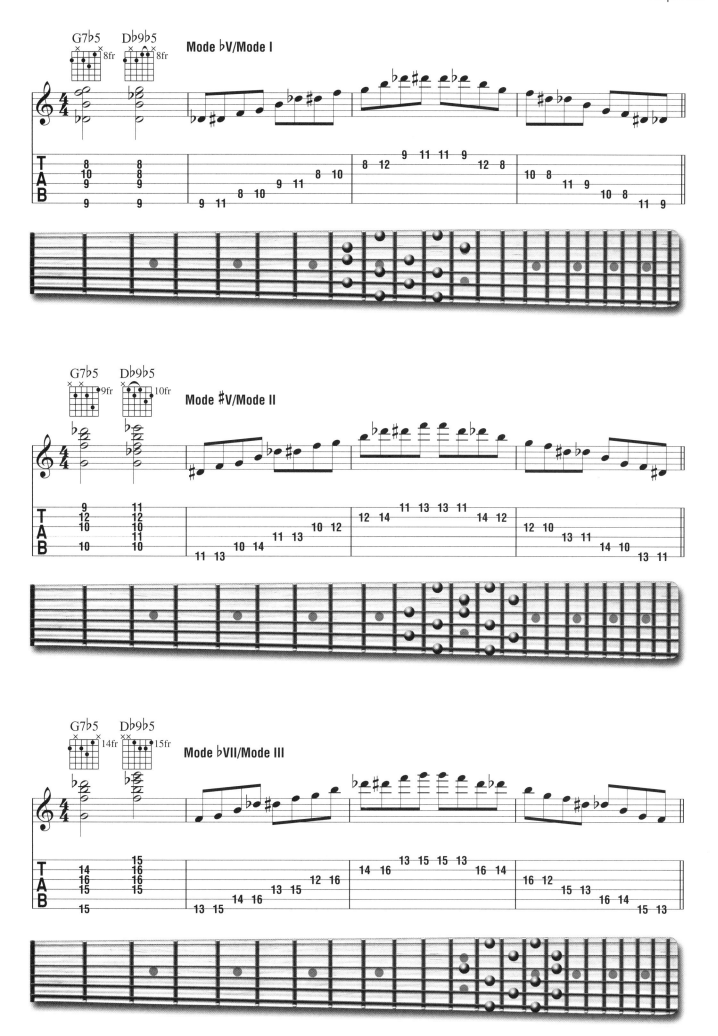

Fig. 20B shows the five fingerings for the D♭7/G9 whole tone pentatonic scale in music and tab notation, along with a fretboard diagram. Each pattern follows the two-notes-per-string rule. The initial chords are suggested voicings that are a good fit for each of the five patterns with respect to sound and proximity.

The scale consists of the following five scale tones (notes):

D♭7 (Mode I):	D♭	F	G	A	B
	Root	3rd	♭5th	♯5th	♭7th
G9 (Mode ♭V):	G	A	B	D♭	F
	Root	2nd	3rd	♭5th	♭7th

Fig. 20B
D♭7/G9 Whole Tone Pentatonic Scale

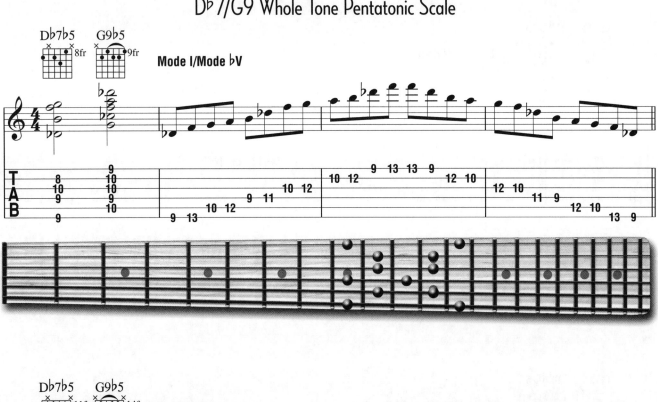

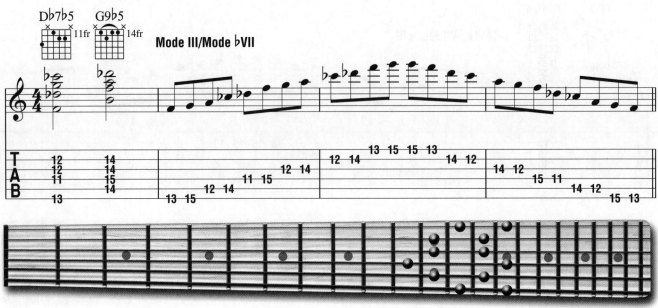

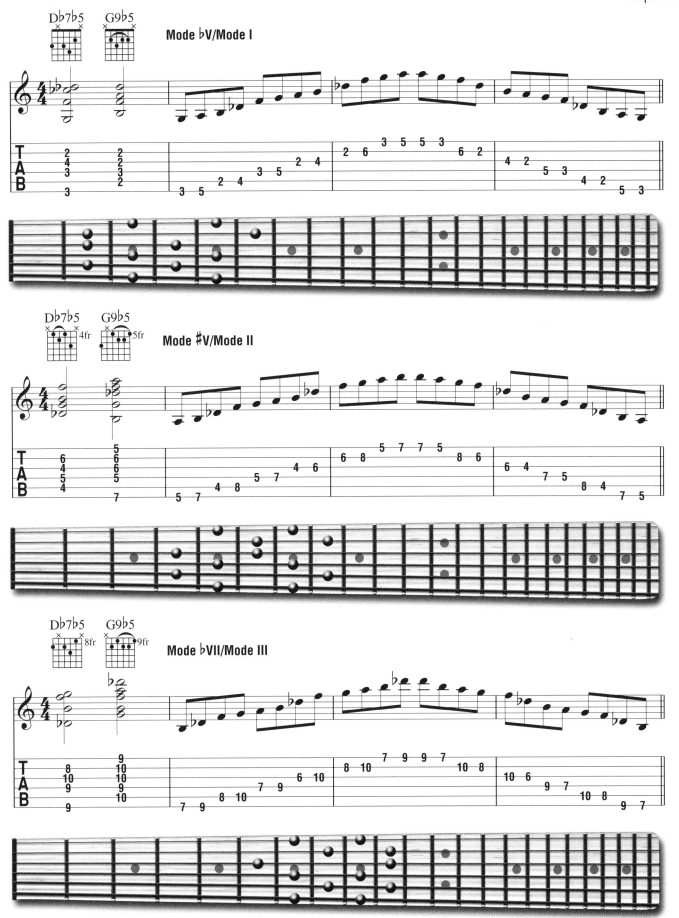

The whole tone pentatonic scale is useful in several ways. First, it covers the 7♭5 chord that occurs very frequently in jazz. Second, this scale is a great source of chromatic notes for connecting the scale tones. Because of the symmetrical nature of the scale, almost any chromaticism will sound good. Third, and most importantly, this scale can also be used for a 7♭5 chord that is a ♭5th (six frets) above or below the root chord. Even better, while the same scale can be used for two distinct 7♭5 chords (e.g., G7♭5 and D♭7♭5), it sounds different for each chord.

The G7 whole tone pentatonic scale below for Mode I (i.e., starts at the root) is the same scale as Mode ♭V of the D♭9 whole tone pentatonic scale.

G7♭5 Whole Tone Pentatonic Scale

(Mode I):	G	B	D♭	D♯	F
	Root	3rd	♭5th	♯5th	♭7th

D♭9 Whole Tone Pentatonic Scale

(Mode ♭V):	D♭	D♯	F	G	B
	Root	9th	3rd	♭5th	♭7th

Since the notes are exactly the same, the fingerings are also the same. However, the same scale will offer different colors, depending on the chord over which you are improvising.

Over a G7 chord, you will get both altered 5th colors (♭5th and ♯5th). Over a D♭7 chord, you will get the sound of higher extensions (9th), as well as emphasis on the ♭5th.

Specifically, Mode I of the G7 whole tone pentatonic scale can be called Mode ♭V of the D♭9 whole tone pentatonic scale. The reverse is also true: Mode I of the D♭9 whole tone pentatonic scale can be called Mode ♭V of the G7 whole tone pentatonic scale

Once again, both scales have the same notes and same fingerboard patterns. However, each scale will function in a different way for both related chords.

Look at what happens when we start with the D♭7 whole tone pentatonic scale (Mode I):

1–3–♭5–♯5–♭7 (D♭–F–G–A–B)

Notice below that the notes are the same, but the color tones for each chord have been switched.

D♭7 Whole Tone Pentatonic Scale

(Mode I):	D♭	F	G	A	B
	Root	3rd	♭5th	♯5th	♭7th

G9 Whole Tone Pentatonic Scale

(Mode ♭V):	G	A	B	D♭	F
	Root	9th	3rd	♭5th	♭7th

To show these relationships more clearly, the two whole tone pentatonic scales are grouped together below based on their root notes.

G7 Whole Tone Pentatonic Scale

(Mode I of G7♭5):	G	B	D♭	D♯	F
	Root	3rd	♭5th	♯5th	♭7th

G9 Whole Tone Pentatonic Scale

(Mode ♭V of D♭7♭5):	G	A	B	D♭	F
	Root	9th	3rd	♭5th	♭7th

D♭7 Whole Tone Pentatonic Scale

(Mode I of D♭7♭5):	D♭	F	G	A	B
	Root	3rd	♭5th	♯5th	♭7th

D♭9 Whole Tone Pentatonic Scale

(Mode ♭V of G7♭5):	D♭	D♯	F	G	B
	Root	9th	3rd	♭5th	♭7th

By playing the same pattern at two different locations on the fretboard, you get two different "color" variations of a 7♭5 chord.

For example, if you play Mode I of the G7 whole tone pentatonic scale, you would start at the third fret, playing the sound of a G7♭5♯5 chord. Now if you play the exact same pattern at the ninth fret (Mode I of the D♭7 whole tone pentatonic scale), you would get the sound of a G9♭5 chord and Mode ♭V of the G9 whole tone pentatonic scale.

The same relationship holds true for the D♭7♭5 chord. If you play Mode I of the D♭7 whole tone pentatonic scale, you would start at the ninth fret, playing the sound of a D♭7♭5♯5 chord. Now if you play the exact same pattern at the third fret (Mode I of the G7 whole tone pentatonic scale), you would get the sound of a D♭9♭5 chord and Mode ♭V of the D♭9 whole tone pentatonic scale.

These relationships are summarized below:

D♭7 Whole Tone Pentatonic Scale = G9 Whole Tone Pentatonic Scale

and

G7 Whole Tone Pentatonic Scale = D♭9 Whole Tone Pentatonic Scale

This can be a bit confusing at first, but with a little practice you get a really powerful improvising tool with this concept. Below is a simple exercise to help you get a basic feel for what is going on.

Improvise with Mode I (third position) of the G7 whole tone pentatonic scale over the G7♭5–D♭7♭5–G7♭5–D♭7♭5 chord progression in **Fig. 20C**.

Fig. 20C
Improvising with the G7 Whole Tone Pentatonic Scale

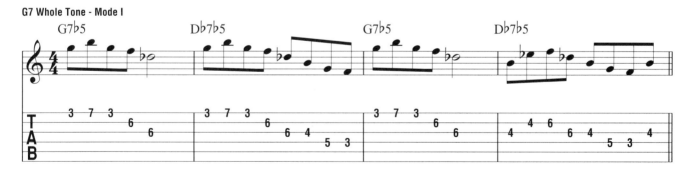

Even though the chords are both simple 7♭5 chords, the scale sounds different over each chord. In particular, the D♭7♭5 has a more complex 9th sound.

Now try to improvise with Mode I (ninth fret) of the D♭7 whole tone pentatonic scale over the same chord progression [Fig. 20D].

Fig. 20D

Improvising with the D♭7 Whole Tone Pentatonic Scale

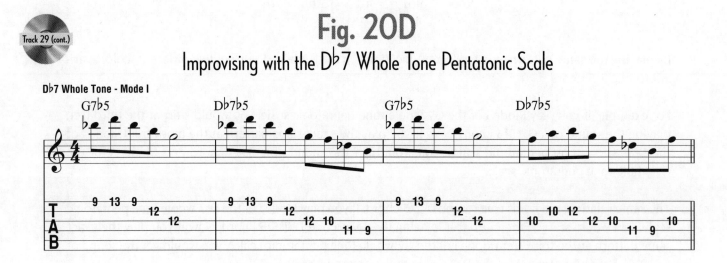

Once again, the scale sounds different over each chord. Now the G7♭5 has the 9th sound.

The added bonus is that you can cover 7♭5 chords by using the same patterns for the two whole tone pentatonic scales at different locations on the fretboard. This gives you tremendous flexibility when soloing. This is especially important for 7♭5 chords because they form the basis for much of the chord substitutions used in jazz.

Another way to get a feel for these relationships is to apply them to a real chord progression. Below is the standard chord progression that was described in Chapter 10, for which the D Lydian Dominant pentatonic scale was used to cover the D7♭5.

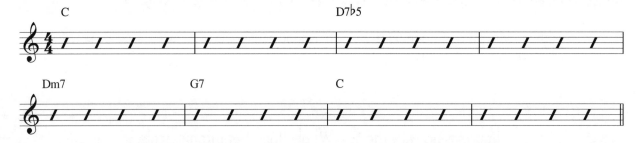

Fig. 20E demonstrates using the D7 (A♭9) whole tone pentatonic scale for the D7♭5 chord. **Fig. 20F** demonstrates using the A♭7 (D9) whole tone pentatonic scale for the D7♭5 chord.

Fig. 20E

D7 Whole Tone Pentatonic Scale: Chord Progression Example

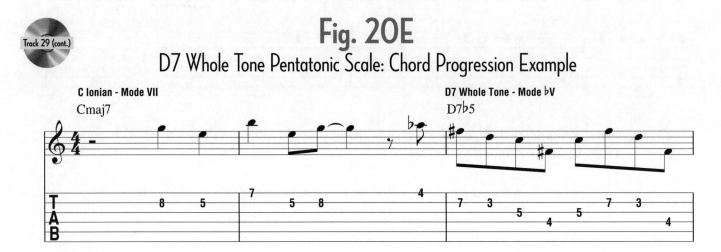

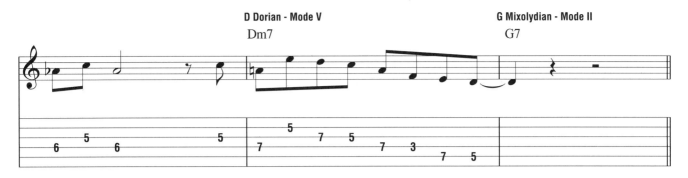

The D7 (A♭9) whole tone pentatonic scale will give the D7♭5 chord the colors of a ♭5th and a ♯5th.

Fig. 20F

A♭7 Whole Tone Pentatonic Scale: Chord Progression Example

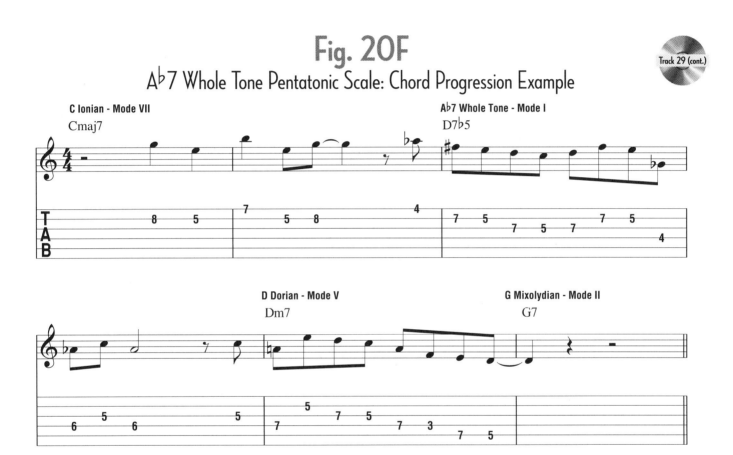

The A♭7 (D9) whole tone pentatonic scale will give the D7♭5 chord the colors of a 9th and a ♭5th and is the better choice in this situation.

Once again, the fingering patterns for the five modes of the D7♭5 whole tone pentatonic scale are identical to the fingering patterns for the five modes of the A♭7♭5 whole tone pentatonic scale. The only difference is that the corresponding modes start on different frets. For example, Mode I for the D7♭5 whole tone pentatonic scale starts at the tenth fret. Mode I for the A♭7♭5 whole tone pentatonic scale (which uses the exact same fingering pattern) starts at the fourth fret.

As was described for the Lydian Dominant pentatonic scale in Chapter 10, there are many songs for which the whole tone pentatonic scale is very useful. For example, songs like "Girl from Ipanema," "Take the A Train," and " Desifinado" start with a Imaj7 chord that moves to a II7 (dominant) chord. Many jazz methods suggest using a Mixolydian scale over the II7 chord. However, this does not really sound "correct." If you are going to use a seven-note scale, the Lydian Dominant seven-note scale (Mixolydian scale with a ♯4th) is a better choice because of the ♯4th leading tone. However, the whole tone pentatonic scale is more "guitar friendly" because it requires fewer notes and can easily be played in two-notes-per-string patterns. Most importantly, you will always have two whole tone pentatonic scales from which to choose, or you can even use (switch between) both.

Below is a comparison of the seven-note G Lydian Dominant scale and the related whole tone pentatonic scales. These scales could be used over any 7♭5 chord (in this case, a G7♭5 chord).

G Lydian Dominant	G	A	B	C♯/D♭	D		E	F
G7 Whole Tone Pentatonic (Mode I)	G		B	D♭/C♯		D♯		F
D♭9 Whole Tone Pentatonic (Mode ♭V)	G		B	D♭/C♯		D♯		F
D♭7 Whole Tone Pentatonic (Mode ♭V)	G	A	B	D♭				F
G9 Whole- Tone Pentatonic (Mode I)	G	A	B	D♭				F

The whole tone pentatonic scale is extremely useful for jazz tunes. As shown above, it can be used to cover 7♭5 chords.

Even more importantly, the whole tone pentatonic scale can be used as a ♭5 substitution scale for any dominant seventh chord. For example, below is a standard turnaround chord progression:

The A7 is a VI7 dominant chord, and the G7 is a V7 dominant chord. However, both can be covered by two different whole tone pentatonic scales. The chart below summarizes the relationships between the A7 (VI7) and G7 (V7) chords and the two discrete whole tone pentatonic scales that can be used to improvise over each chord. Once again, notice that the related whole tone pentatonic scales have the same notes.

A7 Chord	A		C♯		E		G
A7 Whole Tone Pentatonic Scale (Mode I)	A		C♯	E♭		F	G
E♭9 Whole Tone Pentatonic Scale (Mode ♭V)	A		C♯	E♭		F	G
E♭7 Whole Tone Pentatonic Scale (Mode ♭V)	A	B	C♯	E♭			G
A9 Whole Tone Pentatonic Scale (Mode I)	A	B	C♯	E♭			G

G7 Chord	G		B		D		F
D♭7 Whole Tone Pentatonic Scale (Mode ♭V)	G	A	B	D♭			F
G9 Whole Tone Pentatonic Scale (Mode I)	G	A	B	D♭			F
G7 Whole Tone Pentatonic Scale (Mode I)	G		B	D♭		D♯	F
D♭9 Whole Tone Pentatonic Scale (Mode ♭V)	G		B	D♭/D♭		D♯	F

In this example, there are two dominant chords in the progression. However, they have different functions. The A7 is a VI7 chord and is moving to a Dm7 (iim7) chord. The G7 is a V7 chord and is moving to a Cmaj7 (Imaj7) chord. Basically, this means that they have different "qualities." While either of the two whole tone pentatonic scale options will work for each chord, one sounds more "inside," depending on the function of the dominant seventh chord. **Fig. 20G** demonstrates these sounds.

Fig. 20G
Turnaround Using Whole Tone Pentatonic Scale Over Dominant Chords

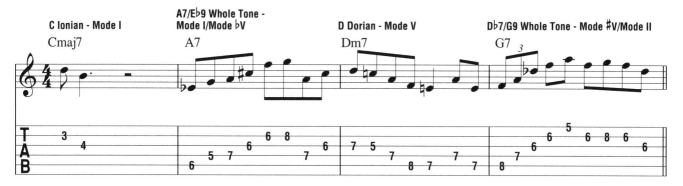

For the A7 (VI7) chord, the A7/E♭9 whole tone pentatonic scale sounds more "inside" because it has an F note that gives the A7 a ♯5th sound that leads nicely to a minor chord, which, in this case, is a Dm7.

For the G7 (V7) chord, the D♭7/G9 whole tone pentatonic scale sounds more "inside" because the only altered note is a ♭5th (D♭). This provides a strong resolution to a major chord, which, in this case, is a Cmaj7. However, the related whole tone pentatonic scales can be interchanged to get different resolution approaches for the dominant chords in this example.

Substitute Scale for the Whole Tone Pentatonic Scale

Recall from in Chapter 19 that, instead of a diminished pentatonic scale, two of the basic pentatonic scales in Section 1—the Mixolydian ♭9 pentatonic scale (Chapter 9) or major blues pentatonic scale (Chapter 11)—are used to cover diminished chords. The whole tone pentatonic scales described in this chapter can also be substituted with a basic pentatonic scale from Section 1—the Lydian Dominant pentatonic scale from Chapter 10. This scale can be used instead of the whole tone pentatonic scale. In fact, in most cases it is more desirable to use the Lydian Dominant pentatonic scale, especially if you want a less-dissonant sound.

The whole tone pentatonic scale and the Lydian Dominant pentatonic scale are compared below for a G7♭5 chord.

G7♭5 Chord	G		B	D♭			F
G7 Whole Tone Pentatonic Scale (Mode I)	G		B	D♭	D♯		F
G Lydian Dominant Pentatonic Scale (Mode II)		A		D♭	D	E	F

Notice that the G Lydian Dominant pentatonic scale is richer in higher-extension color tones such as the 9th (A) and 13th (E). Even though the Lydian Dominant pentatonic scale does not contain a root or 3rd, it is still better for conveying the "jazzy" sound of a 7♭5 chord when improvising because the notes clearly imply that the scale is built on the melodic (jazz) minor scale, as described in Chapter 10. Our ears have become accustomed to the sound of the melodic minor scale in jazz. In fact, the melodic minor scale is often referred to as the "jazz minor" scale.

To demonstrate these different sounds, **Fig. 20H** uses the E♭ Lydian Dominant and D♭ Lydian Dominant pentatonic scales to replace the A7/E♭9 whole tone and D♭7/G9 whole tone pentatonic scales from Fig. 20G.

Track 29 (cont.)

Fig. 20H
Turnaround Variation Using Lydian Dominant Over Dominant Chords

Summary

The Lydian Dominant pentatonic scale is most effective over a dominant 7♭5 chord. However, the whole tone pentatonic scale provides tremendous additional flexibility when dealing with 7♭5 chords and other altered dominant chords.

SECTION 4

Other Pentatonic Scales

This section describes five additional pentatonic scales that are useful in specific

situations. These scales provide additional options for soloing over a tonic minor

chord, a Lydian major seventh chord, or an altered dominant chord.

CHAPTER 21
MINOR (MAJOR SEVENTH) (im[maj7])
PENTATONIC SCALE

m(maj7) Chord Description

The minor triad (root–3rd–5th) is the most basic minor sound. However, this basic sound can be enhanced by adding a major 7th note to the triad to make it a four-note tonic minor chord.

One problem is deciding how to write this chord. There are many variations, some of which are presented below:

Am/Maj7	Am/maj7	Amin/maj7	AmMaj7	Am(Maj7)	Amin(Maj7)
Am-maj7	Am-Maj7	A-Δ7	AmΔ7	Am7	AminMa7
Ami(MA7)	AmMAJ7	AminMaj7			

For purposes of this book, I have chosen to use the following notation: Am(maj7)

The m(maj7) chord is built on the first degree of either the melodic (jazz) minor or harmonic minor scales. For example, the notes of the A melodic minor and harmonic minor scales are:

Melodic (Jazz) Minor:	A	B	C	D	E	F♯	G♯
Harmonic Minor:	A	B	C	D	E	F	G♯

> Notice that the only difference is the sixth degree of the scales. This difference is very important when soloing, because each scale fits a specific situation. For example, this book uses the following modes in each minor scale:
>
> | | | | |
> |---|---|---|---|
> | **Harmonic Minor:** | Mode V | Mixolydian ♭9 Pentatonic Scale | (Chapter 9) |
> | **Melodic (Jazz) Minor:** | Mode IV | Lydian Dominant Pentatonic Scale | (Chapter 10) |

However, Mode I of either scale can be used to build the im(maj7) chord.

The im(maj7) chord is built on the following degrees of either the melodic or harmonic minor scales:

$$1{-}{\flat}3{-}5{-}7$$

In the A melodic and harmonic minor scales, the notes for the im(maj7) chord are:

$$A{-}C{-}E{-}G{\sharp}$$

In addition to a m(maj7) voicing, any tonic minor triad voicing that you use will sound good. In fact, the im(maj7) chord is relatively rare. When it is designated in music, it will most often be part of the following minor chord sequence:

$$m{-}m(maj7){-}m7{-}m6$$

Using an Am chord, the following is an example of a basic chord sequence that includes the m(maj7) chord:

$$Am{-}Am(maj7){-}Am7{-}Am6$$

The first four measures of "My Funny Valentine" use this sequence.

Other related minor chords are m(maj9) and m(add9)—for example, Am(maj9) and Am(add9). They can be substituted freely, subject to desired bass leading and chord voicing movements.

A Minor (Major Seventh) Pentatonic Scale Description

The minor (major seventh) pentatonic scale can be used to cover the m(maj7) chord. It works well in combination with other tonic minor chords. It can also be used as a substitute scale for a dominant seventh flat five chord.

Fig. 21A shows the five fingerings for the A minor (major seventh) pentatonic scale in music and tab notation, along with a fretboard diagram. Each pattern follows the two-notes-per-string rule. The initial chords are suggested voicings that are a good fit for each of the five patterns with respect to sound and proximity.

The scale consists of the following five scale tones (notes):

$$1-{\flat}3-4-5-7 \quad (A–C–D–E–G{\sharp})$$

Fig. 21A
Am(maj7) (im[maj7]) Scales

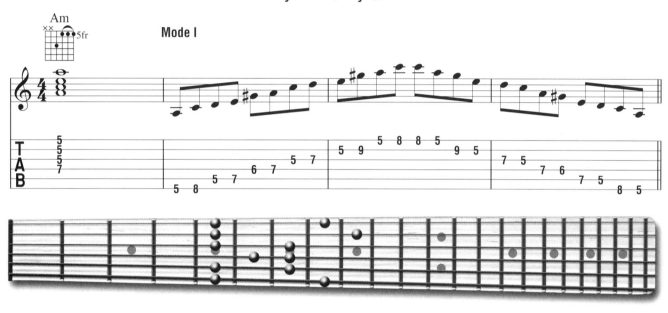

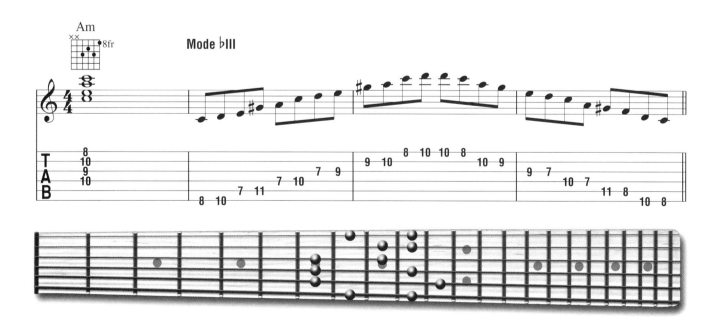

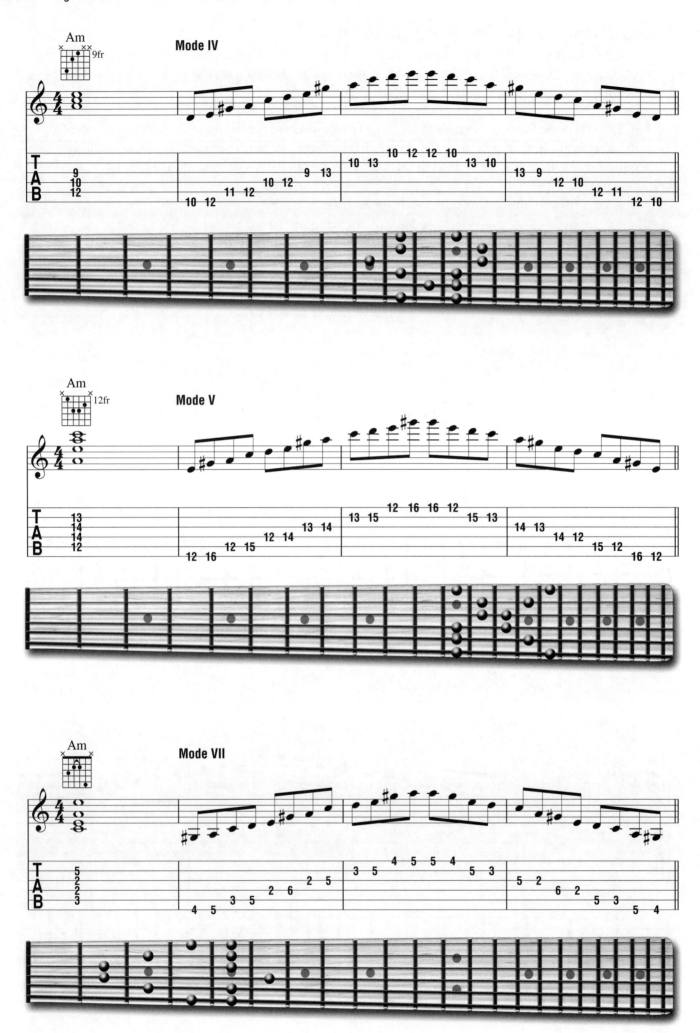

Fig. 21B contains three four-bar example solos that use the A minor-major seventh pentatonic scale.

Fig. 21B
Improvising with the Am(maj7) Pentatonic Scale

Track 30

The unique quality of this scale is the natural 7th, which makes it fit perfectly over a m(maj7) chord. It will also fit well over a tonic minor chord.

This scale is similar to the Phrygian pentatonic scale that was presented in Chapter 4 and the minor pentatonic scale that was presented in Chapter 1. The only difference is the major 7th note, which replaces the ♭7th note in the Phrygian and minor pentatonic scales.

These three scales are compared below:

A Minor (Major Seventh) Pentatonic Scale:	A	C	D	E	G♯
A Phrygian Pentatonic Scale:	A	C	D	E	G
A Minor Pentatonic Scale:	A	C	D	E	G

The interesting thing to note is that all three scales can be used for a minor tonic chord. In addition to its use in a minor (major 7th) vamp, as shown in Fig. 21B, the minor (major seventh) pentatonic scale sounds best as a temporary color scale for the im chord in a minor-tonality tune such as "Summertime" or "Black Orpheus."

For example, below is a common minor vamp progression. Play this progression with the root in the bass on the fourth string so that you get a downward chromatic bass movement.

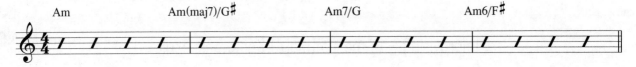

Fig. 21C is an example solo over this progression. Notice how the G♯, G, and F♯ notes are used in the solo to define the chord progression.

Fig. 21C
Improvising with the Am(maj7) Pentatonic Scale: Common Am Vamp

Am(maj7) - Mode I

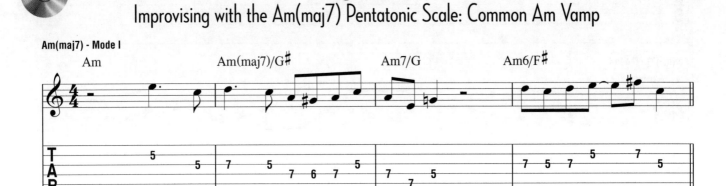

Substitute Scale for a Dominant Seventh Flat Five Chord

The minor (major seventh) pentatonic scale can also be used as a substitute scale for a dominant seventh flat five chord that is a 4th (five frets) above. For example, the A minor (major seventh) pentatonic scale can be used as a substitute scale for a D7♭5 or D9♯11 chord.

Pentatonic scales for the dominant seventh flat five chord were presented earlier in this book. These included the Lydian Dominant pentatonic scale (Chapter 10) and two related tritone (D7 and A♭7) whole tone pentatonic scales (Chapter 20). A comparison of these scales to the A minor (major seventh) pentatonic scale—for a D Lydian Dominant chord (D7♭5)—is shown below.

INTERVALS -	♭5th/♯11th	5th	♯5th	13th	♭7th	root	9th	3rd
D7♭5 Chord	A♭				C	D		F♯
A Minor (Major Seventh) Pentatonic Scale (D9♯11)	G♯ (A♭)	A			C	D	E	
D Lydian Dominant Pentatonic Scale (D13♯11)	G♯ (A♭)	A		B	C		E	
D Whole Tone Pentatonic Scale (D9alt)	A♭		A♯		C	D		F♯
A♭ Whole Tone Pentatonic Scale (D9♭5)	A♭				C	D	E	F♯

Which scale is "best" for a D7♭5 Lydian Dominant chord?

Once again, it all depends on what "color" you want to give the D7♭5 chord. All of the scales contain the characteristic ♭5/♯11 tone; however, you decide if you want a ♯5th, 9th, 13th, or ♯11th "color" in your solo. **Fig. 21D** is a Imaj7–II7–iim7–V7 chord progression in the key of C that uses the A minor (major seventh) pentatonic scale for the II7 chord.

Fig. 21D

Am(maj7) Pentatonic Scale: Substitute for D Lydian Dominant Pentatonic Scale

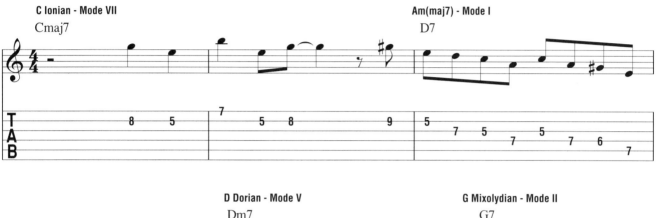

By learning all of these pentatonic scales, you have a tremendously expanded palette of possibilities to add as much depth as you want to your solos. All of these colors sound good, so the point is to try them all and see which ones you like the best in specific situations.

Summary

The minor (major seventh) pentatonic scale in this chapter can be used to cover a minor (major seventh) chord and a dominant seventh flat five chord that is a 4th (five frets) above. For the dominant seventh flat five chord, the minor (major seventh) pentatonic scale is an alternative to the pentatonic scales presented in Chapters 10 and 20.

CHAPTER 22
LYDIAN ♯4 (IVmaj7♯4) PENTATONIC SCALE

maj7♯4 Chord Description

The sound of the Ionian major seventh (Imaj7) chord was discussed in Chapter 2. The basic IVmaj7 chord can be voiced identically to the Imaj7 chord:

$$1-3-5-7$$

For an Fmaj7 chord in the key of C, for example, the notes are:

$$F-A-C-E$$

However, the sound of the major seven ♯4 (IVmaj7♯4) chord is very different—albeit very important—in jazz. It has a characteristic "Lydian" sound that makes a simple major seventh chord sound very "jazzy."

The IVmaj7♯4 chord is built on the following notes of the major scale:

$$Root-3rd-♯4th-5th-7th$$

In the key of C, the notes of the Fmaj7♯4 (IVmaj7♯4) are:

$$F-A-B-C-E$$

Voicing this chord can be a challenge because it does not lie well on the guitar fretboard. However, in most cases, a ♯4th voicing is not even needed. A regular major seventh chord will work in most situations. Unless it is the melody note or desired color note in a chord progression, the ♯4th note is not really necessary.

The only related major chord that works well is the maj9♯11. It can be substituted freely with the maj7♯4, maj7, or maj9, subject to desired bass leading and chord voicing movements. A maj9♯11 chord works especially well as a substitute for a major seventh chord at the end of a song.

This chord is notated in many different ways, including the following:

Fmaj7♯4	Fmaj7+4	Fmaj7aug4	Fmaj7♭5	Fmaj7-5
Fmaj7♯11	Fmaj7+11	Fmaj7aug11	Fmaj9♭5	Fmaj9♯11

Many times the following notations are used interchangeably:

♯4	+4	aug4	♯11	+11	aug11	♭5	-5

However, there are important theoretical differences in these notations. An overview of these differences is shown in Appendix D (Enharmonic Notes and Intervals). For purposes of this chapter, these terms are used interchangeably.

F Lydian Seven-Note Scale

Soloing on a Lydian IVmaj7 chord can be very challenging. The usually recommended scale is the seven-note Lydian scale, which is built on the fourth degree of the major scale. In the key of C, the following F Lydian scale could be used to cover an Fmaj7 or Fmaj7♯4:

$$F-G-A-B-C-D-E$$

The important distinguishing note is the ♯4 (the note B in the above F Lydian scale). This note establishes the very bright-sounding "Lydian" tonality. Also, notice that the F Lydian scale is the same as the C major scale, only it starts on the note F. This has potentially very important implications. If we start the C major scale on the F note, we have the Lydian scale (F–G–A–B–C–D–E). While the notes of the C Ionian scale and the F Lydian scale are the same, they *are not* the same scale. The difference is in the fourth note of each scale. In the C Ionian scale, the fourth note is F, which is a perfect 4th interval (five half steps) from C. However, in the corresponding F Lydian scale, the fourth note of the scale is a B, which is an augmented 4th interval (six half steps) from F. This gives the Lydian major seventh chord a characteristic maj7♯4 sound.

According to George Russell's *Lydian Chromatic Concept of Tonal Organization*, this Lydian scale—*not the major scale*—is the true harmonic representative of the tonality of its tonic major chord. Mr. Russell's entire system of chord/scale relationships is based on this concept. I highly recommend this book for anyone serious about theoretical approaches to improvisation and tonal organization. His model is very detailed and deep but opens your mind to a different way of thinking about chords and scales.

However, to greatly simplify his theory as it applies to a Cmaj7, you would not use the C Ionian major scale for soloing. Instead, you would use the C Lydian scale (the G Ionian scale starting on C). This would give you the ♯4 tone (F♯) to color the sound of the Cmaj7 chord. This color tone (F♯) is indeed very jazzy sounding over a Cmaj7 chord. In fact, after you get used to it, you will find that adding it to solos over any maj7 chord will significantly open up your sound.

The pentatonic modal approach in this book greatly simplifies the application of Lydian theory and provides you with several useful pentatonic substitute scale options for soloing over Lydian major chords. The basic Lydian pentatonic scale was discussed in Chapter 5. In Chapter 15, six additional Lydian pentatonic scale substitutions were presented. Below are two additional Lydian pentatonic scale alternatives for the IVmaj7 chord.

F Lydian ♯4 Pentatonic Scale Description

Fig. 22A shows the five fingerings for the F Lydian ♯4 pentatonic scale in music and tab notation, along with a fretboard diagram. Each pattern follows the two-notes-per-string rule. The initial chords are suggested voicings that are a good fit for each of the five patterns with respect to sound and proximity.

The scale consists of the following five scale tones (notes):

1–3–♯4–5–7 (F–A–B–C–E)

Fig. 22A
F Lydian ♯4 Pentatonic Scale

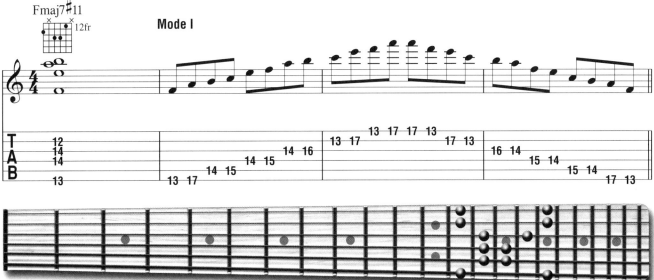

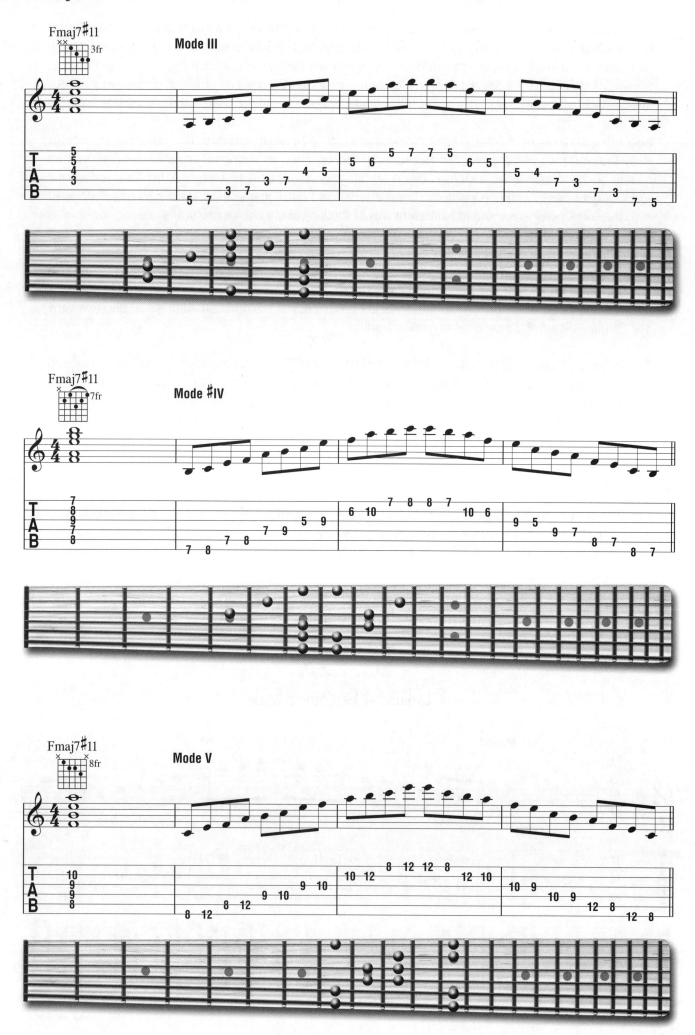

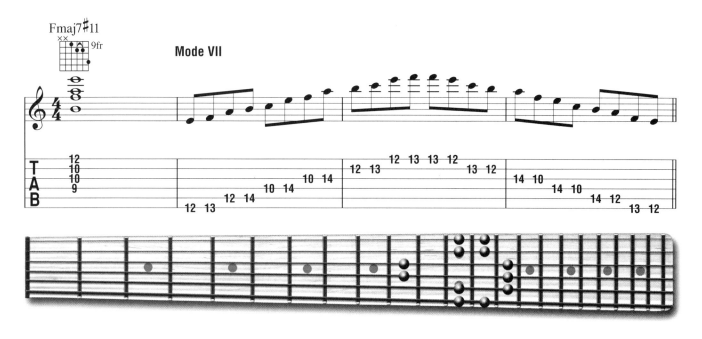

Fig. 22B presents two four-bar solos using the F Lydian ♯4 pentatonic scale. Notice that these solos are variations of the first two solos in Fig. 5D, which use the F Lydian pentatonic scale. The ♯4 note (B) in Fig. 22B adds the great Lydian quality to these solos.

Fig. 22B
Improvising with the F Lydian ♯4 Pentatonic Scale

The main advantage of the Lydian ♯4 pentatonic scale is that you get a true Lydian sound that is not harsh because the scale includes both the 5th and the ♯4th (♭5th). Additionally, this scale can be used very effectively for playing non-diatonic maj7 chords (ones that are not in the key of the progression).

F Lydian #11 Pentatonic Scale Description

A variation of the F Lydian #4 pentatonic scale is the F Lydian #11 pentatonic scale. **Fig. 22C** presents the five fingerings for the F Lydian #11 (IVmaj9#11) pentatonic scale in music and tab notation, along with a fretboard diagram. The #11th is the same note as a #4th, only it is one octave higher and implies a higher chord extension that includes the 9th.

Each pattern follows the two-notes-per-string rule. The initial chords are suggested voicings that are a good fit for each of the five patterns with respect to sound and proximity.

The scale consists of the following five scale tones (notes):

1–2–3–#11(#4)–7 (F–G–A–B–E)

Fig. 22C
F Lydian #11 Pentatonic Scale

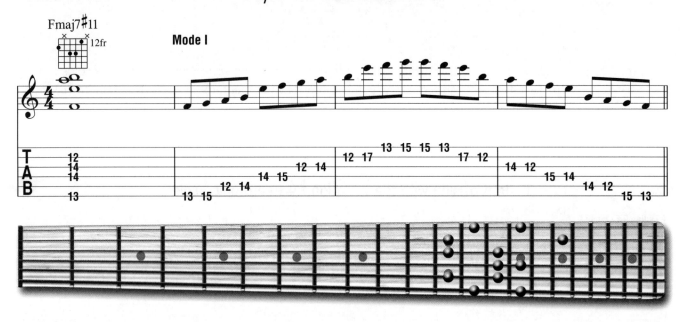

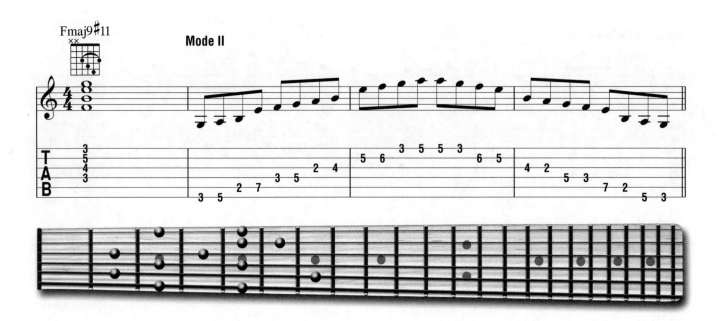

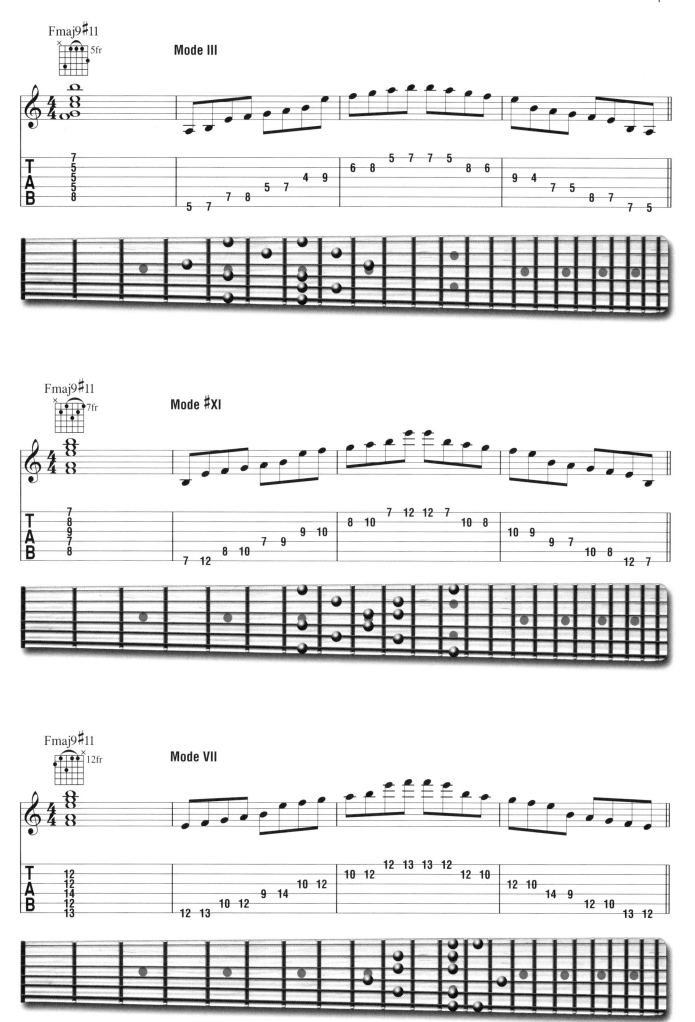

Notes of the F Lydian ♯11 Pentatonic Scale	Fmaj7 chord
F	Root
G	9th
A	3rd
B	♯11th
E	7th

The advantage of this scale is that the sound of the scale is clearly Lydian and rich with color tones, especially the major 9th and ♯11th.

The disadvantage of this scale is that it requires awkward patterns and finger stretches (five frets) to maintain the two-notes-per-string approach. However, this scale does provide a very "open" and modern jazz sound.

Comparing the F Lydian ♯4 and F Lydian ♯11 Pentatonic Scales

Fig. 22D demonstrates the use of the F Lydian ♯4 pentatonic scale in a Cmaj7–Fmaj7 progression, while **Fig. 22E** demonstrates the use of the F Lydian ♯11 pentatonic scale. Notice how both pentatonic scales imbue a much more modern sound than the F Lydian pentatonic scale from Chapter 5.

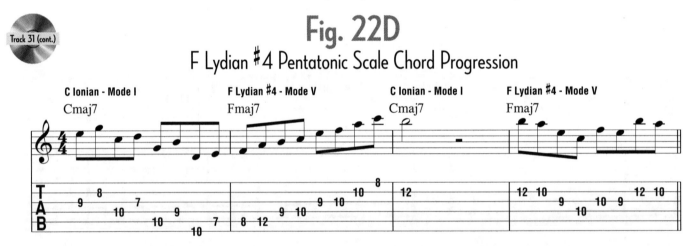

Track 31 (cont.)

Fig. 22D
F Lydian ♯4 Pentatonic Scale Chord Progression

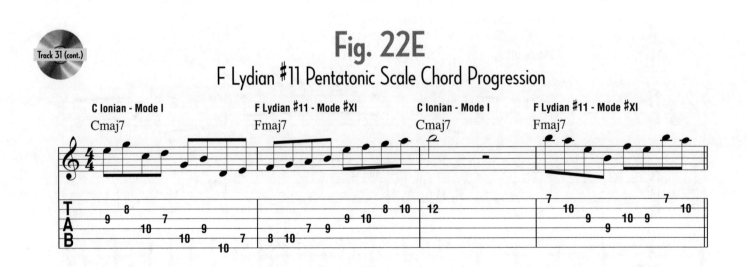

Track 31 (cont.)

Fig. 22E
F Lydian ♯11 Pentatonic Scale Chord Progression

Substitution for a V7 Chord

Both the IVmaj7#4 and IVmaj7#11 can serve as substitutes for a V7 chord. The IVmaj7#4 gives the V7 chord a suspended 4th or suspended 11th sound. The IVmaj7#11 gives the V7 chord a nice, unaltered dominant 13th sound.

The two scales are shown below with respect to a G7 (dominant) chord.

Notes of the F Lydian #4 Pentatonic Scale	G7 Chord	Notes of the F Lydian #11 Pentatonic Scale	G7 Chord
F	7th	F	7th
A	9th	G	Root
B	3rd	A	9th
C	11th	B	3rd
E	13th	E	13th

Fig. 22F illustrates these two scales being used as substitute scales for the G7 chord in the context of a ii–V–I chord progression in the key of C.

Fig. 22F
F Lydian #4 and F Lydian #11 Pentatonic Scales: Substitutes for G7 (V7) Chord

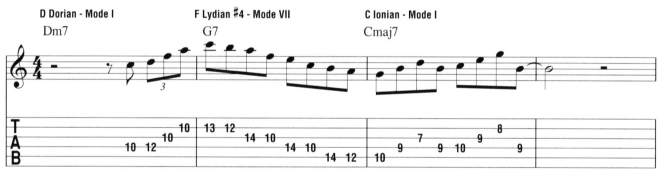

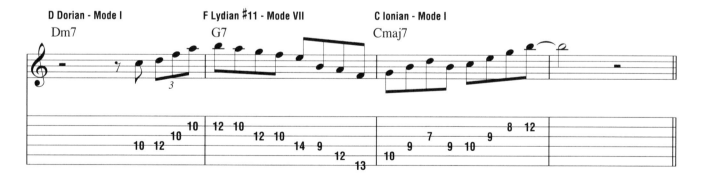

Summary

This chapter covered a wide range of soloing possibilities for a maj7#4 chord. The choice depends on personal taste, practicality of using various patterns, and the tone colors that are desired. Because facility with the Lydian "sound" is important, all of the alternatives that have been presented should be investigated. However, the recommended choice is the Lydian #4 (IVmaj7#4) pentatonic scale. Also, the Lydian #4 pentatonic scale can be used as a practical substitution for a suspended dominant chord.

CHAPTER 23
MIXOLYDIAN ♯9 (V7♯9) PENTATONIC SCALE

7♯9 Chord Description

The sound of the Mixolydian ♯9 (V7♯9) chord is very distinctive. It is sometimes referred to as the "Jimi Hendrix" chord, as it's featured in the classic riff chord of "Purple Haze." This chord is also used quite a bit in funk/dance tunes, such as "Funky Town" by Lipps, Inc. In jazz, the V7♯9 chord is often used in "funky" group vamps or as a substitute V7 chord moving to a i minor chord. The V7♯9 is also used in "advanced" jazz tunes, such as the first two measures in "ESP" by Miles Davis.

The V7♯9 chord can be built from several scales. For example, in G, the following scales contain the G7♯9 chord:

G7♯9 Chord	G		B♭/A♯	B			D			F
Diminished scale (half step/whole step)	G	A♭	B♭	B		D♭	D		E	F
A♭ Melodic Minor, Mode VII (G Super Locrian or G Diminished Whole Tone)	G	A♭	B♭	B		D♭		E♭		F
E♭ Harmonic Major, Mode III	G	A♭	B♭	B			D	E♭		F
G Blues scale	G		B♭		C	D♭	D			F

All of these scales will work with a G7♯9 chord. Notice that they all include B♭, which is the ♯9th tone of the chord. Each scale has different "colors" associated with it, thus deciding which scale to use is a matter of taste. In general, most jazz methods recommend using Mode VII of the melodic minor scale (a.k.a. the Super Locrian or diminished whole tone scales). For example, using Mode VII of the A melodic minor scale over a G7♯9 chord will create a very rich and jazzy sound. The reason is that, in addition to the sound of the ♯9th, this scale also provides the sound of the ♭9th, ♯5th, and ♭5th. This is a very interesting altered-dominant sound that is common in jazz.

The notes of a G7♯9 chord are:

$$
\begin{array}{ccccc}
G & B & D & F & A\sharp(B\flat) \\
\text{Root} & \text{3rd} & \text{5th} & \flat\text{7th} & \sharp\text{9th}
\end{array}
$$

Inversions with the root or 5th in the bass sound the best.

Any other altered dominant chord (e.g., G7♭9, G7♭9♭5, G7♭9♯5, G7♯9♭5, G7♯9♯5, G7♯9♭13, or G13♭9) can be substituted freely, subject to desired bass leading and chord voicing movements.

G Mixolydian ♯9 Pentatonic Scale Description

Fig. 23A shows the five fingerings for the G Mixolydian ♯9 pentatonic scale in music and tab notation, along with a fretboard diagram. Each pattern follows the two-notes-per-string rule. The initial chords are suggested voicings that are a good fit for each of the five patterns with respect to sound and proximity.

The scale consists of the following five scale tones (notes):

1–♯9(♯2)–3–5–7 (G–A♯–B–D–F)

Fig. 23A

G Mixolydian ♯9 Pentatonic Scale

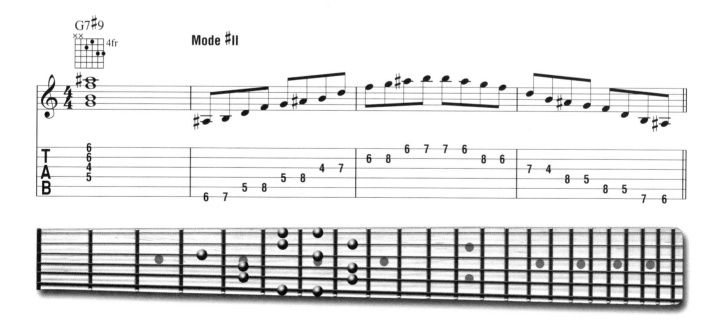

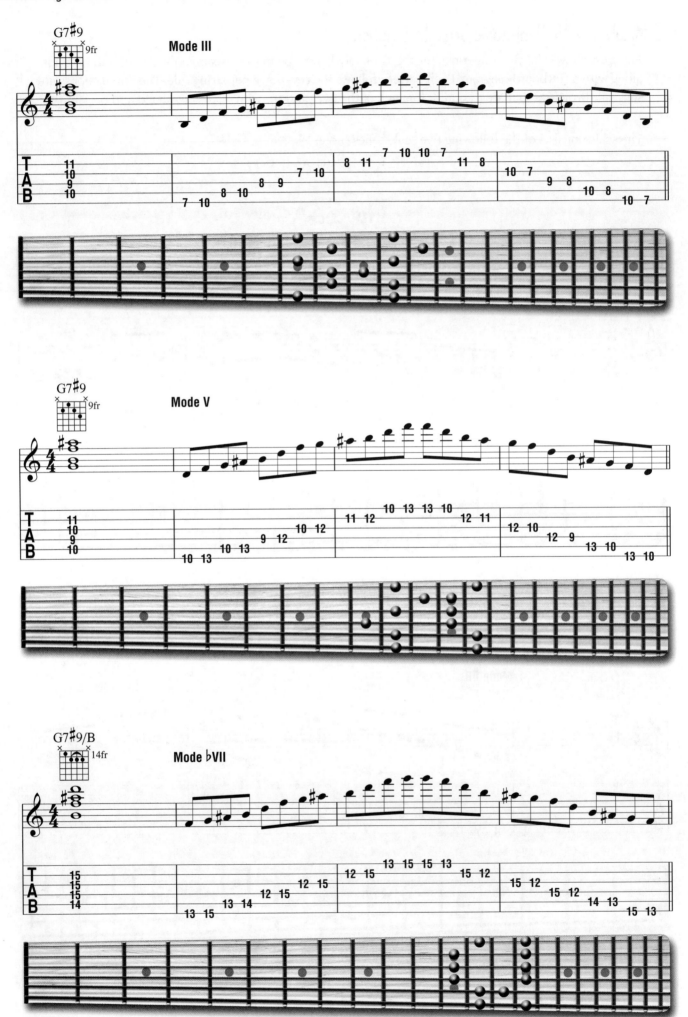

Fig. 23B is a 12-bar solo, made up of three four-bar phrases, using the G Mixolydian ♯9 pentatonic scale over a static G7♯9 vamp. This scale is great in a vamping situation because it contains both the major 3rd note (also found in the Mixolydian scale) and the minor 3rd note (found in the G minor pentatonic blues scale and the G minor pentatonic scale). In other words, this scale has the best of all worlds.

Fig. 23B

Track 32

Improvising with the G Mixolydian ♯9 Pentatonic Scale

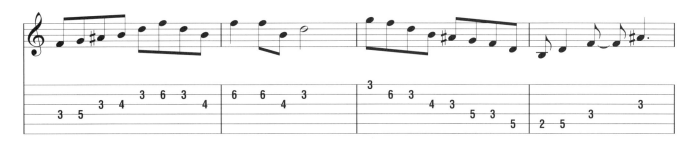

The Mixolydian ♯9 pentatonic scale also should be practiced moving to the tonic minor chord of the key, as shown in **Fig. 23C**. The Mixolydian ♯9 pentatonic scale also works while moving to the tonic major chord, as shown in **Fig. 23D**.

Fig. 23C

Track 32 (cont.)

Improvising with the G Mixolydian ♯9 Pentatonic Scale: Moving to a Cm7 Chord

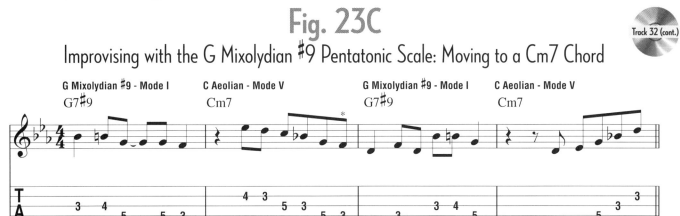

*Not in mode

Fig. 23D
Improvising with the G Mixolydian ♯9 Pentatonic Scale: Moving to a Cmaj7 Chord

Substitute Scale for a Dominant Seventh Chord

The Mixolydian ♯9 pentatonic scale is best suited as a substitute for a pentatonic scale that includes an altered 9th, such as the Mixolydian ♭9 pentatonic scale (Chapter 9). It can also work as a substitute scale for any dominant chord in which the ♯9th tone does not conflict with the melody note (e.g., 2nd/9th).

Summary

The Mixolydian ♯9 pentatonic scale is a very useful tool to have available, particularly for vamping over a static dominant chord. In addition to providing the dominant seventh tonality, the ♯9th essentially adds a ♭3rd "blue note" sound to the scale.

CHAPTER 24
MIXOLYDIAN ♯5 (V7♯5) PENTATONIC SCALE

7♯5 Chord Description

The sound of the Mixolydian ♯5 (V7♯5) chord is very important because of its signature "augmented" sound. The V7♯5 transitions nicely to a minor chord, a major chord, or another dominant chord. It is particularly useful when moving to a minor chord because the ♯5 note reinforces the minor tonality.

The V7♯5 chord is built on Mode 5 of the harmonic minor scale. In the key of A minor, for example, the harmonic minor scale is:

$$A–B–C–D–E–F–G♯$$

Therefore, Mode 5 would start on the note E of the A harmonic minor scale, as shown below:

$$E–F–G♯–A–B–C–D$$

The V7♯5 chord is built on the following degrees of Mode 5 of the harmonic minor scale:

$$1–3–♯5–♭7$$

In the key of Am, the notes of an E7♯5 chord are:

E	G♯	B♯/C	D
Root	3rd	♯5th	♭7th

Inversions with the root or 7th in the bass sound the best.

Any other altered dominant chord can be substituted freely, subject to desired bass leading and chord voicing movements.

The V7♯5 chord is notated in several different ways. Below are several ways an E dominant ♯5 chord might be notated:

E7♯5	E7+5	E7+	E7aug	E+7	Eaug7

E Mixolydian ♯5 Pentatonic Scale Description

Fig. 24A shows the five fingerings for the E Mixolydian ♯5 pentatonic scale in music and tab notation, along with a fretboard diagram. Each pattern follows the two-notes-per-string rule, except for an alternate pattern for Mode ♯V. In this particular situation, an alternate pattern is shown with one note on the second string and three notes on the first string. While this deviates from the strict two-notes-per-string rule, this pattern is less awkward than the two-notes-per-string version. The initial chords are suggested voicings that are a good fit for each of the five patterns with respect to sound and proximity.

The scale consists of the following five scale tones (notes):

$$1–3–5–♯5–♭7 \quad (E–G♯–B–C–D)$$

Fig. 24A
E Mixolydian #5 Scale

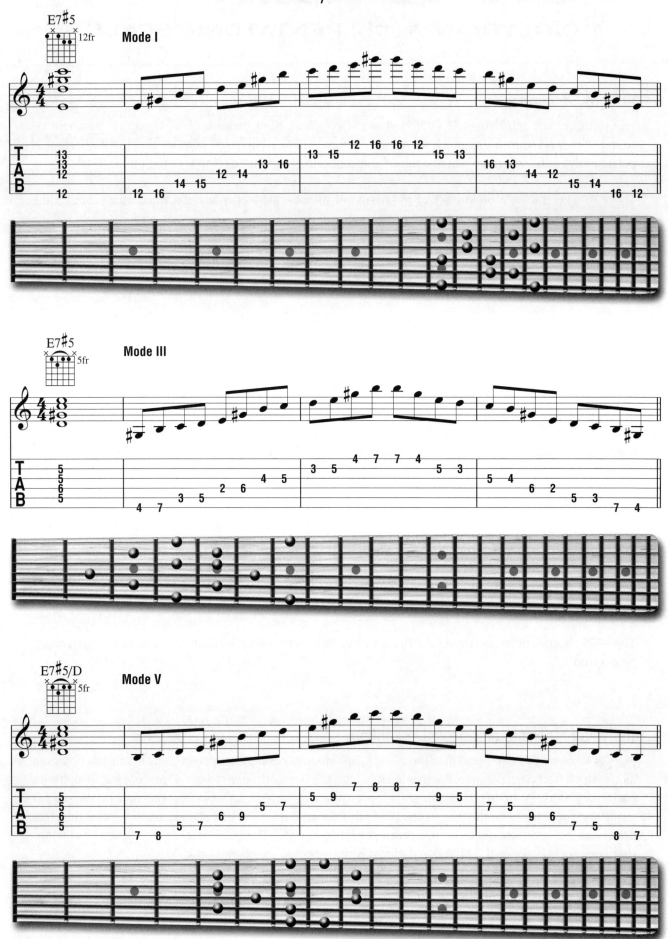

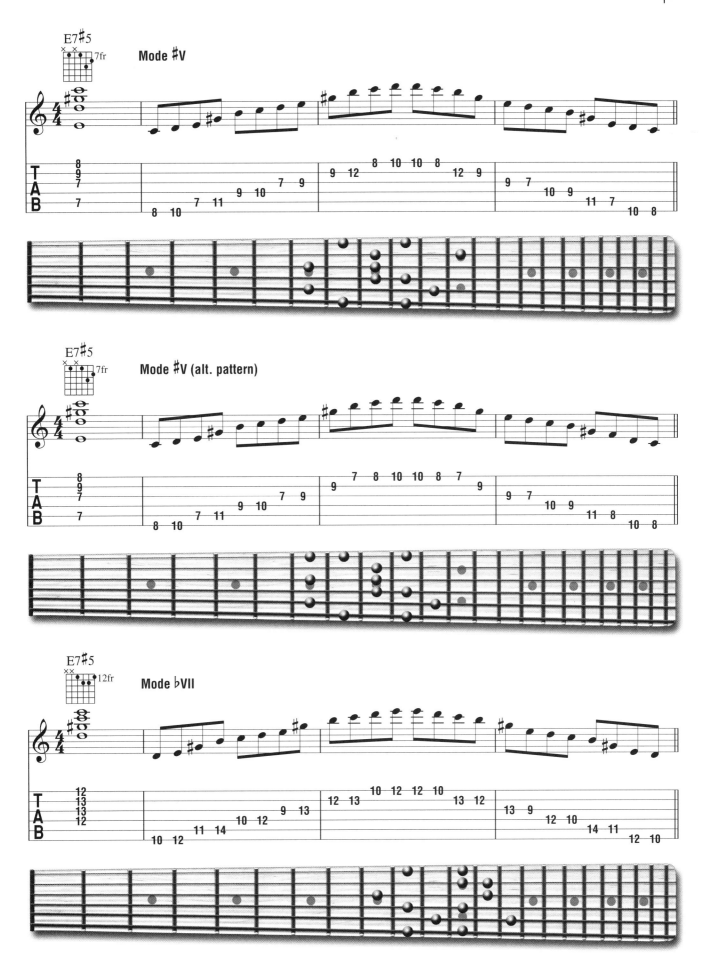

The absence of higher extensions like a 9th or 13th keeps the scale sounding very "inside." Also, the lack of altered notes like a ♭9th, ♯9th, or ♭5th maintains the focus on the "augmented" nature of this scale.

Resolution to Minor Chords

The following chord progressions demonstrate the Mixolydian ♯5 pentatonic scale making nice transitions to minor tonalities.

The Mixolydian ♯5 pentatonic scale sounds particularly good moving up a 4th to a minor chord [**Fig. 24B**]. The E Mixolydian ♯5 pentatonic scale is used in measures 1 and 3.

Fig. 24B

Track 33

Improvising with the Mixolydian ♯5 Pentatonic Scale: Resolving to a Tonic Minor Chord

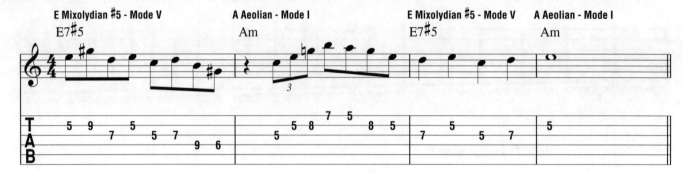

Fig. 24C demonstrates movement to a iim7 chord. This example uses the A Mixolydian ♯5 pentatonic scale in measure 2.

Fig. 24C

Track 33 (cont.)

Improvising with the Mixolydian ♯5 Pentatonic Scale: Resolving to a iim7 Chord

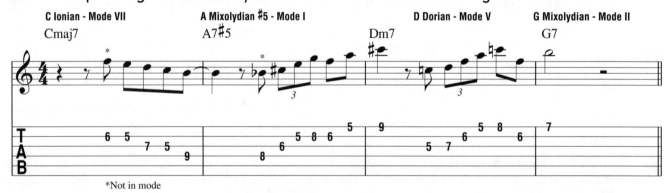

*Not in mode

Fig. 24D demonstrates movement to a iiim7 chord. This example uses the B Mixolydian ♯5 pentatonic scale in measure 2.

Fig. 24D

Track 33 (cont.)

Improvising with the Mixolydian ♯5 Pentatonic Scale: Resolving to a iiim7 Chord

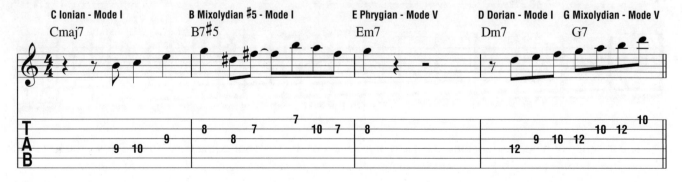

Resolution to Major Chords

The following chord progressions demonstrate the Mixolydian #5 pentatonic scale making smooth transitions to major chords.

Fig. 24E demonstrates movement to a Imaj7 chord. This example uses the G Mixolydian #5 pentatonic scale in measure 2.

Fig. 24E
Improvising with the Mixolydian #5 Pentatonic Scale: Resolving to a Tonic Major Chord

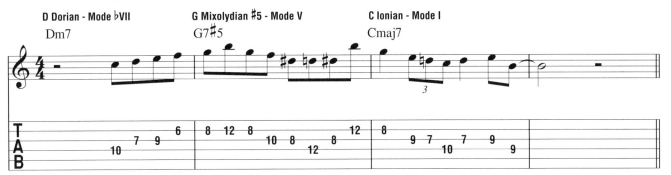

Fig. 24F demonstrates movement to a I6 chord. This example uses the C Mixolydian #5 pentatonic scale in measure 2.

Fig. 24F
Improvising with the Mixolydian #5 Pentatonic Scale: Chord Vamp

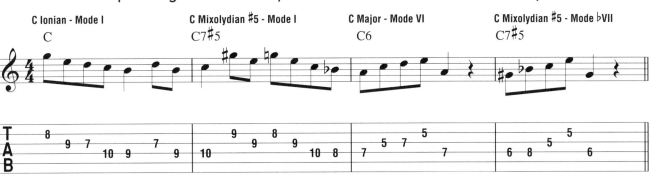

Substitute Scale for a Dominant Seventh Chord

The Mixolydian #5 pentatonic scale is best suited as a substitute for a pentatonic scale that is built from the harmonic minor scale, such as the Mixolydian ♭9 pentatonic scale (Chapter 9). It can also work as a substitute scale for any dominant chord where the augmented sound of the #5th is desired.

Summary

The Mixolydian #5 pentatonic scale is very useful for providing an augmented sound to a dominant chord scale. The #5 note in the scale provides very nice voice leading into the next chord or chord scale, especially when moving to a minor tonality.

CHAPTER 25
MIXOLYDIAN 13♭9 (V13♭9) PENTATONIC SCALE

13♭9 Chord Description

The sound of the Mixolydian 13♭9 (V13♭9) chord is useful in chord-melody soloing and comping on slower songs. It works best as an altered V7 in a ii-V progression that moves to a Imaj7 or iiim7 (substitute Imaj7) chord.

The notes and intervals for a G13♭9 chord, for example, are:

G	B	D	F	A♭	E
Root	3rd	5th	♭7th	♭9th	13th

Because of the inherent limitations of the guitar fretboard, there are no practical chords that use all six of the notes. Therefore, notes need to be excluded in order for the chord to be playable. There are really only three useful inversions, which are shown below for G13♭9 in the context of iim7–V–Imaj7 progressions.

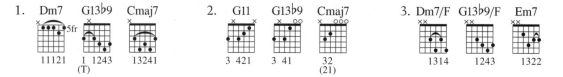

The first two progressions resolve nicely to Cmaj7 (Imaj7). The third progression resolves to an Em7 (iiim7) substituting for a Cmaj7 (Imaj7) chord.

Any other altered dominant chord (e.g., G7♭9, G7♭9♭5, G7♭9♯5, G7♯9♭5, G7♯9♯5, G7♯9♭13, or G13♭5) can be substituted freely for the G13♭9, subject to desired bass leading and chord voicing movements.

The V13♭9 chord can be built from two scales, as demonstrated below with a G13♭9 chord.

G13♭9 Chord	G	A♭		B		D	E	F
G Diminished (half step/whole step):	G	A♭	B♭	B	D♭/C♯	D	E	F
G Dorian ♭9 (Mode II of F Melodic Minor):	G	A♭	B♭		C	D	E	F

Both of these scales will work for a G13♭9 chord; they just have different "colors" associated with them. It is a matter of personal taste. For example, for a G13♭9 chord, Mode II of the F melodic minor scale will give the chord a very rich and jazzy sound. The reason is that, in addition to the sound of the 13th, this scale also provides the sound of the ♭9th, ♯9th, and 11th. This is a very interesting altered dominant sound that is common in jazz. Since this scale lacks the 3rd (instead, it has the 11th), it also gives a nice "suspended" color. The diminished (half step/whole step) scale does include the 3rd, as well as the ♭9th, ♯9th, ♭5th, and 13th.

G Mixolydian 13♭9 Pentatonic Scale Description

Fig. 25A shows the five fingerings for the G Mixolydian 13♭9 pentatonic scale in music and tab notation, along with a fretboard diagram. Each pattern follows the two-notes-per-string rule. The initial chords are suggested voicings that are a good fit for each of the five patterns with respect to sound and proximity.

The scale consists of the following five scale tones (notes):

♭2–3–5–13–♭7 (A♭–B–D–E–F)

There are two important things to note about this scale. First, it does not contain the root. With a six-note chord and a five-note pentatonic scale, one note needs to be eliminated. The two initial choices are the root and the 5th. In general, the root is not necessary since there is an assumption that the bass will cover it. The 5th is also expendable since it is a "neutral" tone and does not really contribute to the color of the chord. In this case, the root was omitted for ease in fingering the scale. Also, the unaltered 5th in the scale more strongly implies movement to a tonic major chord.

The second important point is that this scale has already been covered—but under a different name. The Mixolydian 13♭9 pentatonic scale shares the exact same scale pattern as the Mixolydian ♭9 pentatonic scale (Chapter 9), only a minor 3rd (three frets) lower. For example, the G Mixolydian 13♭9 pentatonic scale is exactly the same as the E Mixolydian ♭9 pentatonic scale. Thus, no new fretboard pattern needs to be learned. If you want to get the sound of a G13♭9, you just need to play an E Mixolydian ♭9 pentatonic-scale pattern.

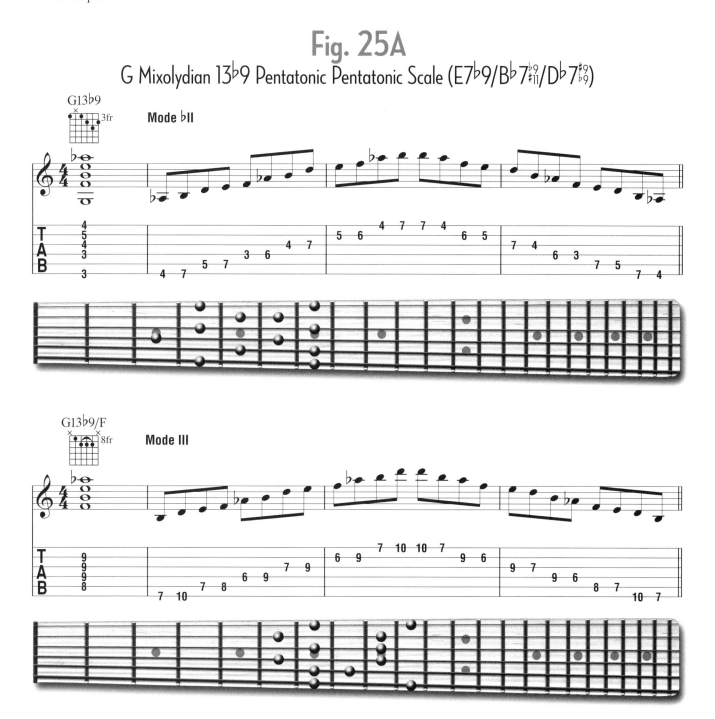

Fig. 25A
G Mixolydian 13♭9 Pentatonic Pentatonic Scale (E7♭9/B♭7♭9#11/D♭7#9♭9)

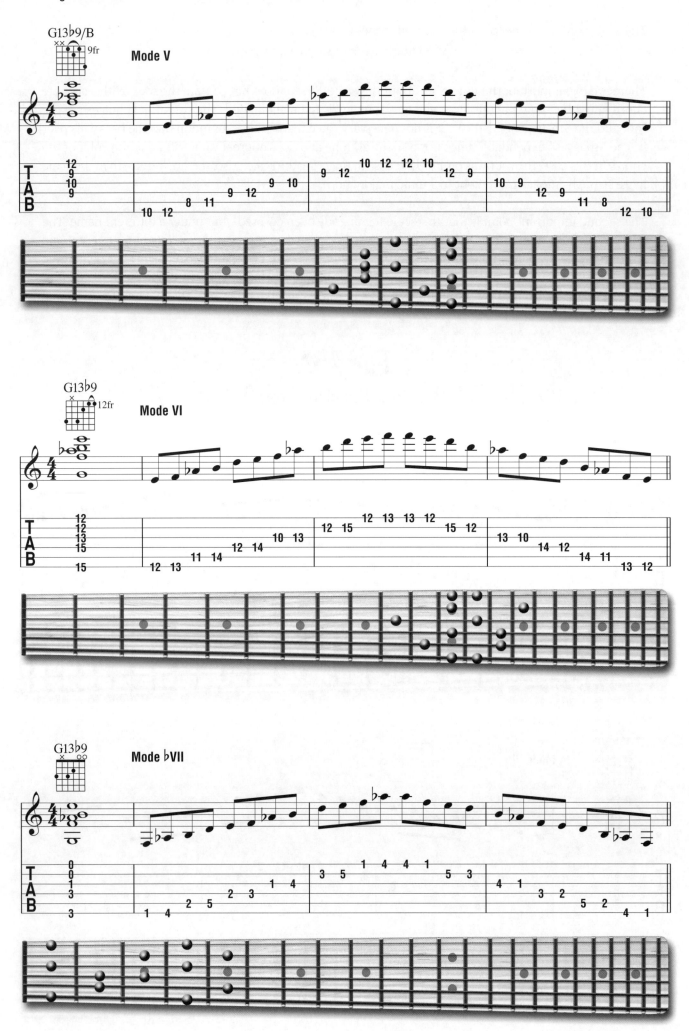

Below is a comparison of the notes of the G Mixolydian 13♭9 pentatonic scale and its relationships to the intervals of a G13♭9 and corresponding E7♭9 chord.

G Mixolydian 13♭9 Pentatonic Scale/ E Mixolydian ♭9 Pentatonic Scale	A♭	B	D	E	F
G13♭9	♭9th	3rd	5th	13th	♭7th
E7♭9	3rd	5th	♭7th	Root	♭9th

The same notes and patterns are used for both chords. The only difference is the names of the Modes that define the chord degree on which the scale starts. These are shown below:

Scale Note:	A♭/G♯	B	D	E	F
G Mixolydian 13♭9 Pentatonic Scale	Mode ♭II	Mode III	Mode V	Mode VI	Mode ♭VII
E Mixolydian ♭9 Pentatonic Scale	Mode III	Mode V	Mode ♭VII	Mode I	Mode ♭II

This is a very important concept. For example, the G Mixolydian 13♭9 pentatonic scale can be used to transition smoothly to a Cmaj7 *or* to an Amaj7 chord (where it would function as a pentatonic scale for an E7♭9 chord).

It gets better: This same scale can also be used for a B♭7alt chord (e.g., B♭7♭9♯11) and a D♭7alt chord (e.g., D♭7♯9♭9). This means that one scale can be used to smoothly transition to four different major tonal centers and two minor tonal centers.

These relationships are illustrated below.

Pentatonic Scales (with the Same Notes)	Implied Chord	Resolution Major Chord	Resolution Minor Chord
G Mixolydian 13♭9/ E Mixolydian ♭9	G13♭9	Cmaj7	
G Mixolydian 13♭9/ E Mixolydian ♭9	E7♭9	Amaj7	Am
G Mixolydian 13♭9/ E Mixolydian ♭9	B♭7♭5♭9	E♭maj7	
G Mixolydian 13♭9/ E Mixolydian ♭9	D♭7♯9♭9	G♭maj7	G♭m

Review the progression below, which demonstrates the flexibility of the Dominant 13♭9 pentatonic scale.

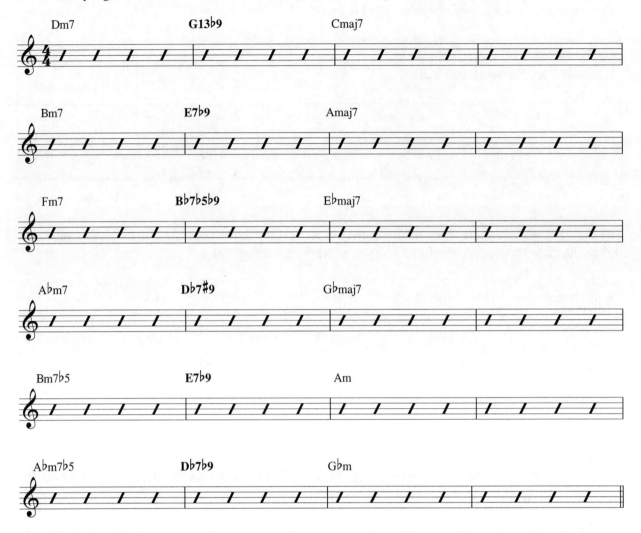

All of the dominant chords in the progression above (in **bold**) can be covered by the E Mixolydian ♭9 pentatonic scale from Chapter 9 or the G13♭9 pentatonic scale from this chapter—they are the same multi-purpose scale.

Fig. 25B is an example solo that demonstrates the versatility of the Mixolydian 13♭9 pentatonic scale. While all of the notes for the minor and major chords need to be adjusted for each chord change, the exact same notes, scale, and mode can be used for all six dominant chords in this progression—even though the chord progression moves through six unrelated keys. In this example, the exact same phrase, based on the G Mixolydian 13♭9 pentatonic scale (Mode ♭II), is used for each dominant chord in the six different (four major and two minor) key centers.

Fig. 25B

Track 34

Using Identical Mixolydian 13♭9 Pentatonic Scales in Six Different ii-V-I Progressions

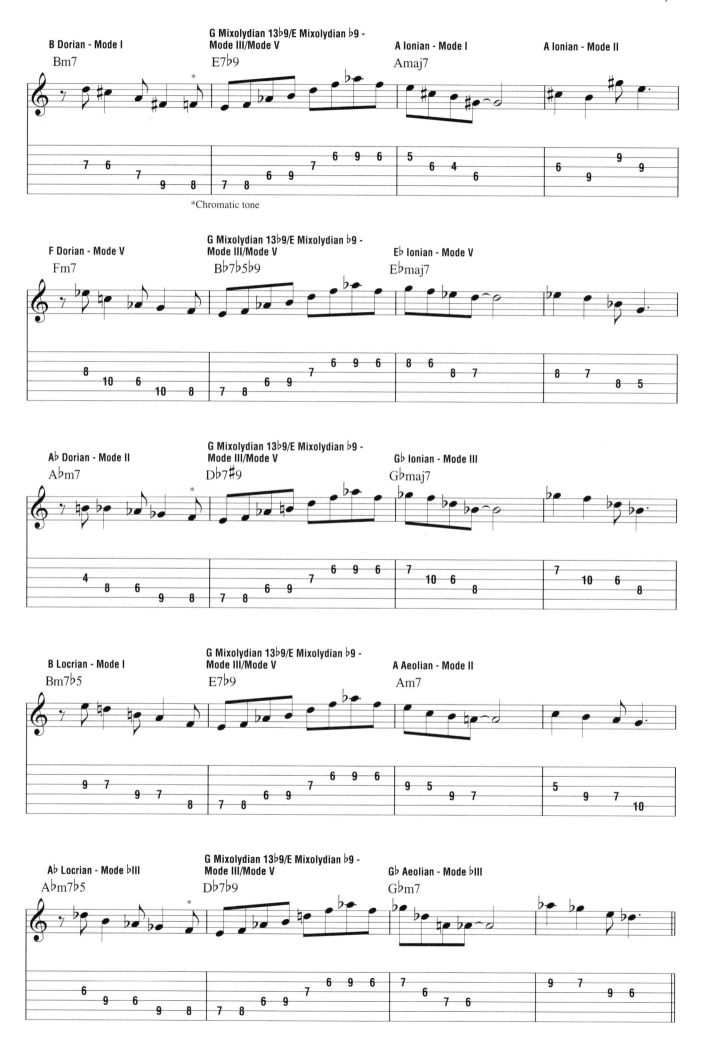

*Chromatic tone

The reason that the Mixolydian 13♭9 flows smoothly into only two minor tonal centers has to do with the nature of the upper extensions in the dominant chord being reflected in the Mixolydian 13♭9. In general, the following rules apply for dominant chords:

- 13ths move to major

- ♯5ths move to minor but can also move to major

- ♭5ths move to major

- 9ths move to major but, in specific cases, may move to minor

- ♭9ths move to major or minor equally well

- ♯9ths move to minor (more strongly) or major

Therefore, a G Mixolydian 13♭9 pentatonic scale that implies a G13♭9 chord does not move smoothly to a Cm chord. Also, the G Mixolydian 13♭9 pentatonic scale that implies a B♭7♭5♭9 does not move smoothly to an E♭m chord.

Summary

By using scale patterns that have already been learned, the Mixolydian 13♭9 pentatonic scale provides a very useful altered dominant tonality. Essentially, the Mixolydian 13♭9 pentatonic scale is the Mixolydian ♭9 pentatonic scale a minor 3rd (three frets) higher. The Mixolydian 13♭9 pentatonic scale is extremely versatile and can be used as the V7 chord for four different major chords and two minor chords.

SECTION 5

Chord Progressions

This section focuses on applying the individual pentatonic chord scales to the common chord progressions that characterize jazz music. The most important components of chord in jazz are the ii–V, ii–V–I, and iim7♭5–V7–i progressions. These are the foundation of the language of jazz, as virtually all standard jazz tunes are built around them. The pentatonic chord scale approach to mastering these important progressions is demonstrated.

This section also focuses on the preeminent song forms in jazz: the blues, rhythm changes, standards, and "Coltrane changes." The pentatonic chord scale approach described in this book is utilized to master these important jazz song forms. The final chapter demonstrates how the pentatonic chord scale approach can be utilized in several ways to enable you to master the most challenging of all jazz compositions—"Giant Steps" by John Coltrane.

I am confident that completion of this section will validate the claims made at the beginning of the book regarding the effectiveness of the pentatonic modal approach to jazz guitar improvisation.

CHAPTER 26
ii-V PROGRESSIONS

The ii-V chord sequence is the most important progression in jazz, pop, and Latin. The ability to solo through ii-V changes defines your ability as a jazz musician. Virtually every jazz standard contains ii-V changes.

Fig. 26A summarizes, for a ii-V chord progression in a major key, the options presented in Sections 1–4. The key of C is used in this example; however, it is important that you become familiar with this chord progression in all 12 keys. Focus especially on the "jazz keys" of E♭, B♭, A♭, F, G, and D♭.

Fig. 26A
ii-V Pentatonic Scale Options in a Major Key

SECTION 1

Dm7 - D Dorian, C Major, C Major Blues

G7 - G Mixolydian, C Major, C Major Blues, C Minor, C Minor Blues

SECTION 2

Dm7 - F Lydian, D Minor, A Minor, A Aeolian, E Minor, B Locrian

G7 - B Locrian, G Major (E Minor), G Mixolydian ♭9, G Lydian Dominant, D♭ Lydian Dominant, F Locrian, D♭ Mixolydian ♭9, D Locrian

SECTION 3

Dm7 - None presented in Section 3

G7 - G7 Whole Tone, D♭7 Whole Tone

SECTION 4

Dm7 - F Lydian ♯4, F Lydian ♯11

G7 - D Minor (Major Seventh), G Mixolydian ♯5, F Lydian ♯4, F Lydian ♯11, G Mixolydian ♯9, G Mixolydian 13♭9

The ii-V progression is used in many different ways in jazz. What this means is that not every combination of ii-Vs in Fig. 26A will work in all situations—it depends on how the ii-V progression is being used in the context of the tune. Following are two examples of how a ii-V progression might function in a song.

1. As a repeating ii–V for an entire song. This pattern is characteristic of "groove"-type jazz songs like "Listen Here" by Eddie Harris or Latin songs like "Oye Como Va" by Tito Puente. The repeating progression can either be one or two measures long, as shown below.

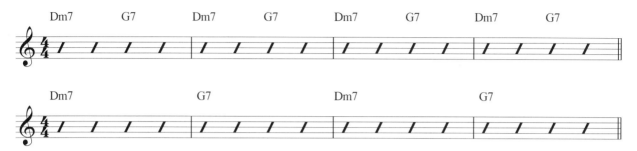

In these cases, it's best to approach the song as a modal tune. This means to start by "thinking" in terms of one tonal center that can be embellished by pentatonic chord scales from Section 1. In the previous examples, the tonal center is essentially D (minor) Dorian. This means that a solo should be based on the D minor pentatonic scale (D–F–G–A–C) and the seven-note D Dorian scale (D–E–F–G–A–B), which is probably what you are already doing.

Now start to selectively add the D Dorian pentatonic scale from Chapter 3 to cover the Dm7 chord. Make sure that your ear can hear the different nuances that the three scales (D minor pentatonic scale, D Dorian scale, and D Dorian pentatonic scale) bring to the Dm7 chord.

Next, begin to selectively add the G Mixolydian pentatonic scale from Chapter 6 to the G7 chord. Notice how this scale "accents" the sound of the G7 chord.

Once again, for a repeating ii–V chord progression, focus on the minor pentatonic scale, using the pentatonic chord scales from Chapter 3 (D Dorian Pentatonic Scale) and Chapter 6 (G Mixolydian Pentatonic Scale) to embellish your solos.

Fig. 26B is an example solo that incorporates these ideas.

Fig. 26B
ii–V Solo

175

2. Different types of ii-V sequences in a song. This situation is characteristic of jazz songs like "Satin Doll," with repeating ii-V cycles and different types of ii-V sequences within the song, as shown below.

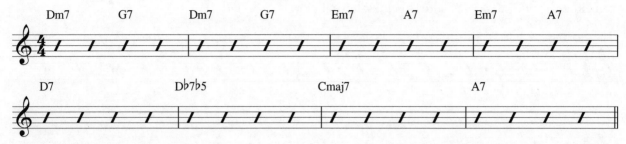

While the Dm7-G7 and Em7-A7 repeating patterns both appear to be ii-V progressions, it is very important to understand that they serve different functions within the overall chord progression. The Em7-A7 progression is really a iiim7-VI7 progression. The "key" is to try to identify how the V7 chord of a ii-V sequence is functioning in the chord progression. In this case, the A7 is a VI7 chord in the key of C. This means that it is serving as a secondary dominant VI7 chord; that is, it contains an implied ♭9th (Note: The same would be true for a III7 or VII7 chord). Furthermore, any dominant chord can be replaced by a ii-V chord sequence. That means that in the previous progression, the D7 (measure 5), D♭7 (measure 6), and the A7 (measure 8) chords can also be considered ii-V sequences. With these replacements the chord progression becomes primarily ii-Vs, as follows:

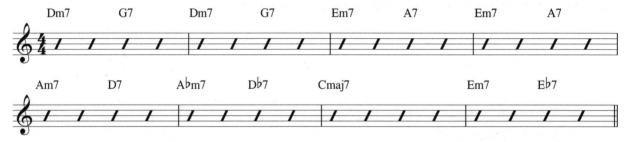

The Am7-D7 and A♭m7-D♭7 progressions are also different types of ii-V progressions. In the dominant chord, they imply the sound of the ♭5th.

> The previous chord progression demonstrates the four basic types of major-key ii-V progressions that you will encounter in jazz:
>
> | ii-V7 | ii-V7♭5 |
> |-------|---------|
> | ii-V7♭9 | ii-♭II7 |

Fig. 26C incorporates these ideas is an example solo over the previous chord progression.

Track 35 (cont.)

Fig. 26C
Jazz Standard Solo Based on Several ii-V Progressions

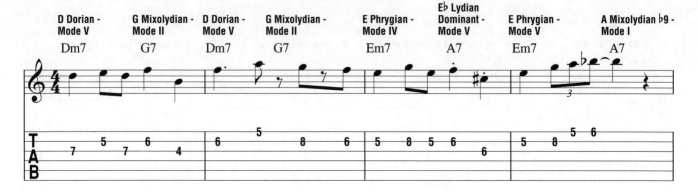

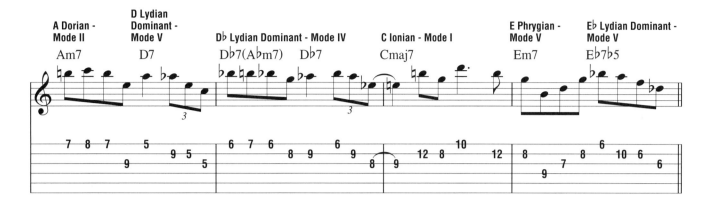

To simplify the distinctions, the focus will be on the different types of dominant chords. The ii chord can be considered a basic minor seventh chord (iim7). The chart below indicates representative ii–V combinations for each of the four types of ii–V chord variations described above.

ii–V Variations	Example Chord Change, Key of C	ii Pentatonic Scale	V Pentatonic Scale
ii–V7	Dm7–G7	D Dorian	B Locrian*, G Mixolydian, G Major, G Mixolydian ♯5, F Lydian ♯4, F Lydian ♯11
ii–V7♭9	Dm7–G7♭9	D Dorian	G Mixolydian ♭9, D Locrian, G Mixolydian ♯9, G Mixolydian13♭9
ii–V7♭5	Dm7–G7♭5	D Dorian	G Lydian ♭5, G7 Whole Tone, D Minor (Major Seventh)
ii–♭II7	Dm7–D♭7	D Dorian	D♭ Lydian ♭5, D♭ Mixolydian ♭9, F Locrian D♭7 Whole Tone

*IMPORTANT NOTE: For ii–V combinations with unaltered dominant chords, I recommend the use of the Locrian pentatonic scale to cover the V7 chord. It has a "jazzier" sound than the corresponding Mixolydian pentatonic scale and is a perfect match for the Dorian pentatonic scale. Therefore, for a Dm7–G7 progression I recommend using a D Dorian–B Locrian combination. In regard to a formula, just remember to match a Dorian pentatonic scale with the Locrian pentatonic scale that is three half steps (three frets) lower. Also, get used to *not* changing hand position. For example, if you play the D Dorian pentatonic scale in Mode V at the fifth position, play the B Locrian pentatonic scale at the fifth position as well (Mode ♭VII).

You can "mix and match" the D Dorian pentatonic scale with any pentatonic scale in the fourth column from the chart—they will all sound correct. To fully gain an appreciation for the vast resources that you now have available for pentatonic soloing over a ii–V progression, you should spend time with as many of the combinations from the chart as possible.

The first combination to focus on is the D Dorian pentatonic scale–B Locrian pentatonic scale combination. Use the following pentatonic scale exercises to gain proficiency with this important combination.

1. Whole steps, descending:

2. Whole steps, ascending:

3. Half steps, descending:

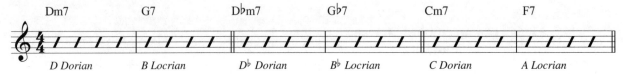

4. Half steps, ascending:

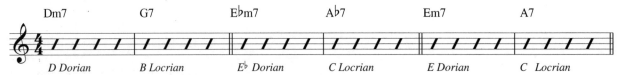

5. Three half steps, ascending:

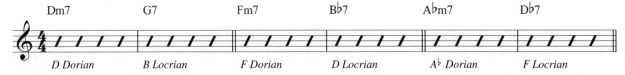

6. Three half steps, descending:

7. Circle of 4ths (Important!):

I know that this seems like a lot of work, and... it is. However, this is how other jazz instrumentalists like sax, trumpet, and keyboard players internalize these changes and appear to play so effortlessly through complex chord changes.

Now you are ready for the next combinations. While you can skip around and pick any ii–V combinations that you wish, you should try to have some type of systematic approach. I recommend that you go through the previous seven exercises using the first combinations from each of the four ii–V categories. Then go on to the second, and then the third, etc. This means you would systematically go through the seven exercises using the following ii–V combination sequence:

D Dorian Pentatonic Scale–B Locrian Pentatonic Scale

D Dorian Pentatonic Scale–G Mixolydian ♭9 Pentatonic Scale

D Dorian Pentatonic Scale–G Lydian ♭5 Pentatonic Scale

D Dorian Pentatonic Scale–D♭ Lydian ♭5 Pentatonic Scale

D Dorian Pentatonic Scale–G Mixolydian Pentatonic Scale

D Dorian Pentatonic Scale–D Locrian Pentatonic Scale

D Dorian Pentatonic Scale–G7 Whole Tone Pentatonic Scale

D Dorian Pentatonic Scale–D♭ Mixolydian ♭9 Pentatonic Scale

etc.

Don't forget you are a guitar player. That means that you also have to practice these combinations using different patterns for each pentatonic scale. Remember, each pentatonic scale has five fingerboard positions. Thus, to thoroughly practice just the D Dorian pentatonic scale–B Locrian pentatonic scale combination, you have five different positions to work on. Effectively, this means that the previous exercises need to be multiplied by a factor of 5 to account for a thorough coverage of the basic combination possibilities!

If this seems beyond your motivation, you can always just practice the specific combinations, at the specific fretboard positions, that interest you. Once again, I strongly recommend developing proficiency with the Dorian pentatonic scale–Locrian pentatonic scale combinations.

Summary

Proficiency with the ii–V chord progression is absolutely essential for playing jazz. The exercises provided in this chapter will be of great assistance while playing through virtually any standard jazz tune.

CHAPTER 27
ii-V-I PROGRESSIONS

The ii–V–I chord sequence is the logical extension of the ii–V progression presented in Chapter 26. As with the ii–V progression, the ability to solo through ii–V–I changes essentially defines your ability as a jazz musician. Virtually every jazz standard contains multiple ii–V–I changes. The ii–V–I progression is used in several ways in a tune, including the following:

- As the basis for an entire tune
- As an intro
- As an outro
- As a transition between verses
- As a transition from a bridge to a verse
- As a transition to a new key center within a song

Fig. 27A summarizes, for a ii–V–I chord progression in a major key, the options presented in Sections 1–4. The key of C is used in this example; however, it is important that you become familiar with this progression in all 12 keys. Focus on the "jazz keys" of E♭, B♭, A♭, F, G, and D♭.

Fig. 27A
ii-V-I Pentatonic Scale Options in a Major Key

Dm7   G7   Cmaj7

SECTION 1

Dm7 - D Dorian, C Major, C Major Blues

G7 - G Mixolydian, C Major, C Major Blues, C Minor, C Minor Blues

Cmaj7 - C Ionian, C Major, C Major, C Major Blues

SECTION 2

Dm7 - F Lydian, D Minor, A Minor, A Aeolian, E Minor, B Locrian

G7 - B Locrian, G Major (E Minor), G Mixolydian ♭9, G Lydian Dominant, D♭ Lydian Dominant, F Locrian, D♭ Mixolydian ♭9, D Locrian

Cmaj7 - E Phrygian, A Aeolian, C Major, B Minor (Lydian sounds for endings)

SECTION 3

Dm7 - None presented in Section 3

G7 - G7 Whole Tone, D♭7 Whole Tone

Cmaj7 - None presented in Section 3

SECTION 4

Dm7 - F Lydian #4, F Lydian #11

G7 - D Minor (Major Seventh), G Mixolydian #5, F Lydian #4, F Lydian #11, G Mixolydian #9, G Mixolydian 13♭9

Cmaj7 - D Minor (Major Seventh), G Mixolydian #5, F Lydian #4, F Lydian #11, G Mixolydian #9, G Mixolydian 13♭9

The following are suggested approaches for becoming familiar with the pentatonic soloing options on a ii–V–I progression.

You can "mix and match" any of the columns in Fig. 27A—they will all sound correct. To fully gain an appreciation for the vast resources that you now have available for pentatonic soloing, you should spend time with as many combinations as possible, focusing on gaining proficiency with the chord scales in Section 1.

A good way to start is by simply ignoring the chord changes and playing only the C major (A minor) pentatonic scale [**Fig. 27B**].

Fig. 27B
ii–V–I Solo: Major Pentatonic Scale

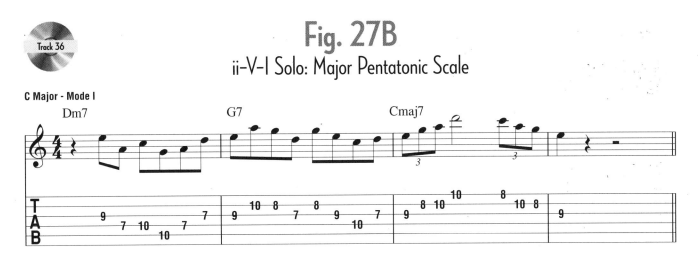

Now use pentatonic chord scales from Section 1 for all three chords [**Fig. 27C**].

Fig. 27C
ii–V–I Solo: Pentatonic Chord Scales

Next, experiment with various substitute and/or reharmonized pentatonic scales. **Fig. 27D** is an example solo that uses substitute scales with altered and higher chord extensions from Fig. 27A.

Fig. 27D
ii–V–I Solo: Substitute Pentatonic Scales

Now branch out on your own and try different combinations of chord scales from Fig. 27A. Even when you use the more "dissonant" pentatonic scales from Fig. 27A, they will still sound "correct" in the context of the progression.

> **IMPORTANT NOTE:** While Sections 2, 3, and 4 provide you with a wealth of pentatonic options from which to choose, the eleven pentatonic scales from Section 1 should cover the vast majority of your soloing situations.

CHAPTER 28
iim7♭5–V7–i PROGRESSIONS

The iim7♭5–V7–i chord sequence is the minor-key version of the ii–V–I progression that was presented in Chapter 27. As with the ii–V–I progression, the ability to solo through iim7♭5–V7–i changes is extremely important in playing jazz music. The iim7♭5–V7–i progression is used in several ways in a tune, including the following:

- As a basic chord progression within a song
- As an intro
- As an outro
- As a temporary key change to a minor tonality within a song

Fig. 28A summarizes, for a iim7♭5–V7–i chord progression in the key of C minor (E♭ major), the options presented in Sections 1–4. It is important that you become familiar with this progression in all 12 keys. Focus especially on the common jazz keys of Gm, Fm, Am, Dm, F♯m, and Em.

Fig. 28A
iim7♭5–V7–i Pentatonic Scale Options in a Minor Key

SECTION 1
Dm7♭5 - D Locrian, F Minor

G7♭9 - G Mixolydian ♭9, C Minor Blues

Cm - C Minor, C Aeolian, C Minor Blues

SECTION 2
Dm7♭5 - F Dorian, A♭ Lydian ♯4

G7♭9 - D♭ Lydian Dominant, F Locrian, D♭ Mixolydian ♭9, D Locrian

Cm - None presented in Section 2

SECTION 3
Dm7♭5 - None presented in Section 3

G7♭9 - G7 Whole Tone, D♭7 Whole Tone

Cm - None presented in Section 3

SECTION 4
Dm7♭5 - None presented in Section 4

G7♭9 - G Mixolydian ♯5, G Mixolydian ♯9

Cm - C Minor (Major Seventh)

The following are suggested approaches for becoming familiar with the pentatonic soloing options available for a iim7♭5–V7–i progression

You can "mix and match" any of the columns in Fig. 28A—they will all sound correct. To fully gain an appreciation for the vast resources that you now have available for pentatonic soloing, you should spend time with as many combinations as possible, focusing especially on gaining proficiency with the chord scales in Section 1. These are your "bread and butter" changes, as they always sound good and are relatively easy to remember. Make sure you get familiar with the Section 1 changes in all five positions of the i chord.

A good way to start is by simply ignoring the chord changes and play only the C minor pentatonic scale [**Fig. 28B**].

Fig. 28B
iim7♭5-V7-i Solo: Minor Pentatonic Scale

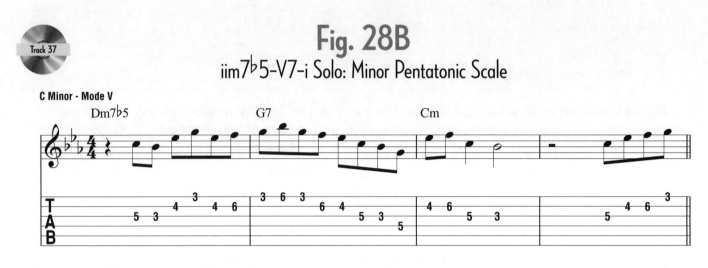

Next use pentatonic chord scales from Section 1 for all three chords [**Fig. 28C**].

Fig. 28C
iim7♭5-V7-i Solo: Pentatonic Chord Scales

Fig. 28D uses scales with altered and higher chord extensions from Fig. 28A.

Fig. 28D
iim7♭5-V7-i Solo: Pentatonic Substitute Chord Scales

Now branch out on your own and try different combinations of chord scales from Fig. 28A. Even when you use the more "dissonant" pentatonic scales from Fig. 28A, they will still sound "correct" in the context of the progression.

While Sections 2, 3, and 4 provide you with a wealth of pentatonic options from which to choose when soloing over a iim7♭5-V7-i chord progression, the eleven pentatonic scales from Section 1 should cover the vast majority of your soloing situations.

The following are the first eight measures of a standard jazz chord progression:

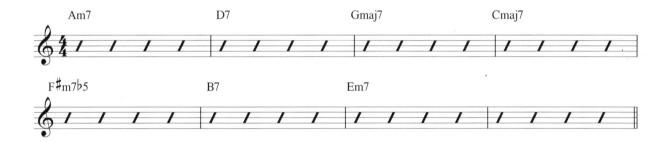

Notice that measures 5–8 are simply a iim7♭5-V7-i chord progression in the key of E minor. While the song is in a major key, this iim7♭5-V7-i progression is a temporary switch to a minor tonality, which is very common in many jazz standards. As a matter of fact, the entire chord progression for this tune, including the bridge, is primarily made up of major and minor II–V–I progressions. This makes the song very easy to solo over, using only the pentatonic scales in Section 1. For review, Fig. 11O is a sample solo over this chord progression, using only the basic pentatonic chord scales. Fig. 11P–X demonstrate how to incorporate blues pentatonic scales into this chord progression.

After you have gained facility for soloing over a iim7♭5-V7-i chord progression with the scales from Section 1, you can gradually incorporate the scales described in Sections 2–5; the possibilities are really limitless! Also, don't forget: You don't need to stay exclusively with pentatonic scales from this book. You can also choose to use them selectively to complement whatever current approach you might have for soloing over iim7♭5-V7-i changes.

CHAPTER 29

THE BLUES

This chapter focuses on applying pentatonic chord scales to the four basic blues forms—standard blues, jazz blues, minor blues, and bebop blues.

Standard Blues

Chapter 11 presented an overview of how various combinations of pentatonic scales covered in Section 1 can be used to solo over standard 12-bar blues changes. Standard blues is the form that is used in traditional blues and rock songs. The form is shown below.

Notice the last four measures: Standard blues is characterized by a V7–IV7–I7–V7 progression in the last four measures.

Four options were presented in Chapter 11 for using pentatonic scales over the following 12-bar standard blues progression in the key of C.

Option 1: Use the C minor pentatonic scale (Chapter 1) for the entire progression (see Fig. 11B).

Option 2: Use the C minor blues pentatonic scale (Chapter 11) for the entire progression (see Fig. 11C).

Option 3: Use the C major blues pentatonic scale (or A minor blues pentatonic scale) for the C7 chord and the C minor blues pentatonic scale for the other chords (see Fig. 11D).

Option 4: Use combinations of both blues pentatonic scales and both major/minor pentatonic scales (see Fig. 11E).

The next step is to add pentatonic chord scales as options for soloing over the individual chords. Notice that in this standard blues version of the 12-bar blues, all of the chords are dominant seventh chords. This provides a lot of opportunity to utilize the harmonic richness of their associated pentatonic chord scales. For example, the chart below contains a standard blues chord progression in the "jazz" key of B♭. Two variations of a pentatonic scale solo are included.

= Variation 1
= Variation 2

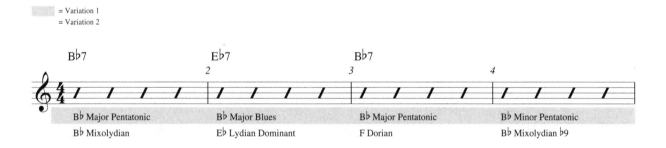

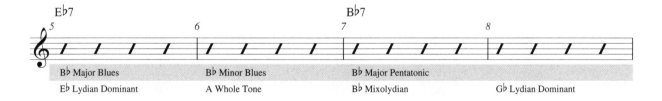

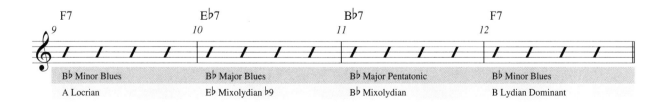

Fig. 29A uses major, minor, major blues, and minor blues pentatonic scales. **Fig. 29B** consists of suggested pentatonic chord-scale alternatives to the first variation.

Track 38

Fig. 29A
Standard Blues Changes: Variation 1

*Not in mode

Fig. 29B
Standard Blues Changes: Variation 2

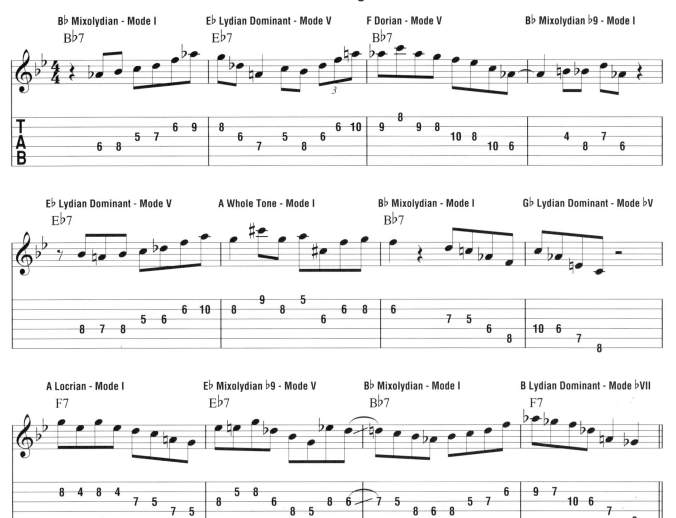

Notice that even though only pentatonic chord scales are used, the unmistakable quality of the blues is clearly evident.

The next step is to "mix and match" the two sets of pentatonic scales in the chart. Focus on the first variation, adding the chord scales from the second variation very selectively. When the chord scales are used for "spice" rather than used for the entire song, more attention is brought to them. The point is that you have a wealth of pentatonic material that you can draw upon.

Jazz Blues

Jazz blues is a variation of the standard blues form. It differs from the standard blues in three important ways:

1. It uses more harmonic complexity (measures 2, 4, 6, 7–8);

2. It uses a ii–V7 progression in measures 9–10 instead of a V7–IV7 progression; and

3. The last two measures (measures 11–12) consist of a turnaround (I7–VI7–ii–V7) instead of a simple I7–V7 progression

The following example shows the following:

- general form of a jazz blues chord progression in Roman numerals

- typical jazz blues chord progression in the key of B♭

- suggested pentatonic scales

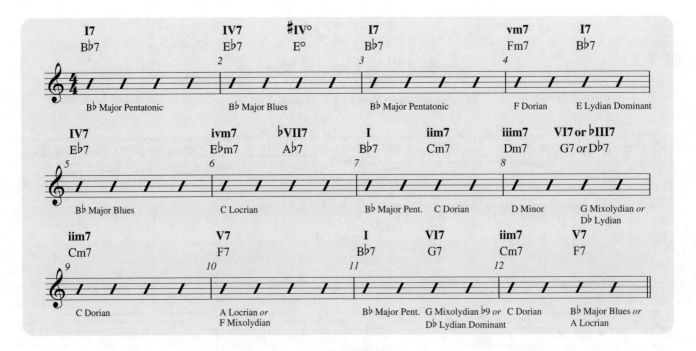

An example solo over this progression is shown in **Fig. 29C**. Once again, each scale flows melodically into the next; there are no "wrong" notes. Although there are some "outside" notes, they sound "jazzy."

Track 40

Fig. 29C
Jazz-Blues Changes

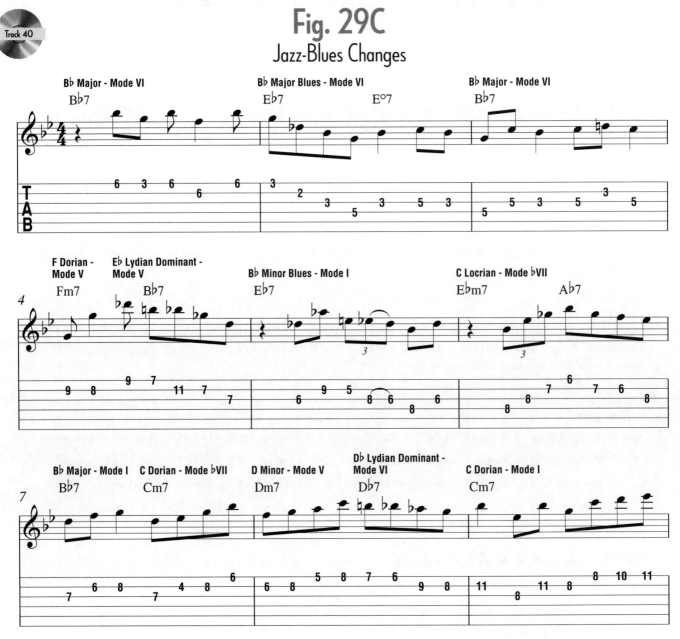

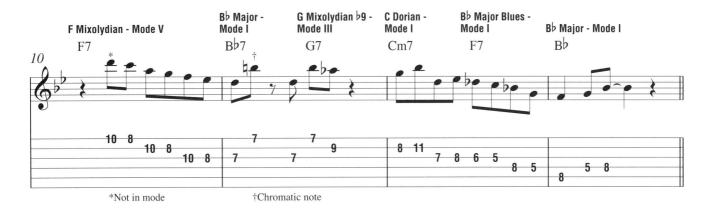

*Not in mode   †Chromatic note

For a jazz blues chord progression, it is preferable to minimize the use of the pentatonic chord scales so that you keep the focus on the blues form (see Fig. 11F). Grant Green was a master of playing straight-ahead blues lines while adding jazz "flavors" to certain parts of his solos. For example, try playing the progression in the chart with a more "B.B. King"-type of feeling. However, in measures 7–8, use the example pentatonic chord scales before going back to the "B.B. King" style in measure 9. All of a sudden you get that great "Grant Green" or "Barney Kessel" jazz vibe in a simple blues tune. Next, do the same thing but, in addition to using the example pentatonic chord scales in measures 7–8, add pentatonic chord scales to measures 11–12. Now you should be getting the type of sound that jazz saxophone or piano players get when they solo over the blues.

Now try different combinations of your style and the pentatonic chord scales. The number of options available to you is truly limitless.

Here are some other options:
- Try different tempos
- Try staying in the third position
- Try staying in the sixth position
- Try all five positions
- Try different keys, focusing on the "jazz" keys of B♭, F, G, A♭, and E♭
- Try different styles of blues (swing, shuffle, boogie-woogie, straight eighth notes, etc.)

Even though you need to practice as many variations as you can, remember that, especially in the blues, "less is more." Think of the pentatonic chord scales as "seasoning" on a salad—don't overdo it! You never want to play everything you know in the first chorus; instead, play simple melodic lines. Then spice up your blues melodies with the pentatonic chord scales. The contrast between simple blues melodies (focusing on the standard blues scale) and the harmonic complexity of the pentatonic chord scales will give your solos a truly professional sound.

Minor Blues

Minor blues is another basic form of the blues. It is used as a progression to "jam" on and is also the basis for minor blues jazz tunes like "Equinox" by John Coltrane. There are several chordal variations of the basic 12-bar minor blues form, four of which are presented in the following examples.

Fig. 29D is the simplest version, with no turnaround in the last measure.

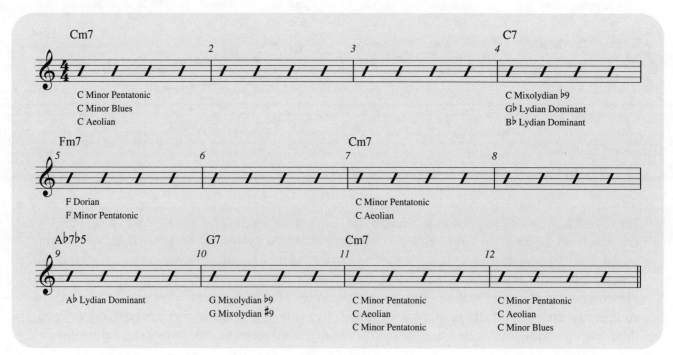

Fig. 29D
Minor Blues Changes: Variation 1

Track 41

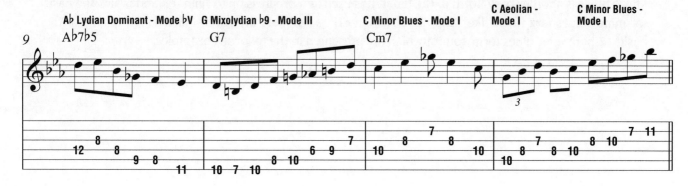

Fig. 29E introduces the "Equinox" change (G7 to D♭9) in measure 10. This variation also uses a C7 chord in measure 4 to lead to the Fm7 chord, as well as a V7 chord in measure 12 to return to the top of the progression.

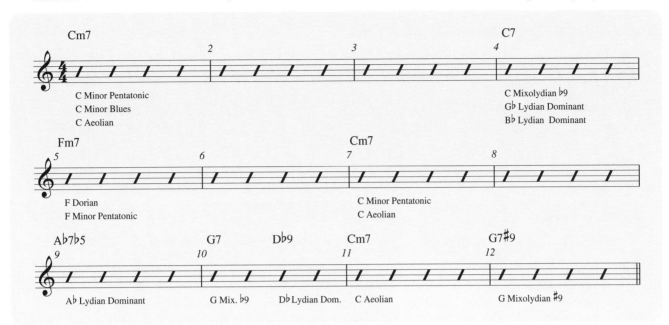

Fig. 29E
Minor Blues Changes: Variation 2

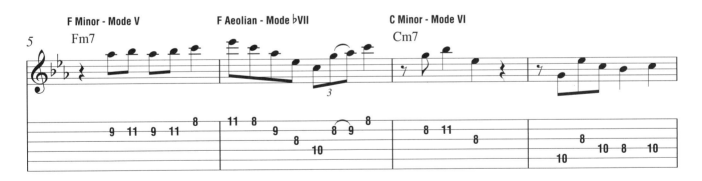

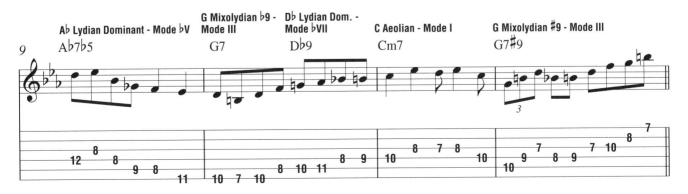

Fig. 29F demonstrates the "tritone" substitution of Db7b5 for G7 in measure 10. Also, measures 11–12 incorporate a minor-key turnaround to return to the top of the progression.

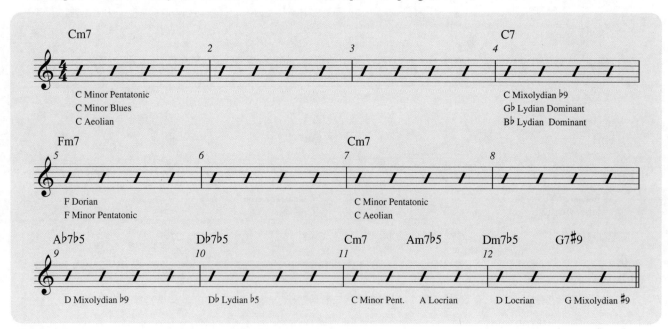

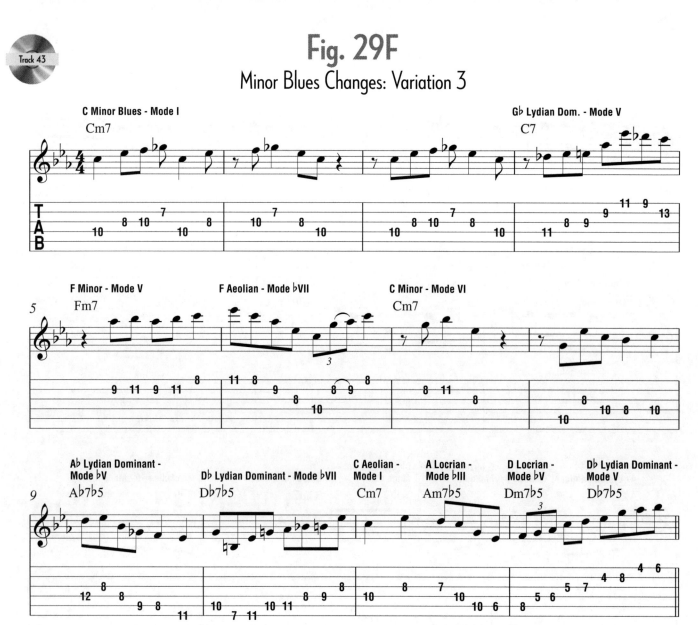

Fig. 29F
Minor Blues Changes: Variation 3

Fig. 29G is really an alternate approach to measures 9–10. Notice that, in this variation, the V7 (G7♭9) chord is used in measure 9 instead of the ♭VI7 chord as in the other three variations.

Fig. 29G

Minor Blues Changes: Variation 4

Track 44

The variations can be "mixed and matched," as each scale flows melodically into the next; there are no "wrong" notes. Although there are "outside" notes, they sound "jazzy."

As with standard blues and jazz blues, the key is to minimize the use of the pentatonic chord scales so that you keep the focus on the blues form. For example, try playing the progression in the chart using a "B.B. King"-type of feeling. Think in terms of "The Thrill Is Gone." In measure 4, use the pentatonic chord scales before going back to the "B.B. King" style in measure 5. Next, do the same thing but, this time, add pentatonic chord scales to measures 11–12. The result is the same type of sound that jazz saxophone or piano players get when they solo over a minor blues. Here are some other options:

- Try different combinations of your style and the pentatonic chord scales
- Try different tempos
- Try staying in the third position
- Try staying in the eighth position
- Try all five positions
- Try different keys, focusing on the "jazz" minor keys of Cm (example in the chart), Am, Gm, Fm, and Em
- Try different styles of minor blues (6/8, swing, shuffle, straight eighth notes, etc.)

Even though you need to practice as many variations as you can, remember that, in the blues, "less is more." Therefore, play simple, melodic lines. Then spice up your minor blues melodies with the pentatonic chord scales. The contrast between simple minor blues melodies (focusing on the standard minor and minor blues scales) and the harmonic complexity of the pentatonic chord scales will give your solos a truly professional sound.

Bebop Blues

This blues variation is associated with alto saxophone legend Charlie Parker. In fact, these changes are often referred to as "Bird blues" ("Bird" was a nickname of Charlie Parker) or "'Confirmation' blues" (a Charlie Parker song that uses similar changes).

The following chart is an example of the chord changes to and suggested pentatonic scale variations for soloing over a bebop blues song in the key of F.

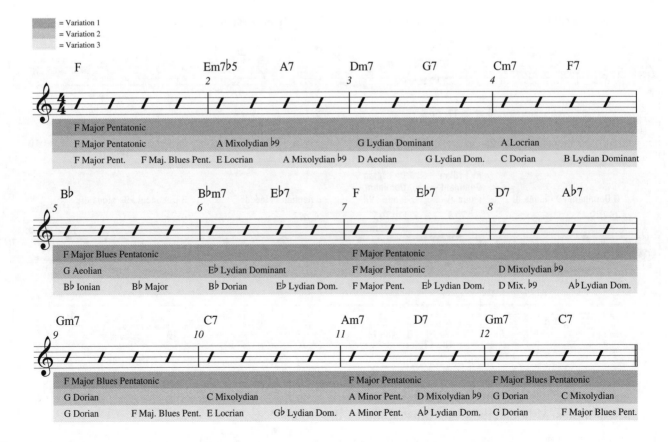

The main difference in this blues form is measures 2–4, where a cycle of descending ii–V progressions resolve to the IV chord (B♭) in measure 5. This cycle provides a nice vehicle to add a lot of harmonic content to the first four measures. Actually, there are many other ii–V progressions in this tune. In addition to measures 2–4, measure 6, measure 8 (Am7–D7 can be substituted for the D7), measures 9–10, measure 11, and measure 12 contain ii–V progressions. In fact, this entire progression is also known as "ii–V Blues".

Fig. 29H is an example of how these changes can be handled very simply by using only the F major pentatonic and F major blues pentatonic scales.

Fig. 29H
Bebop Blues Changes: Variation 1

Fig. 29I uses the pentatonic chord scales that closely match the chord progression of the song.

Fig. 29I
Bebop Blues Changes: Variation 2

Track 46

Fig. 29J is an example of using a different pentatonic scale in every measure.

Fig. 29J
Bebop Blues Changes: Variation 3

Track 47

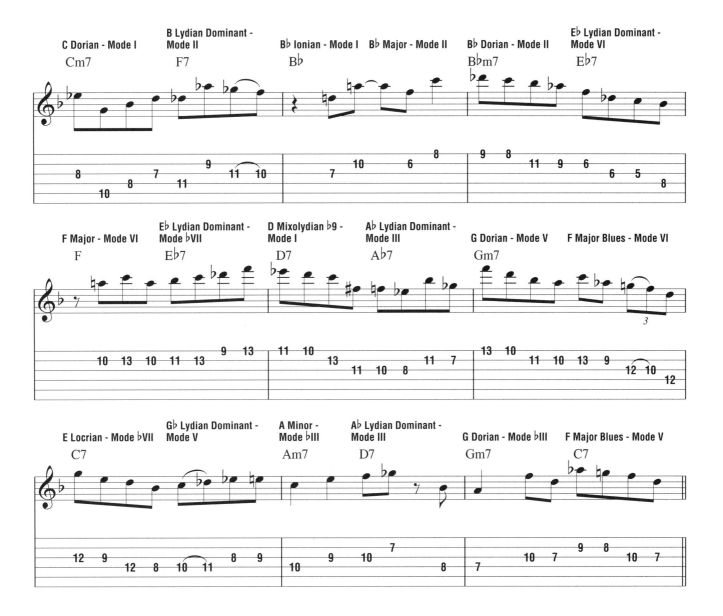

As suggested in the previous sections, you should also try adding different combinations of the pentatonic chord scales to your style. Here are some additional approaches to experiment with:

- Try different tempos
- Try staying in the third position
- Try staying in the sixth position
- Try all five positions
- Try different keys, focusing especially on the keys of B♭, G, C, A♭, and E♭
- Try different styles of bebop blues (swing, fast bebop, straight eighth notes, etc.)

As was also stated previously, even though you need to practice as many variations as you can, remember that "less is more." Think of the pentatonic chord scales as "seasoning" on a salad—don't overdo it! You never want to play everything you know in the first chorus; instead, play simple, melodic lines with two—or even one—of the basic pentatonic scales. Then spice up your blues melodies with the pentatonic chord scales. The contrast between simple blues melodies and the harmonic complexity of the pentatonic chord scales gives this blues progression its signature sound.

Summary

The blues is the foundation of all jazz. Proficiency in playing through blues changes is an absolute requirement for a jazz musician. This chapter presented the pentatonic scale approach to soloing over the four basic types of blues changes:

1. Standard Blues
2. Jazz Blues
3. Minor Blues
4. Bebop Blues

The focus is to develop a good balance between the basic pentatonic scale patterns presented in Chapters 1 and 11 with the pentatonic chord scales in the rest of the book.

Also, emphasis was given to the following:

- Continue to develop pentatonic scale variations in addition to those provided in the examples
- Try different combinations of your current playing style and the pentatonic chord scales
- Try different tempos
- Try staying in third position
- Try staying in sixth position
- Try all five positions
- Try different keys
- Try different styles of blues (swing, fast bebop, straight eighth notes, etc.)

In addition to proficiency in soloing over the four blues formats presented in this chapter, the ultimate goal is to be able to interject blues elements into virtually any chord progression.

CHAPTER 30
RHYTHM CHANGES REVIEW AND
THE BRIDGE CHORD PROGRESSION

Chapter 11 presented an overview of how various combinations of pentatonic scales covered in Section 1 can be used to solo over "Rhythm Changes". "Rhythm Changes" refers to a standard chord progression that is based on the song "I've Got Rhythm," composed by George Gershwin.

As noted in Chapter 11, many jazz tunes, especially bebop songs, are based on this progression. A few examples include "Oleo," "Anthropology," and "Moose the Mooche." Being able to solo over these changes is an absolute requirement for playing jazz. The difficulty is that, in addition to chords that change every two beats, Rhythm Changes are usually played at fast-to-ridiculously-fast speeds.

Overall Chord Progression

This progression follows a standard 32-bar AABA format, which means that there are two verses, followed by a bridge, followed by a third verse. Then the tune just keeps repeating.

The basic chord changes for the song are shown below.

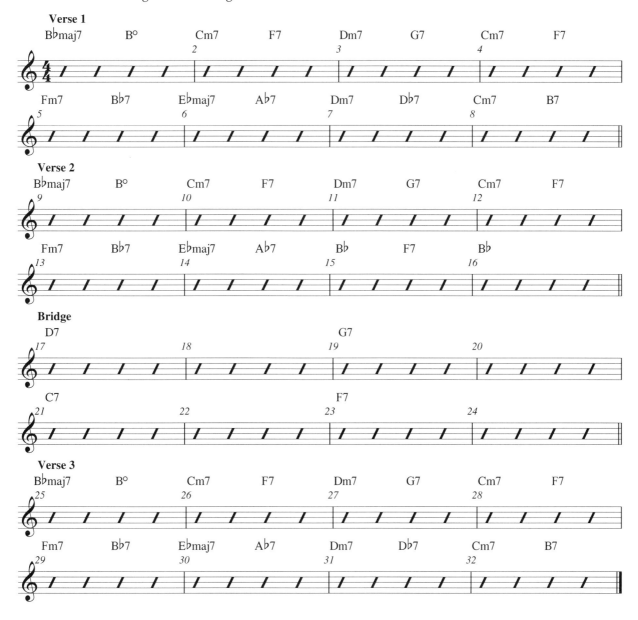

The Verses

Notice that the verses are characterized by changing chords every two beats. As described in Chapter 11, instead of trying to play the changes (i.e., playing a different scale over each chord), you can use the same approach described in Chapter 29 for playing the blues: use various combinations of the major pentatonic scale and the major blues pentatonic scale for the entire progression.

> The following five steps were suggested in Chapter 11 for developing facility with the verse sections of the tune.
>
> **Step 1:** Use the B♭ major (G minor) pentatonic scale for the entire progression (see Fig. 11G).
>
> **Step 2:** Add arpeggios and chromatics to the solo (see Fig. 11H).
>
> **Step 3:** Add the B♭ major (G Minor) blues pentatonic scale to the progression (see Fig. 11I).
>
> **Step 4:** Use six different (B♭ major, B♭ major blues, B♭ minor, B♭ minor blues, C minor, C minor blues) pentatonic scales in the progression (see Fig. 11J).
>
> **Step 5:** Use pentatonic chord scales for the entire progression (see Fig. 11K).

These five examples only scratch the surface with respect to pentatonic chord-scale options. For example, notice that the example solo in Fig. 11L focuses on the ii–V chord sequences in the progression. These are summarized below:

Measures 2, 4, and 8: Cm7–F7

Measures 3 and 7: Dm7–G7

Measure 5: Fm7–B♭7

Measure 6: E♭m7–A♭7 (implied)

Consequently, you can use the resources in Chapter 26 (ii–V Progressions) for many more pentatonic chord-scale ideas for these particular measures. Now let's turn our attention to the bridge changes for this tune.

The Bridge

As described at the beginning of the chapter, Rhythm Changes follows the AABA form, with a bridge after the second verse. The bridge is shown below.

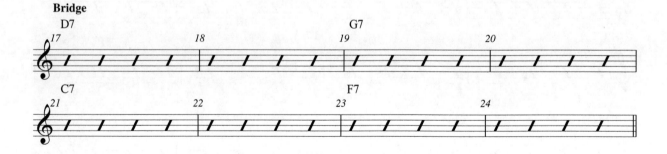

Since each chord in the bridge is two measures long, you have a lot of flexibility when playing over these changes.

Below is a sample of pentatonic scales that can be "mixed and matched."

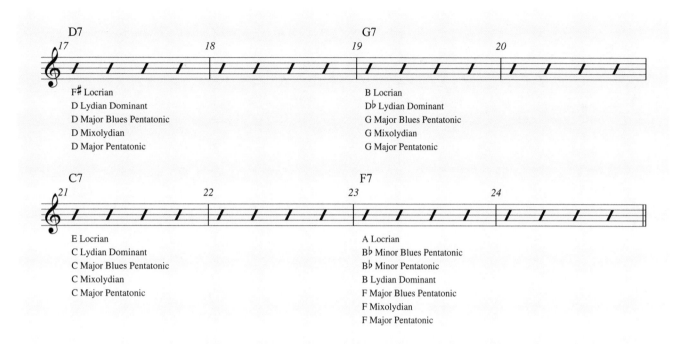

This list can be further expanded by choices from Chapter 16 (substitute dominant seventh pentatonic scales) and all of Section 4 (Other Pentatonic Scales). All these scales will sound correct no matter how you mix them. However, there should be some type of consistency of sound. To start, I recommend using the substitute Locrian Pentatonic Scales for the D7, G7, C7 and F7 chords. **Fig. 30A** is an example solo using substitute Locrian pentatonic scales over the bridge changes.

Fig. 30A
"Rhythm Changes" Bridge: Variation 1

Track 48

Another approach is to treat each chord of the bridge as a ii–V progression. This opens up a lot of other nice combinations of pentatonic scales from Chapter 26.

The following are a few of the more "straight ahead" alternatives:

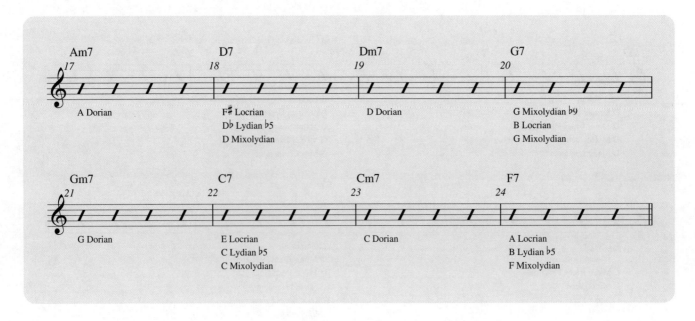

Fig. 30B is an example solo using the ii–V changes approach. Try different combinations of the ii–V examples in the above chart over the bridge changes. All of them will sound good.

Fig. 30B
"Rhythm Changes" Bridge: Variation 2

Track 48 (cont.)

For a more "jazzy" sound, try using the substitute Lydian Dominant pentatonic scales over the bridge chord progression.

Fig.30C is an example solo using this approach. Notice that the solo also uses the B♭ minor blues penta-tonic scale in the last measure to provide a nice, bluesy transition back to the song's third verse.

Fig. 30C
"Rhythm Changes" Bridge: Variation 3

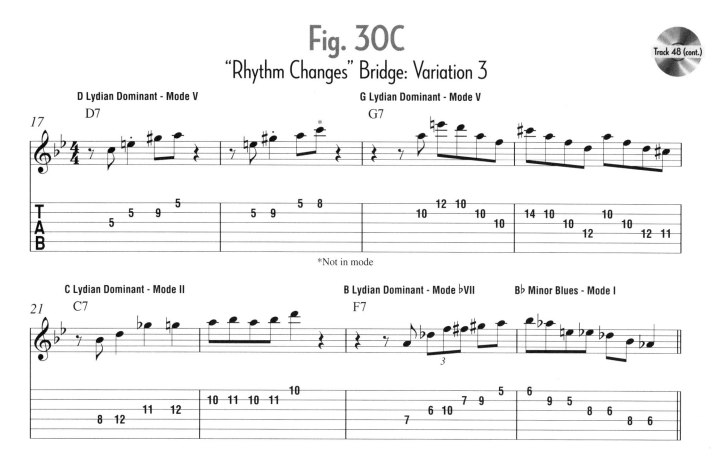

*Not in mode

Summary

This chapter presents a wealth of pentatonic scale options for playing over Rhythm Changes. The examples are provided to give you an idea of the range of options that are available. As with the chapter on the blues, your solo should not be cluttered with every pentatonic scale that you can squeeze in; instead, focus primarily on using the B♭ major pentatonic scale, especially in the verses, and color your solo with occasional use of the B♭ major blues pentatonic scale. The pentatonic chord scales sound best when used in measures 5–8. Here are some additional options:

- Try different tempos
- Try staying in third position
- Try staying in sixth position
- Try all five positions
- Try different keys, especially focusing on the keys of F, E♭, and A♭

Even though you need to practice as many variations as you can, remember that, just as in the blues, "less is more." Think of the pentatonic chord scales as "seasoning" on a salad—don't overdo it! You never want to play everything you know in the first choruses; instead, play simple, melodic lines with the basic B♭ major pentatonic scale. Then spice up your melodies with the pentatonic chord scales. However, for the bridge, focus strictly on pentatonic chord scales. The contrast between simple melodies in the verses and the harmonic complexity of the pentatonic chord scales in the bridge will give your solos a truly professional sound.

CHAPTER 31

STANDARDS

Chapter 11 covered an approach to soloing over standards that combines pentatonic chord scales with blues pentatonic scales. The importance of including elements of the blues in soloing over non–blues based tunes was emphasized as well. Once again, it is strongly suggested that you carefully listen to the great blues players and the great "bluesy" jazz players to ensure that you have the sound of the blues firmly engrained in you soul.

Three "rules" were presented for developing a soloing approach for standards:

Rule #1: You can use the blues pentatonic scale in standards over tonic (and/or temporary tonic) major and/or minor chords in the progression.

The chord changes to "Autumn Leaves" were used to demonstrate the use of the blues pentatonic scale for tonic major/minor chords and pentatonic chord scales for all other chords.

Rule #2: You can use the blues pentatonic scale in standards over turnarounds in 1) verses, 2) the bridge, 3) intros, 4) outros, 5) connecting verses, and even 6) entire tunes.

Turnarounds are a basic component of standards. Incorporating the blues pentatonic scale into the various types of turnarounds that appear in a standard was presented with several examples.

Rule #3: You can use the blues pentatonic scale for entire non-turnaround tunes.

The major blues pentatonic scale is so versatile that it can be used in any diatonic chord progression, in any part of a song. In fact, it can even form the basis for soloing over the entire tune.

The following are two examples of using the pentatonic approach to soloing over "standards" changes. The first example demonstrates a fast-tempo song, while the second example demonstrates a slow-tempo song.

Fast-Tempo Chord Progression

To supplement the material on standards in Chapter 11, below is the chord progression to a standard fast-tempo chord progression and two variations of suggested pentatonic scales for soloing over its changes.

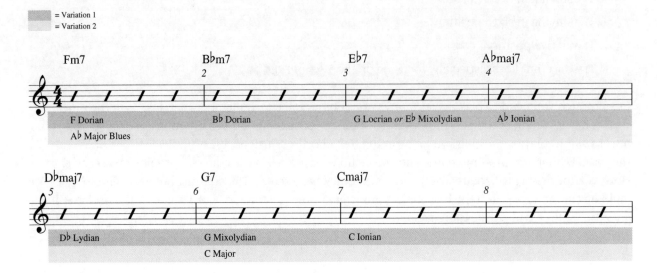

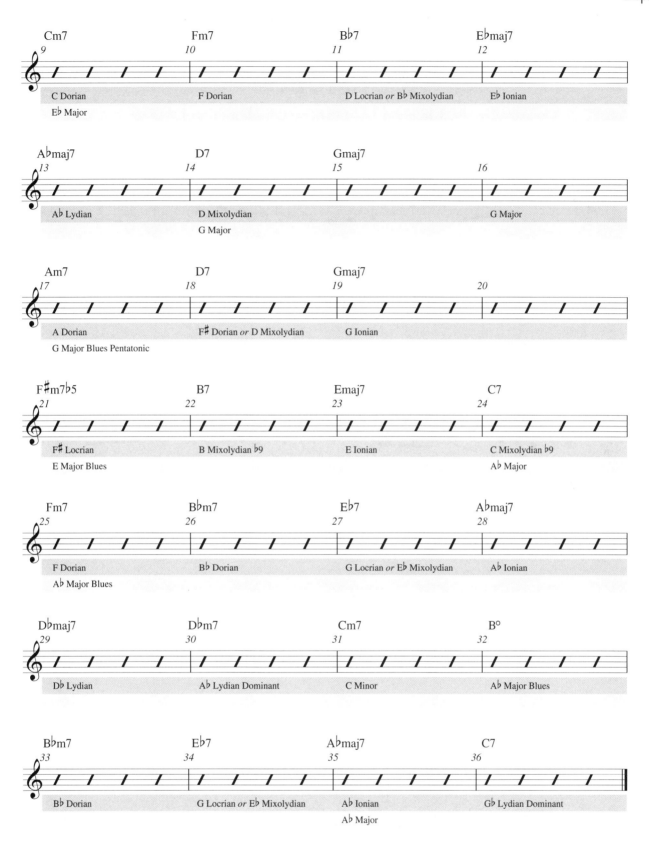

The changes to this song represent a few common characteristics of standards:

- Several ii–V progressions
- Several ii–V–I progressions
- Shifting tonal centers (measures 1–5=A♭, measures 6–8=C, measures 9–13=E♭, measures 14–20=G, measures 21–23=E, measures 24–36=A♭)

Two pentatonic soloing variations are provided. **Fig. 31A** uses pentatonic chord scales exclusively.

Fig. 31A
Fast-Tempo Chord Progression: Variation 1

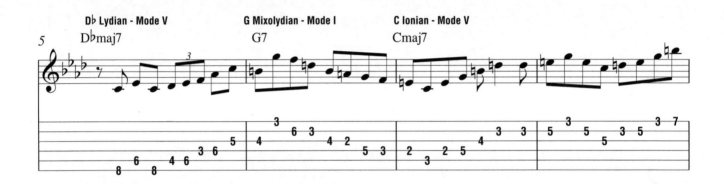

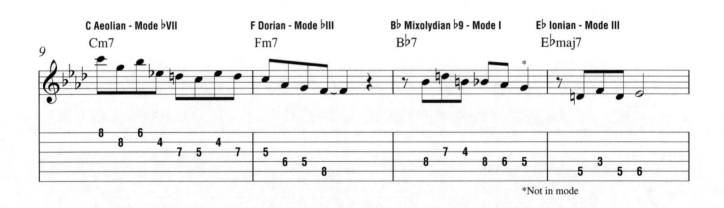

*Not in mode

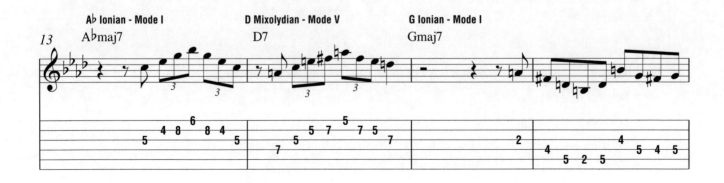

*Chromatic note

Fig. 31B uses only the major pentatonic scale and the major blues pentatonic scale for each of the song's five tonal centers (A♭, C, E♭, G, and E).

Fig. 31B
Fast-Tempo Chord Progression: Variation 2

*Not in mode

Practice both variations until you are comfortable with the five tonal centers within the changes. Then create your own variations by combining the pentatonic chord-scale approach of Fig. 31A with the more bluesy approach of Fig. 31B.

Slow-Tempo Chord Progression

The following is a standard slow-tempo chord progression and two variations of suggested pentatonic scales for soloing over its changes.

Fig. 31C is an example solo that uses various combinations of pentatonic scales from the chart to cover the changes.

Fig. 31C
Slow-Tempo Chord Progression

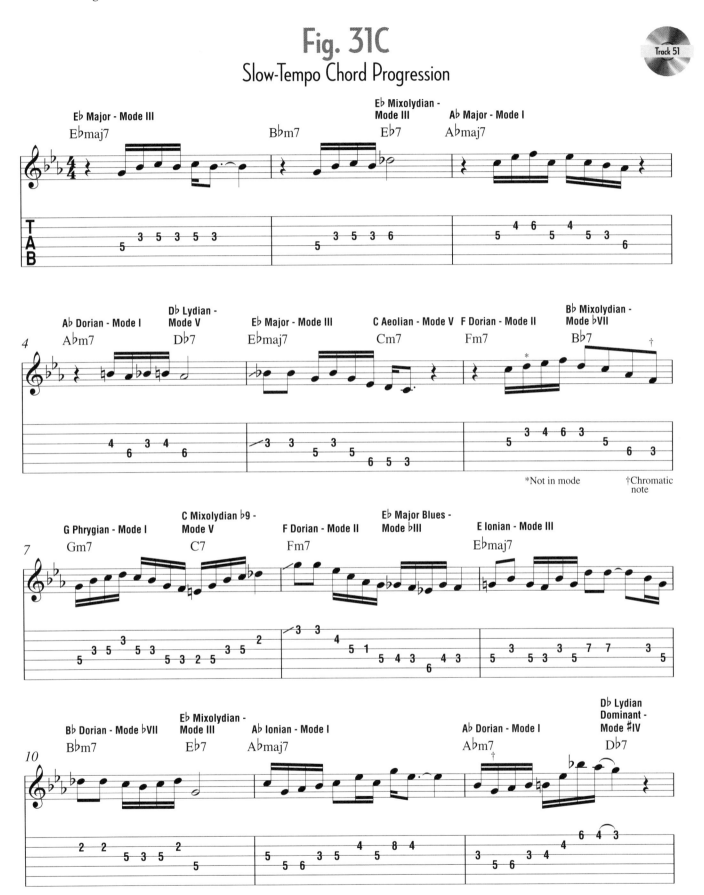

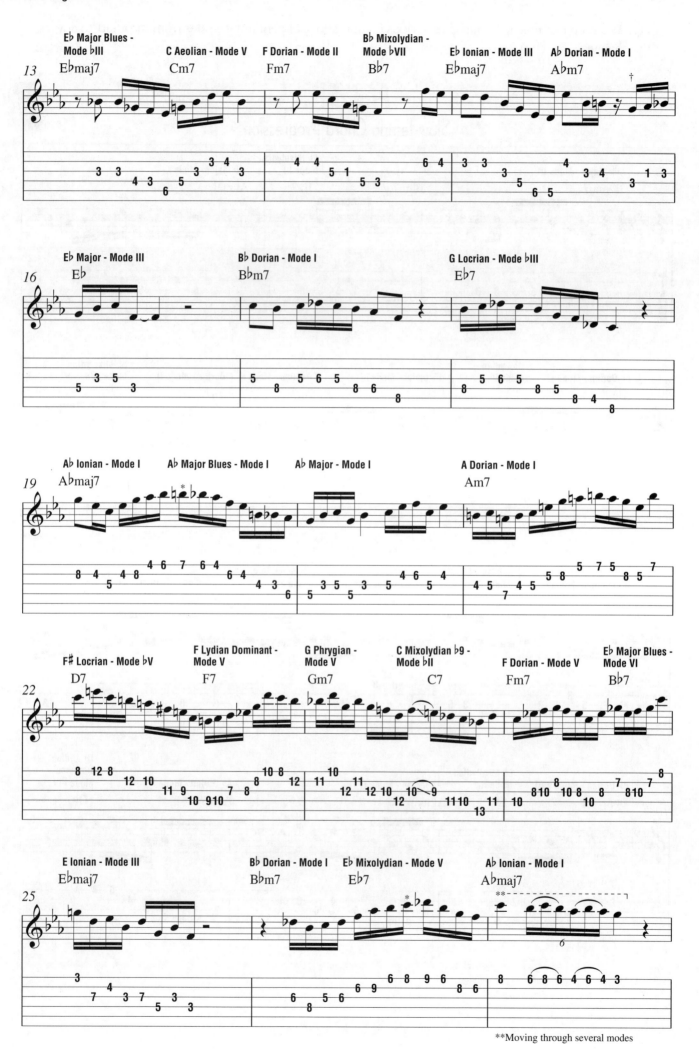

**Moving through several modes

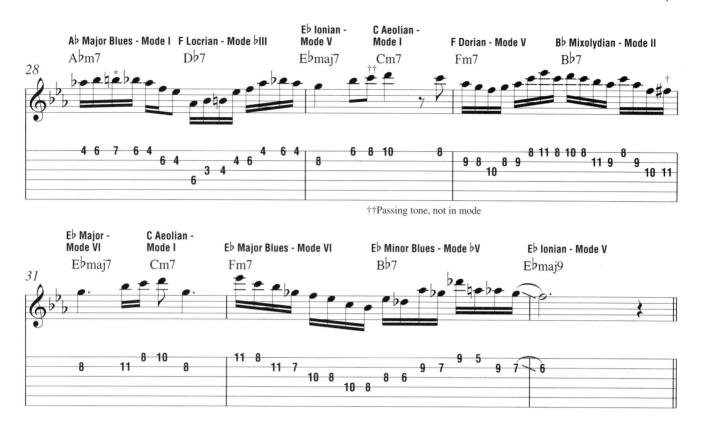

††Passing tone, not in mode

The changes to this song represent several common characteristics of slow-tempo standards:

Verses

- ii–V progressions
- ii–V–I progressions
- Shifting tonal centers (measure 1=E♭, measures 2–3=A♭, measure 4=G♭, measures 5–9=E♭)

Bridge

- ii–V progressions
- ii–V–I progressions
- Shifting tonal centers (measures 17–20=A♭, measures 21–22=G, measure 23–25=E♭)

Also, notice the use of blues pentatonic scales to add the important "blues" element to this standard slow-tempo chord progression.

Next, try the changes at different tempos. For example, these changes can also be played as a bossa nova or even at a fast-swing tempo. Here are some other options:

- Try staying in third position
- Try staying in sixth position
- Try playing in all five positions
- Try different keys, focusing particularly on the keys of F, B♭, C, and G

Summary

This chapter presents the pentatonic scale approach to soloing over standards. The "rules" (from Chapter 11) for developing a soloing approach for standards are demonstrated in the two variations presented for each example song (fast tempo and slow tempo). The pentatonic scale approach works well with any song, at any tempo. The examples are provided to give you an idea of the range of options that are available. As with the chapter on the blues, your solo should not be cluttered with every pentatonic scale that you can squeeze in. Also, pay particular attention to the sound of the "bluesy" pentatonic scales over chord changes to standards.

Now try the pentatonic scale approach on other standards that you like and/or on bossa-nova tunes. No matter the complexity of the chord changes, this system will always work.

CHAPTER 32
COLTRANE CHANGES AND THE "GIANT STEPS" CHORD PROGRESSION

According to jazz guitar great Joe Diorio, "John Coltrane's composition 'Giant Steps' is without a doubt the most challenging jazz chord progression of the late 20th Century" (*Giant Steps* Diorio, 1997, p. 4). Coming from someone of such stature, this is a profound statement.

"Giant Steps" is generally considered to be the "final exam" for jazz musicians. To be able to navigate the fast chord changes, in three tonal centers, at a blistering speed, with *musicality* is a major accomplishment that very few musicians—including guitar players—are able to achieve.

"Giant Steps" has an almost mystical quality about it. Entire books have been written about the song and its composer, the legendary saxophonist John Coltrane. This particular song is the topic of countless articles and chapters in jazz method books. Many theories have been put forward on how to navigate the changes. Many transcriptions of "Giant Steps" have been published. Many analyses of the transcriptions have been written. Many accomplished jazz artists, including guitarists, have recorded the song in a wide range of styles. An annotated list of book, article, web, and guitar-recording resources are presented in Appendix E.

The Coltrane Changes Formula

"Giant Steps" defined a whole new way of looking at standard chord changes—specifically, the ii–V–I change. In fact, the term "Coltrane changes" or "Coltrane cycle" is an important part of the jazz lexicon. These terms refer to the harmonic approach taken in "Giant Steps," which basically substitutes major seventh chords a major 3rd apart over a standard ii–V–I chord progression.

For example, take a simple C major seventh tonic chord. The standard ii–V–I progression for this chord would be: Dm7–G7–Cmaj7. However, Coltrane used a different approach to get from the Dm7 (ii chord) to the Cmaj7 (I chord): He substituted two tonal centers, a major 3rd apart, between the ii chord and the I chord. For a Cmaj7 I chord, these tonal centers are A♭ and E. He used basic V chords to arrive at (resolve to) these tonal centers. For example, review the following comparison of a standard ii–V–I progression in the key of C with "Coltrane changes."

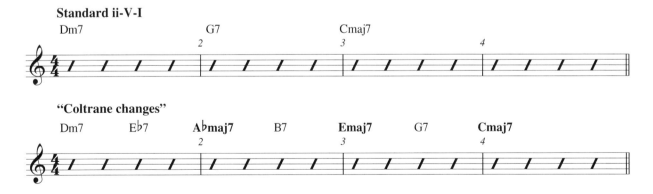

Notice that the three key centers (in **bold**)—A♭, E, and C—are all a major 3rd (four frets) apart. Another way to think about this relationship is that the tonal-center chord letters make up an augmented triad. For example, the notes of a C augmented triad are C, E, and G♯ (A♭). These three notes form the temporary key changes of the "Coltrane changes" formula. This formula gives the basic ii–V–I progression a very "outside"—yet musical—sound. Instead of playing a solo over simple ii–V–I chords whereby there is only one V–I chord movement, there are now three V–I chord movements to navigate within the same amount of time. Also, notice that with the standard four-measure ii–V–I progression, the I chord is reached at the third measure. However, in the "Coltrane changes" substitution, the I chord is delayed till the fourth measure. This gives an additional feeling of delayed resolution that contributes to the "outside" sound of the progression.

Using the "Coltrane changes" to solo over a standard ii–V–I progression will be discussed further at the end of this chapter. First, the implementation of this approach for soloing over the "Giant Steps" chord progression is presented.

Important Preparatory Work for "Giant Steps"

Before working on "Giant Steps," you must first listen to John Coltrane's original 1959 recording, on Atlantic Records. It is available in many CD collections. There is no way to appreciate the mystical beauty of this seminal song without immersing yourself in the original recording. If this is your first time, it will be very difficult to fully appreciate what is going on in the song. Don't worry about it—at some point in your musical development, you will "get it." Just keep listening. If you haven't listened to it in a while, listen again. You will appreciate it even more.

Next, acquire a transcription of the song, which is available in several books of John Coltrane transcriptions. Transcriptions are also available on the web (be sure it is a legal transcription!). As noted in Appendix E, the book by David Demsey, *John Coltrane Plays Giant Steps* (1996), contains a complete transcription of all 96 recorded choruses of "Giant Steps." The book by Scott D. Reeves, *Creative Jazz Improvisation* (2001), contains a transcription of the first four choruses. Following the recording with a transcription gives you even greater appreciation for the artistry of John Coltrane.

Now you are ready to approach this song.

Learning the Song Structure

First, learn to play the chord changes (see the following chord chart).

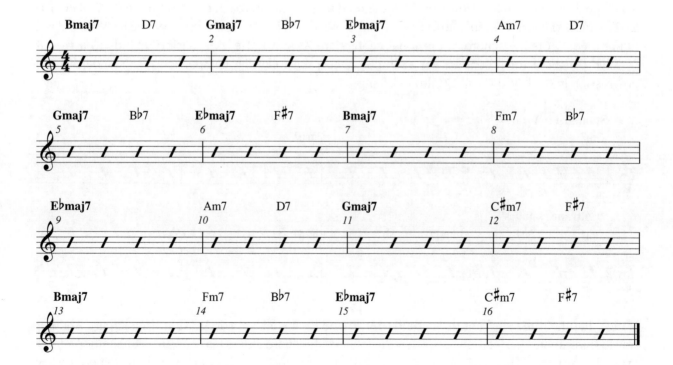

Notice the following:

- There are three tonal centers (in **bold**): B, G, and E♭
- The overall design of the song is that the odd numbered measures (1, 3, 5, 7, 9, 11, 13, and 15) are all related by key centers of ascending major 3rds. This is a very non-standard tone-center movement.
- The first half of the song achieves this overall design with descending major 3rd tonalities.
- The second half of the song achieves this overall design with ascending major 3rd tonalities.

While the chords are nothing more than simple major seventh, minor seventh, and dominant seventh chords, note that three tonal centers (B, E♭, and G) are involved. Also, note the fact that the song is played at a very fast tempo.

Once you have the structure of the song under your fingers, try comping along with the original recording **[Fig. 32A]**. Forget about fancy chord substitutions or extensions—there is no time. Use simple chord shapes. On the original recording, the piano comping of Tommy Flanigan is clearly audible. Notice that he is comping with simple inversions and simple rhythms. Fortunately, the chord changes are easy to hear. This makes it easier to follow along. However, because of the speed of the song, it will be a challenge to keep up with the comping through the whole song. This is OK. After only a few choruses, you will really begin to relate to the legend surrounding this song. Below are some suggested chord shapes.

Fig. 32A
Rhythm-Guitar Chort Chart

Now it is time for you to solo. Don't despair—even the great jazz pianist Tommy Flanigan is having a tough time navigating the changes, as you can hear on the recording.

Record the changes in a sequencer (I highly recommend Band-In-A-Box by PG Music). Set the tempo at approximately 150 beats per minute (about half the speed of the recording). At this speed, you should be able to cleanly play the chord changes. If this is still too fast, just slow the speed and gradually work up to 150 bpm. Next, learn the "head," or melody, of the song (available in many legal "fake" or "real" books). Since the melody is mostly half notes and quarter notes, this should not be a problem. Practice alternating between playing the melody and comping the chord changes. The goal is to really internalize the song.

Now you are ready to begin (or restart) a journey that all jazz musicians must undertake: learning to solo over "Giant Steps." This is an important rite of passage for jazz musicians.

Brief Analysis of the Coltrane Solo

It is way beyond the scope of this book to get into theoretical aspects of what John Coltrane is playing in his solos. However, there are numerous resources available for you to investigate the complexity of this song on your own. As mentioned previously, an annotated description of resources is presented in Appendix E. The chapter on Coltrane substitutions in the book by Reeves (2001) has one of the most concise descriptions of what is going on in John Coltrane's solo. According to Reeves, "Coltrane clearly outlines each of the chords, primarily with three- or four-note groupings too numerous to indicate" (p. 169). This is clearly evident as you follow the transcription. For example, below is a description of the chord solo devices used by Coltrane in the first eight measures of his solo. Notice the emphasis on four-note groupings. The book by Bergonzi (1992) is highly recommended as an excellent and comprehensive reference on using four-note groupings for jazz soloing.

Measure	Chord	Chord Solo Device	3-note grouping	4-note grouping
1	Bmaj7	5–3–1 descending arpeggio	X	
	D7	1–2–3–5 pattern		X
2	Gmaj7	1–5–3–1 descending arpeggio		X
	B♭7	9–7–6–5 pattern		X
3	E♭maj7	E♭ major scale		X
4	Am7	5–3–1–7 descending arpeggio		X
	D7	3–♭9–1–7 pattern		X
5	Gmaj7	3–5–1–3 ascending arpeggio		X
	B♭7	3–5–7–9 ascending arpeggio		X
6	E♭maj7	1–2–3–5 pattern		X
	F♯7	7–9–3–5 pattern		X
7	Bmaj7	Descending Ionian scale	X	
8	Fm7	Descending chromatic scale		X
	B♭7	Descending Mixolydian scale		X

While the various devices that Coltrane uses in his solo are simple at the individual chord level, the way that he permutates and combines them into coherent melodies, at a ridiculously fast tempo, is what his genius is all about.

Guitarists' Guide to Soloing Over "Giant Steps"

This brings us back to the goal of this book: providing you with a pentatonic approach to soloing over any set of chord changes, including the "Giant Steps" chord progression. The pentatonic approach is important because it is the most familiar, particularly Mode I of the minor pentatonic scale. This is the scale that, in all probability, you can play the fastest. You need the important capability of speed in order to tackle "Giant Steps" at a reasonable level of performance.

It is interesting to note that several guitarists have recorded "Giant Steps" in various styles, including straight-ahead jazz, jazz bossa, chord solo, and even jazz fusion. These recordings are annotated in Appendix E. This is not a comprehensively researched list; I am sure there are other recordings by guitarists. However, these are the recordings that I am familiar with at the time of this writing. All of the recordings show phenomenal musicianship and guitar playing and belong in your CD collection, especially Jimmy Bruno's recording of "Giant Steps" on the album *Burnin'*. It truly captures the virtuosity and musicality of the original recording.

After listening to any of these recordings (especially Jimmy Bruno's), you may be ready to give up jazz guitar playing. However, do not despair—you have come too far to quit. You are now able to solo effectively over virtually any jazz song. As mentioned at the beginning of the chapter, "Giant Steps" is the "final exam" for all musicians. Believe it or not, you are prepared to tackle this song.

The following is the chord progression and three variations of suggested pentatonic scales for soloing over the changes to "Giant Steps."

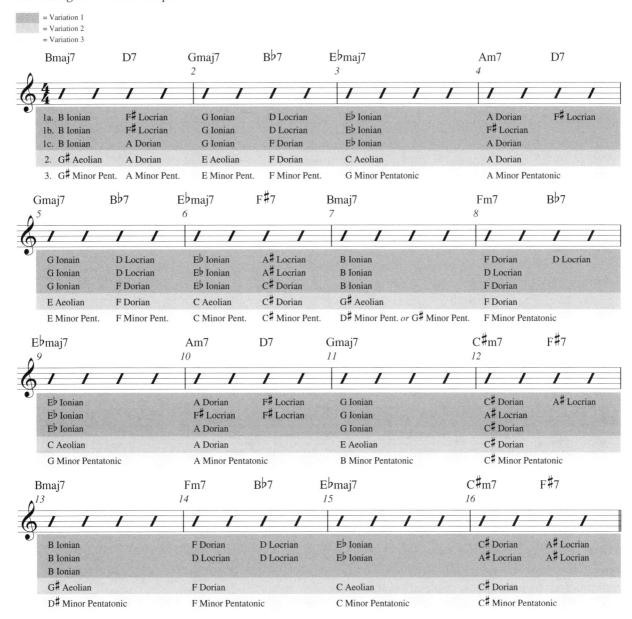

Three pentatonic soloing variations are provided.

Variation1A uses a pentatonic chord scale for each chord change in the song [**Fig. 32B**]. The Ionian pentatonic scale is for all major seventh chords, the Dorian pentatonic scale for all minor sevenths, and the Locrian pentatonic scale for all dominant sevenths.

Fig. 32B
Solo Variation 1A: Ionian, Dorian and Locrian Pentatonic Scales

Therefore, you can play the song with only three pentatonic scales—Ionian, Dorian, and Locrian. Using only three scale shapes greatly simplifies the physical aspects of soloing over these changes while still maintaining the harmonic complexity of the changes.

This variation can be further simplified in two ways by simplifying the chord progression even further. In Variation 1B, the major seventh chords are still covered by the Ionian pentatonic scale [**Fig. 32C**]. However, the minor seventh chords are treated as their related dominant sevenths and therefore are covered by the Locrian pentatonic scale (measures 8, 10, 12, 14, and 16). In other words, all ii–V progressions are treated as simple V chords. Now you can solo through the entire song using only two pentatonic chord scales, Ionian and Locrian, while still maintaining the strong V–I sound of the changing tonal centers.

Fig. 32C
Solo Variation 1B: Ionian and Locrian Pentatonic Scales

Track 54

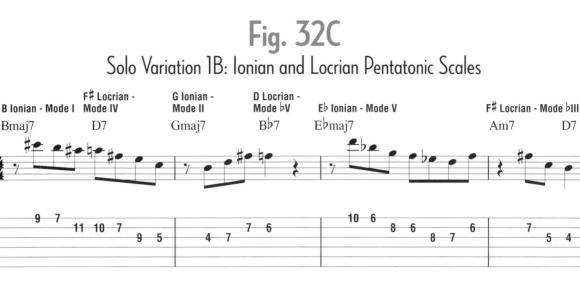

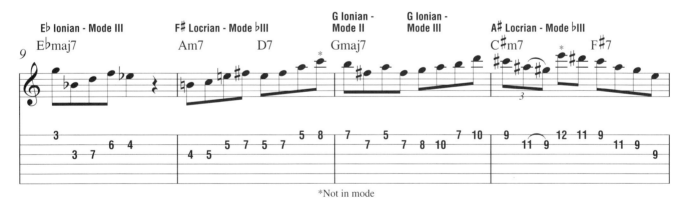

*Not in mode

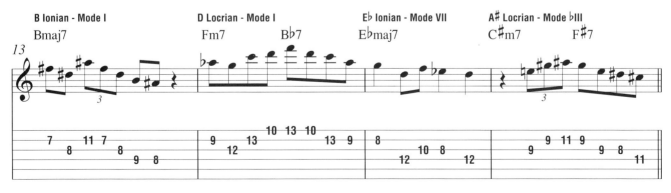

A similar approach is used for Variation 1C [**Fig. 32D**]. The difference is that all V chords and ii–V progressions are treated as ii chords and thus are covered with the Dorian pentatonic scale. Consequently, you can solo through the entire song using only two pentatonic chord scales, Ionian and Dorian, which offer a "suspended" sound to the changing tonal centers.

Fig. 32D
Solo Variation 1C: Ionian and Dorian Pentatonic Scales

*Not in mode

Variation 2 uses the associated Aeolian pentatonic scale for the major seventh chords [**Fig. 32E**]. This gives the major seventh chords a different jazzy flavor than the Ionian pentatonic scale that is used in Variation 1.

Fig. 32E
Solo Variation 2: Aeolian and Dorian Pentatonic Scales

Track 56

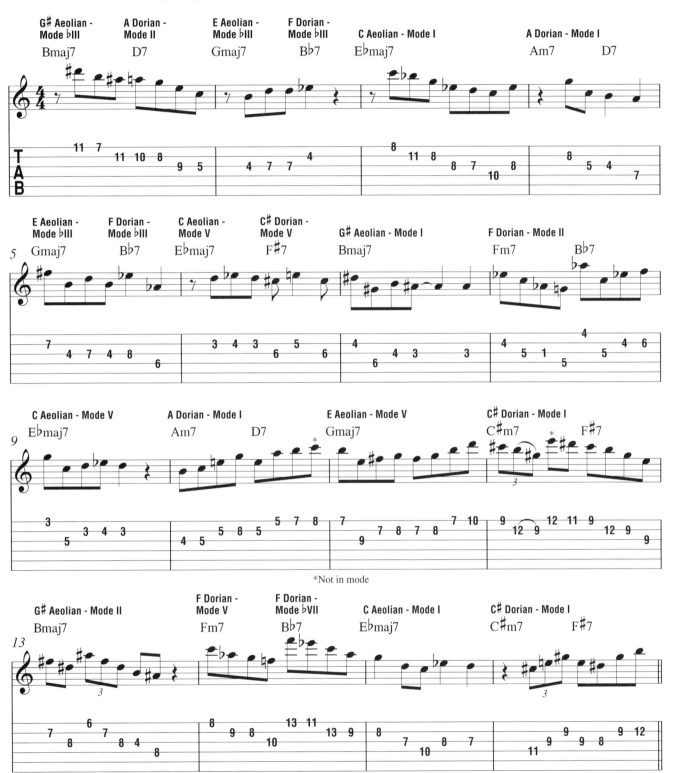

*Not in mode

Note that you can simplify Variation 2 in the same two ways that Variation 1 was simplified. First, you can change all of the ii–V progressions to V chords and use the Locrian pentatonic scale over these changes (measures 8, 10, 12, 14, and 16). Second, as demonstrated in Fig. 32D, you can simplify the progression by treating all V chords and ii–V progressions as ii chords, covering them with the Dorian pentatonic scale. With this approach, you can solo through the entire song using only two "minor" pentatonic chord scales, Aeolian and Dorian.

IMPORTANT NOTE: Since these two pentatonic scales (Aeolian and Dorian) use identical patterns, you are effectively playing the entire solo with just one pentatonic-scale pattern. The next variation takes this approach, using an even easier pentatonic scale pattern—the minor pentatonic scale.

Variation 3 is very interesting and potentially the most powerful [**Fig. 32F**]. I call it the "cheating" way to play "Giant Steps" changes. With this approach, you can play the entire song with *only one pentatonic scale*. Even better, it is the easiest of all the pentatonic scales because it is probably the first one you ever learned—the minor pentatonic scale (Chapter 1). It even gets better: You can play the entire song using only two of the minor pentatonic chord shapes—Mode I and Mode V (see Fig. 1A). These are most likely the first two pentatonic shapes that you ever learned. In fact, even though there are five pentatonic shapes, many guitarists get by using only Mode I and Mode V.

Fig. 32F
Solo Variation 3: Basic Minor Pentatonic Scales

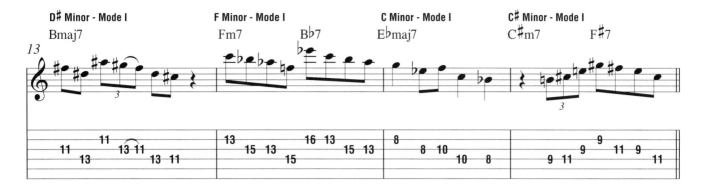

What this all means is that you are able to solo over "Giant Steps" at close to the maximum speed that you are able to play guitar. Why? Because you will only be using the two easiest of all the pentatonic scales and the ones you have been playing the longest.

The structure of Variation 3 is duplicated below and expanded to demonstrate how the entire song can be covered using only two modes (Mode I and Mode V) of the minor pentatonic acale. The Mode name and starting fret position for each is also included.

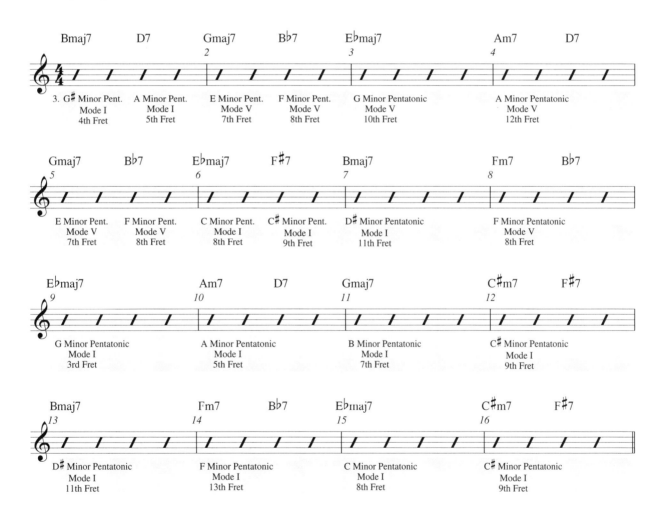

Granted, with this approach you have to move all over the fretboard. However, the position changes allow you maximum use of the same patterns. Also, all of that hand movement actually looks pretty "flashy."

Notice that we have converted all of the chords, including the major sevenths, to minor chords. This gives us the option to use the basic minor pentatonic scales from Chapter 1 for soloing over all of the chords in this progression. This approach is harmonically correct since all that you are doing is substituting the Phrygian pentatonic scale for the major seventh chords, as described in Chapter 12. Also, remember that the Phrygian pentatonic scale is the same scale as the minor pentatonic scale from Chapter 1. For the minor seventh and dominant seventh chords, you are simply substituting the minor pentatonic scale for both.

The second half of the song (measures 9–16) is particularly easy to play since you are simply using the basic Mode I pattern, starting at the third fret, and moving it up by whole steps till you get to the 13th fret. At that point, you just move the shape down to the eighth fret and finish off the sequence at the neighboring ninth fret. Plus, you have a whole measure to solo at each fret position. While the first half of the song requires faster position changes, they are still relatively simple to do since the patterns are close together and ascend in an easy-to-remember pattern.

The "Coltrane Changes" Formula Revisited

As described earlier in this chapter, the "Coltrane changes" formula is a harmonic approach that substitutes major seventh chords a major 3rd apart over a standard ii–V–I chord progression. Also, each major seventh chord is preceded by its relative dominant seventh chord. This formula is used extensively in "Giant Steps" and can be used in any ii–V–I chord progression. Therefore, it is important that you become comfortable playing the "Coltrane changes" as an independent chord sequence so that you can use it as often as you like, especially when you want to make a ii–V–I progression sound "outside."

The following chart superimposes "Coltrane changes" over a standard ii–V–I progression in the key of C.

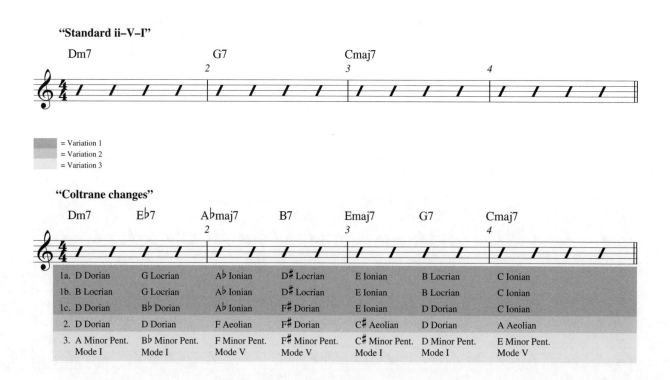

The three variations are the same as those presented in the previous "Giant Steps" chord progression chart. Variation 1A uses pentatonic chord scales for each chord in the "Coltrane changes" [**Fig. 32G**]. Variation 1B limits the pentatonic chord scales to only Ionian and Locrian [**Fig. 32H**]. And Variation 1C limits the pentatonic chord scales to Ionian and Dorian [**Fig. 32I**].

Fig. 32G
ii-V-I Solo Variation 1A: Ionian, Dorian and Locrian Pentatonic Scales

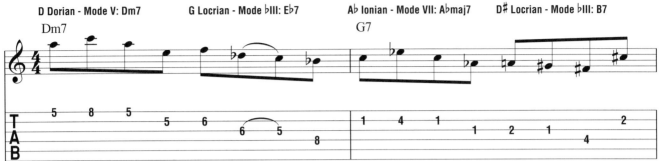

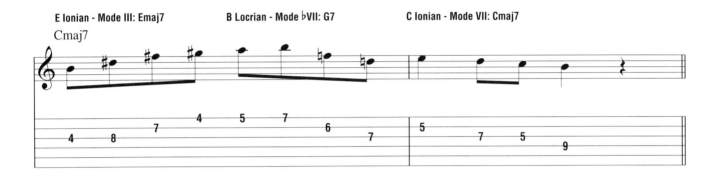

Fig. 32H

ii-V-I Solo Variation 1B: Ionian and Locrian Pentatonic Scales

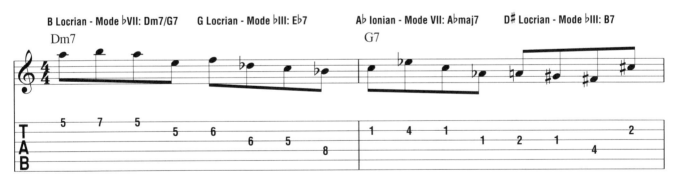

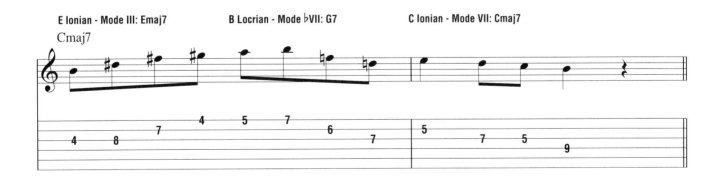

Track 58 (cont.)

Fig. 32I
ii–V–I Solo Variation 1C: Ionian and Dorian Pentatonic Scales

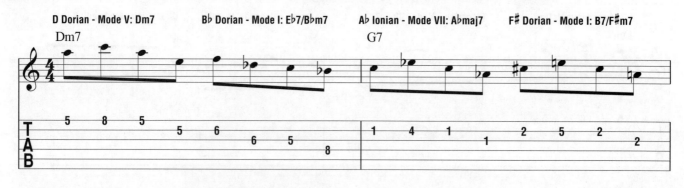

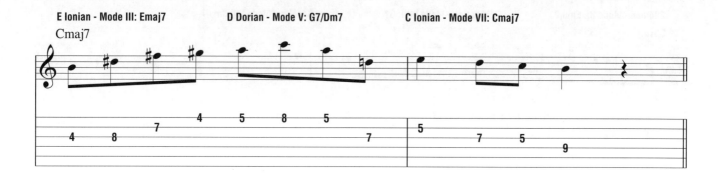

Variation 2 simply replaces the Ionian pentatonic scales with the relative Aeolian pentatonic scales [**Fig. 32J**]. Notice that you are now using only minor pentatonic scales—that all use the same Mode patterns!

Track 58 (cont.)

Fig. 32J
ii–V–I Solo Variation 2: Dorian and Aeolian Pentatonic Scales

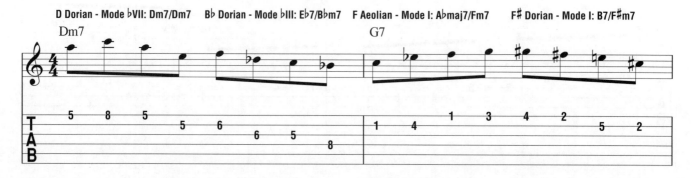

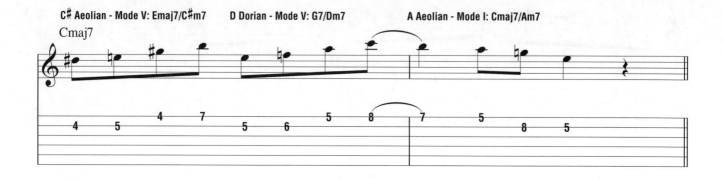

To simplify soloing options even further, Variation 3 demonstrates the option of using only the basic minor pentatonic scales from Chapter 1 [**Fig. 32K**]. In addition, as was shown with the "Giant Steps" chord progression, the entire ii–V–I progression can be played with only Mode I and Mode V of the minor pentatonic scale. You should also practice Variation 3 by minimizing frethand movement. This can be done by focusing on one fretboard position at a time, using the various Modes from the minor pentatonic scale to cover the chord changes.

Fig. 32K

Track 58 (cont.)

ii–V–I Solo Variation 3: Basic Minor Pentatonic Scales

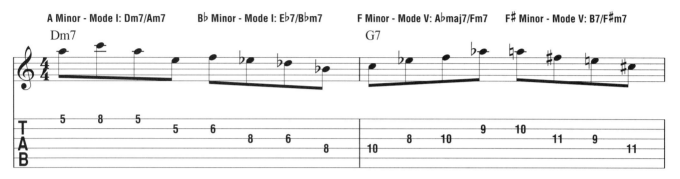

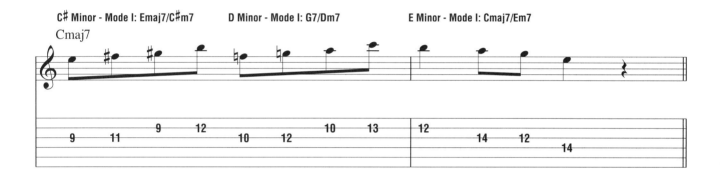

The next step is to play this progression in the other four pentatonic positions on the fretboard.

Finally, it is also very important to get familiar with this progression in all keys so that you can maximize your use of this device independent of the key of the song. Start with the "jazz" keys of E♭, B♭, G, F, and A♭.

Now, for a final bonus, I will show you how to get even more mileage out of this progression.

As demonstrated in Fig. 32L, Variation 3 of the "Coltrane changes" can be used over a static major seventh chord with *no modifications to the pentatonic scale sequence.*

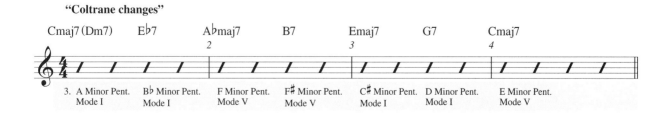

This means that if you are vamping on Cmaj7, you can use all of the devices in Chapter 2 and Chapter 12. In addition, you can now superimpose the "Coltrane changes" minor pentatonic scales over the static Cmaj7 chord [**Fig. 32L**]. This will make your solo sound very "outside" yet melodic at the same time. All that you are doing is placing a temporary ii–V progression inside of a Imaj7 vamp. This is a very common jazz-soloing device.

Track 58 (cont.)

Fig. 32L
"Coltrane Changes" Over a Cmaj7 Vamp: Basic Minor Pentatonic Scales

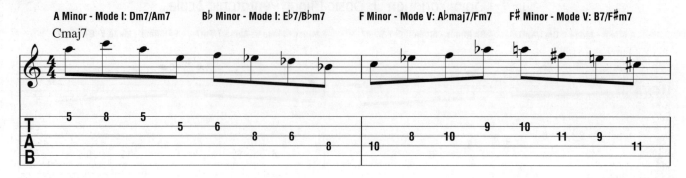

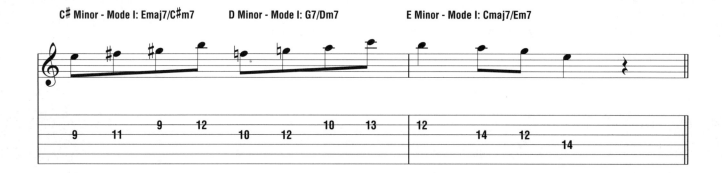

The A minor pentatonic scale in measure 1 works over either a Cmaj7 or a Dm7 chord. As shown in Chapter 1 and Chapter 12, the A minor pentatonic scale (which is the same as the C major pentatonic scale) is a substitute scale for the Cmaj7 (Imaj7) chord. As shown in Chapter 13, the A minor pentatonic scale is also a substitute scale for the Dm7 (iim7) chord.

Summary

This final chapter is a culmination of all the material presented in this book. It presents the pentatonic scale approach for soloing over the most challenging chord progression in jazz—"Giant Steps." This chapter also demonstrates an approach to incorporating "Coltrane changes" over standard ii–V–I changes and static major seventh chords.

At this point, you are prepared to solo effectively over virtually any chord progression. Your solos will have strong melodic content and will sound cohesive. You can play as simple or as "outside" as you choose. Also, because you are focusing on pentatonic scales, you will be able to play close to your maximum speed. Most importantly, the information in this book does not change your style. Instead, it builds upon what you already know, allowing you to continue to grow in any direction that you choose.

The possibilities are truly limitless.

SECTION 6

Appendices

This section provides important background information for the pentatonic chord-scale approach that is used in this book. This approach uses the concept of major- and minor-scale modes to build pentatonic chord scales that are based on these modes.

An overview of the concept of modes is presented in Appendix A.

An overview of the Roman numeral system is described in Appendix B. It is used in this book to describe chords in the context of the key that they are in and also to describe chord progressions that are independent of a key signature.

Appendix C presents an overview of how Roman numerals are used to name the five modes of each pentatonic scale presented in the book.

Appendix D presents an overview of enharmonic notes and intervals as they relate to the chord scales presented in this book.

Lastly, Appendix E is a supplement to Chapter 32. It provides an annotated list of resources for soloing over the chord changes to "Giant Steps."

APPENDIX A
OVERVIEW OF MODES

One of the most mysterious concepts in music, especially to guitarists, is modes. Even if you learn them, what good are they? After you learn that a mode is simply playing the major scale but starting on different notes, what next? The major scale, melodic minor scale, and harmonic minor scale each have seven modes. That's 21 modes to remember. Why are they important to learn? Learning the major and minor scales is hard enough. How will modes help?

When asked by aspiring jazz guitarists, the late legendary studio/jazz/pop guitarist Tommy Tedesco used to say that the only good mode is "pie ala mode."

If you really want to study modes, you can find academic books on music harmony. You can also get information from many guitar and jazz method books. If you want concise explanations of modes, you can check the web. Wikipedia.org (*http://en.wikipedia.org/wiki/Modal_jazz*) is a good place to start. The most practical information I have seen in regard to how modes relate to actual music is Frank Gambale's excellent video, *Modes: No More Mystery* (DCI Music, 1991). I highly recommend this video as it is both instructive and entertaining.

While the theory on modes can get very deep and intimidating, the approach taken in this book is very simple: *modes are the names of chord scales.*

This means that for any given chord, there are different scale/mode possibilities. For example, take a simple minor chord. Within the major scale family alone, there are (as will be explained later) three minor chord modes: Aeolian, Dorian, and Phrygian. In addition to the major scale, there are two minor chord modes in both the melodic minor and harmonic minor scales. That's seven minor chord modes in the basic major and minor scales!

Which mode is best? The answer to that question is what this book is all about.

Major Scale Modes

The easiest way to proceed is to start with the C major scale. The seventh chords derived from the C major scale are as follows:

Cmaj7   Dm7   Em7   Fmaj7   G7   Am7   Bm7♭5

The chord scale for a Cmaj7 is C–D–E–F–G–A–B. This scale is called the Ionian mode. The seven chord scales (modes) for the major scale are shown below.

Chord	Chord Scale	Chord Scale Steps	Mode Name
Cmaj7	C–D–E–F–G–A–B	1–2–3–4–5–6–7	Ionian
Dm7	D–E–F–G–A–B–C	1–2–♭3–4–5–6–♭7	Dorian
Em7	E–F–G–A–B–C–D	1–♭2–♭3–4–5–♭6–♭7	Phrygian
Fmaj7	F–G–A–B–C–D–E	1–2–3–♯4–5–6–7	Lydian
G7	G–A–B–C–D–E–F	1–2–3–4–5–6–♭7	Mixolydian
Am7	A–B–C–D–E–F–G	1–2–♭3–4–5–♭6–♭7	Aeolian
Bm7♭5	B–C–D–E–F–G–A	1–♭2–♭3–4–♭5–♭6–♭7	Locrian

As is apparent from above, all of the modes have the same notes. The difference is that the notes are starting from a different step of the major scale. This observation leads to a real problem with respect to figuring out how to apply modes. You are tempted to believe that if you just stay on the major scale, you will have all seven chords and all seven modes covered. You soon learn that this does you no good when playing music, especially considering that much of jazz improvisation deals with scales other than the major scale. The important column from the previous chart is the one labeled "Chord Scale Steps," which illustrates that each chord scale has a different pattern of scale steps.

For example, look at the Cmaj7 and the Fmaj7. Both chords are major sevenths. However, the C Ionian mode has a natural 4th, while the F Lydian mode has a ♯4th. This has a major impact on how each mode will sound and how it will work (or not work) in a specific chord progression.

Next, look at the three minor chords—Dm7, Em7, and Am7. Notice that they all have different scale steps. This means that, while each chord scale (mode) based on these chords has a minor tonality (they all have steps 1, ♭3, 5, and ♭7), they will each have a different sound because the other steps are different. The only flatted notes for the D Dorian mode are the ♭3rd and the ♭7th. In addition to the ♭3rd and ♭7th, the E Phrygian mode also has a ♭2nd and ♭6th. The A Aeolian mode has a ♭3rd, ♭7th, and ♭6th. Once again, the chord scales (modes) are different.

Think of the modes as chord scales. All modes have unique combinations of whole steps and half steps. This is what makes them sound different from each other.

You may be asking, *"So, for an Am7, which mode is better—Dorian, Phrygian, or Aeolian?"*

The answer: They are all good.

"So, which one should I use?"

It depends on how the chord is functioning in the progression. This is determined by the key of the progression. For example, if the Am7 chord is in the key of G and is moving to a D7 chord, you would use the Dorian mode, since A is the second step of the G major scale. If the Am7 is in the key of F and is moving to a Dm7 chord, you would use the Phrygian mode, since A is the third step of the F major scale. However, if the Am7 is in the key of C and is moving to a Dm7 chord, you would use the Aeolian mode, since A is the sixth step in the key of C.

So, why can't I use the Dorian mode in the last example in which the Am7 chord is moving to a Dm7 chord in the key of C? How do you know that the Aeolian mode is the correct mode?

From the earlier chart, the Dorian mode has the following steps: 1–2–♭3–4–5–6–♭7. For an Am7 chord, this means the following A Dorian scale: A–B–C–D–E–F♯–G. That F♯ note is non-diatonic to the key of C, which has no sharps or flats. On the other hand, the Aeolian mode has the following steps: 1–2–♭3–4–5–♭6–♭7. Notice that it has a ♭6th note. Therefore, the notes of the A Aeolian mode are: A–B–C–D–E–F–G. This scale works perfectly in the key of C.

Making the correct chord scale/mode choices for every chord in any progression is what this whole book is about.

Minor Scale Modes

Because of the complexity of jazz chord progressions, we need more than just the major scale modes; we need modes from the harmonic minor and melodic minor scales. That's the bad news. The good news is that we only need one of the modes from each of these minor scales.

Below are the mode numbers and names for the harmonic minor and melodic minor scales.

Melodic Minor

Mode#	Mode Name
1	Melodic Minor
2	Dorian ♭2, Dorian ♭9, Phrygian 13
3	Lydian Augmented, Lydian ♯5
4	Lydian Dominant, Lydian ♭7
5	Mixolydian ♭6, Mixolydian ♭13, Hindu
6	Locrian 9, Locrian 2
7	Super Locrian, Diminished Whole Tone, Altered

Harmonic Minor

Mode#	Mode Name
1	Harmonic Minor
2	Locrian 6, Locrian Natural 6, Locrian 13
3	Ionian ♯5, Ionian Augmented
4	Dorian ♯4, Dorian ♯11
5	Mixolydian ♭9, Mixolydian ♭9 (♭13), Phrygian Dominant
6	Lydian ♯2, Lydian ♭9
7	Locrian ♭4♭7, Altered ♭♭7 Dominant, Asymmetric Diminished

And you thought learning the mode names of the major scale was tough!

If things weren't hard enough, as you can see from above, most of the modes have more than one name. Various books and methods use different names—it all depends on where you look. I am sure I even missed a few! However, it doesn't matter, since we only need one mode from each scale.

IMPORTANT NOTE: Notice that the modes can be referred to by numbers, which is much easier than trying to remember confusing names. However, *Roman numerals* are used to name the modes of the pentatonic scales presented in this book. (See Appendix C: Overview of Pentatonic Scale Modes.)

From the melodic minor scale, we will be using pentatonic versions of Mode IV, Lydian Dominant. From the harmonic minor scale, we will be using pentatonic versions of Mode V, Mixolydian ♭9.

The mode names and scale steps are shown below.

Scale Name	Mode#	Mode Name	Chord Scale Steps
Harmonic Minor	5	Mixolydian ♭9	1–♭2–3–4–5–♭6–♭7
Melodic Minor	4	Lydian ♭7	1–2–3–♯4–5–6–♭7

These two modes are used for dominant seventh chords. You can see this for yourself since each scale contains a 1, 3, 5, and ♭7, which defines a dominant chord. However, the Mixolydian ♭9 mode has a ♭2 and ♭6. These notes alter the 9th (♭2) and 13th (♭6) of the dominant chord. This means that this scale would work perfectly if you are playing over a G7♭9♭13 chord. On the other hand, the Lydian ♭7 mode has a ♯4. This means that the 4th is altered (♯11th). Therefore, you would use this scale if you were playing over a G7♯11 or G9♯11 chord. Notice that the 9th is not altered in the Lydian ♭7 mode.

Here's how the standard Mixolydian mode compares with these two modes:

Scale Name	Mode#	Mode Name	Chord Scale Steps
Harmonic Minor	5	Mixolydian ♭9	1–♭2–3–4–5–♭6–♭7
Melodic Minor	4	Lydian ♭7	1–2–3–♯4–5–6–♭7
Major	5	Mixolydian	1–2–3–4–5–6–♭7

Notice that the only altered note in the Mixolydian mode is the ♭7. This is the mode to use for an unaltered dominant seventh chord like a G7 or G9.

So, what is the answer to the question, *"What mode is best for a G7 chord?"*

Once again, it all depends.

If you want the sound of an unaltered G7 chord, use the Mixolydian mode. If you want the sound of a G7♭9 chord, use the Mixolydian ♭9 mode. If you want the sound of a G9♯11 chord, use the Lydian ♭7 mode.

This is the approach taken in this book, except that pentatonic versions of the modes are used instead of the seven-note versions that are traditionally used.

Summary

Just remember the following: *modes are the names of chord scales.*

APPENDIX B
OVERVIEW OF ROMAN NUMERAL SYSTEMS

The Roman numeral system is used in this book in three important and distinct ways: 1) to describe chords, 2) to describe chord progressions, and 3) to name the modes of the pentatonic chord scales.

Chords and chord progressions are covered in this Appendix. (Using the Roman numeral system to describe the modes of the pentatonic scales is covered in Appendix C.)

Describing Chords

Instead of lettered chords (e.g., Am7), the Roman numeral system is used to describe chord relationships within the key, chord quality, and chord extension (e.g., vim7).

The C major scale is shown below, along with the degree of each note within the scale.

Note:	C	D	E	F	G	A	B
Scale Degree:	1	2	3	4	5	6	7

A three-note chord (i.e., basic triad) can be built from each note in the major scale. Each of these triads can also be represented by a Roman numeral that corresponds to: 1) the scale degree of the root note in the triad, and 2) the quality of the chord. There are four basic chord qualities: major, minor, diminished, or augmented. Chord qualities may be explicitly stated (e.g., Amaj7, Am7, A7) or implied by upper- or lowercase Roman numerals. Uppercase Roman numerals represent major chords, and lowercase Roman numerals represent minor chords (i.e., uppercase for chords that contain a major 3rd, lowercase for chords that contain a minor 3rd). These relationships are shown below.

Chord:	C	Dm	Em	F	G	Am	B°
Roman Numeral:	I	ii	iii	IV	V	vi	vii°

The triads above are derived by stacking intervals of a 3rd on top of the root note. For example, the G triad consists of the notes G, B, and D. G is the root, or first note. The third note after G is B. The third note after B is D. The same method applies to the formation of the other triads. Now if you stack one more 3rd on top of the triads, you get seventh chords built from the scale tones. These are shown below with the associated Roman numerals.

Chord:	Cmaj7	Dm7	Em7	Fmaj7	G7	Am7	Bm7♭5
Roman Numeral:	Imaj7	iim7	iiim7	IVmaj7	V7	vim7	viim7♭5

Roman numerals offer additional harmonic information about the chord. As shown in the previous figure, the major scale consists of seven notes and seven related seventh chords. Two of the chords are major sevenths, three are minor sevenths, one is a dominant seventh, and one is a half diminished (minor seventh flat five). The minor seventh chords do not function the same way in a chord progression, however. The same is true for the major seventh chords. For example, below are the minor seventh chords in the key of C.

Dm7   Am7   Em7

Each chord serves a different function in the key of C. The Dm7 typically leads to a G7 chord, or it may revert directly back to Cmaj7. The Em7 chord is typically a substitute for a Cmaj7. While the Am7 can also serve as substitute for Cmaj7, it usually follows Cmaj7 or Em7 chords.

What this means is that if you see an Am7 chord, its role in the chord progression depends on the key. For example, the Am7 is part of three keys, as shown below:

KEY	Imaj7	iim7	iiim7	IVmaj7	V7	vim7	viim7♭5
C	Cmaj7	Dm7	Em7	Fmaj7	G7	**Am7**	Bm7♭5
F	Fmaj7	Gm7	**Am7**	B♭maj7	C7	Dm7	Em7♭5
G	Gmaj7	**Am7**	Bm7	Cmaj7	D7	Em7	F♯m7♭5

The Am7 is the vim7 chord in the key of C, the iiim7 chord in the key of F, and the iim7 chord in the key of G. This means that the Am7 chord serves a different function, depending on the key of the progression. This becomes important when you are soloing, as your solo needs to be based on how the chord is functioning in the key and the chord progression. For example, in the key of F, the Am7 is probably serving as a substitute Fmaj7 chord. Over this Am7 chord, your solo will be very different than if you are in the key of G, where the Am7 chord is probably moving to a D7 chord.

Describing Chord Progressions

In addition to describing chords, Roman numerals are also used to describe chord progressions. The reason is that Roman numerals are independent of key. By showing chord progressions with Roman numerals, you do not need to worry about keys. The relationship of the Roman numeral chords will be the same in any key. This makes for quick and easy transposition. For example, below is a standard chord progression in jazz.

If you transpose this to E♭, the progression becomes:

Since there are 12 keys, there are 12 versions of this chord progression, even though the relationship of the chords within each progression is identical across all 12 keys.

Instead, the standard progression above can be identified as follows:

Now you can focus on the chord progression and not the specific key. This is important in jazz because songs and soloing are based on *chord progressions*, and not specific keys.

Roman Numeral Alterations and Extensions

Jazz music involves more than basic chord progressions in the same key. Therefore, modifications to the Roman numeral system are necessary to reflect complexities found in most chord progressions. For example, compare the two common progressions below.

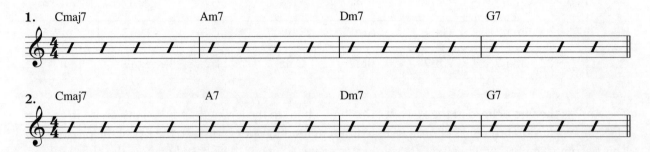

Note that the second chord is different. Technically, the A7 does not belong in the key of C. In harmony theory, it is referred to as a "secondary dominant." Without getting into a lot of harmony theory, modifications to the basic seven Roman numeral chords are done by clearly notating the modification of the chord quality. In the previous example, the two progressions would be notated as follows:

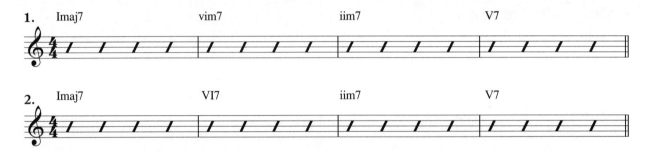

Notice that, in the key of C, a vim7 is an Am7 chord; VI7 is an A7 chord. Remember, since we are using Roman numerals, this relationship holds in any key. For example, in the key of E♭, vim7 is a Cm7 chord; VI7 is a C7 chord.

Modifications are also necessary for chromatic chord designations. For example, review the G major chord progression below.

Notice that the B♭7 and A♭7 chords are not in the key of G. Instead, they represent chromatic movement within the key. Chromatic movement is common in jazz tunes. This chord progression would be notated as follows:

Once again, the advantage of Roman numeral notation is that the progression is independent of key. Your focus is to learn how to play the progression, independent of what key it's in.

Modifications to the Roman numeral system are required for chord extensions, altered chords, substitute chords, and chromatic chords. An overview of typical modifications is shown below.

Chord Extensions

Example Chord	Modification	Meaning
IVmaj7♯4	maj7♯4	major seventh sharp four
IVmaj7♭5, Imaj7♯11	maj7♭5, maj7♯11	major seventh flat five, major seventh sharp eleventh
Imaj6, Imaj9	maj6, maj9	major sixth, major ninth
Imaj6/9	maj6/9	major sixth with added ninth
im(maj7)	m(maj7)	minor (major seventh)
iim11	m11	minor eleventh
ivm6, iim9	m6, m9	minor sixth, minor ninth
V7♭5	7♭5	dominant seventh flat five
V7♯5	7♯5	dominant seventh sharp five
V9	9	dominant ninth
V7♯9	7♯9	dominant seventh sharp nine
V7♭9	7♭9	dominant seventh flat nine
V13♭9	13♭9	dominant thirteenth flat nine
V7alt	7alt	dominant seventh with altered five and nine
i°7	°7	diminished seventh

Chromatic Alterations

Example Chord(s)	Modification	Meaning
♯I7, ♯iii°, ♯iv	♯	raise the chord by one half step
♭III7, ♭VII	♭	lower the chord by one half step

Roman Numeral Conventions for Chords

For purposes of this text, I used the Roman numeral system to identify four pieces of information about the chord: 1) chromatic alterations, if any; 2) the degree of the scale of the chord; 3) the quality of the chord (uppercase for major chords; lowercase for minor); and 4) alterations and/or extensions.

As stated at the beginning of this chapter, this approach results in the following Roman numeral designations of the diatonic major scale chords:

| Imaj7 | iim7 | iiim7 | IVmaj7 | V7 | vim7 | viim7♭5 |

Additional Roman numeral conventions exist, however. Examples are shown below.

I	ii	iii	IV	V	vi	vii	**Triads only**
I	ii	iii	IV	V	vi	vii	**The sevenths are implied**
I7	ii7	iii7	IV7	V7	vi7	vii°7	**The sevenths are shown**
Imaj7	iim7	iiim7	IVmaj7	V7	vim7	viim7♭5	**Combination approach**
I	II	III	IV	V	VI	VII	**Chord quality implied**
IM	IIm	IIIm	IVM	Vx	VIm	VII°	**Chord quality stated**

There are many other variations, including the figured bass approach used in classical music theory. However, I have found that the Roman numeral system used in this book is clear and easy to use.

There are occasions when the shorthand version of the Roman numeral system is used, as shown below.

| I | II | III | IV | V | VI | VII |

Here, the chord qualities are implied, with only uppercase numerals used. For example, it is common to say something like, "The song contains several two-five-one progressions." It is understood that "two-five-one" means "iim7–V7–Imaj7." Learning to "automatically" recognize these patterns (and others) in jazz is essential for understanding how the language of jazz works.

Written		Spoken
ii–V–I	=	"two–five–one"
ii–V	=	"two–five"
V–I	=	"five–one"
I–vi–ii–V	=	"one–six–two–five"
I–IV–V	=	"one–four–five"
iii–vi–ii–V	=	"three–six–two–five"

Summary

The Roman numeral system of describing chords, chord progressions, and the modes of the pentatonic scales is used in this book. The harmony theory behind this approach is deep and beyond the scope of this book. Thus, I have focused on the practical applications of this approach in presenting the concepts covered. I believe that you will find the Roman numeral system described in this chapter to be very useful for describing the music that you play.

APPENDIX C
OVERVIEW OF ROMAN NUMERAL PENTATONIC SCALE MODES

Appendix A presents an overview of modes for the major, harmonic minor, and melodic minor scales. These modes are used to generate specific pentatonic chord scales.

To review, the modes of the major, harmonic minor, and melodic minor scales are as follows:

Mode#	Major	Melodic Minor	Harmonic Minor
1	Ionian	Melodic Minor	Harmonic Minor
2	Dorian	Dorian ♭2	Locrian 6
3	Phrygian	Lydian Augmented	Ionian ♯5
4	Lydian	Lydian Dominant	Dorian ♯4
5	Mixolydian	Mixolydian ♭6	Mixolydian ♭9
6	Aeolian	Locrian 2	Lydian ♯2
7	Locrian	Super Locrian	Locrian ♭4♭7

This book presents pentatonic versions of all seven of the major modes and one each from the melodic minor (Lydian Dominant) and harmonic minor (Mixolydian ♭9) scales.

> **IMPORTANT NOTE:** Notice that the modes can be referred to by numbers. This can be helpful, as it's easier for most people to remember "the 4th mode of melodic minor" than it is to remember specific confusing names. In this book, however, *Roman numerals* are used to name the modes of the pentatonic scales presented.

The pentatonic scales presented in this book consist of five-note scales. Instead of trying to figure out mode names for each step, Roman numerals will be used. For example, below is the familiar A minor pentatonic scale that is presented in Chapter 1.

A Minor Pentatonic Scale	A	C	D	E	G
Interval/Scale Step	1	♭3	4	5	♭7
Mode Name	I	♭III	IV	V	♭VII

Notice that the Mode name relates to the interval represented by the note in the scale. For example, the note G is a ♭7th in the A minor pentatonic scale.

In this book, the mode names of pentatonic scales will be designated by Roman numerals. The Roman numerals represent the starting interval/scale step on the sixth string of the guitar.

For example, Mode ♭III of the A minor pentatonic scale means that you start the scale on the note C (the ♭3rd of Am), which is located at the eighth fret of the sixth string. The rest of this scale is also played from the eighth position, using a two-notes-per-string pattern. The following chart shows the Mode names and corresponding fret positions for all of the notes of the A minor pentatonic scale.

A Minor Pentatonic Scale	A	C	D	E	G
Mode Name	I	♭III	IV	V	♭VII
Fret Position	5th	8th	10th	12th	3rd/15th

Notice that Mode ♭VII shows two positions, 3rd and 15th. This is because if you start the A minor pentatonic scale with the note G, on the sixth string, the scale is playable at both the 3rd and 15th positions on the fretboard. Several of the scale charts will show both a low position and a high position, which represent playable options.

The music notation, tab notation, and fretboard scale diagrams will all use Roman numerals to indicate where on the fretboard each mode of the pentatonic scale should be played.

Summary

The modes of the pentatonic scales in this book are represented by Roman numerals. The Roman numerals indicate the starting scale step and fretboard position for each of the five modes of the pentatonic scales.

APPENDIX D
ANNOTATED LIST OF RESOURCES FOR SOLOING OVER "GIANT STEPS"

The following is an annotated list of resources for an in-depth study of "Giant Steps," as well as soloing approaches to this song. This list is neither exhaustive nor comprehensive—there are many more resources available (check the Web). Nonetheless, this is a select list of resources that I believe are useful and worthwhile. An investigation of these resources will also give you a much greater appreciation of John Coltrane and his significant contributions to music.

Chapter in Book

Scott D. Reeves, "Harmonic Structures and Coltrane Substitutions" *Creative Jazz Improvisation, 3e*, Chapter 12, pp. 163–177, Prentice Hall, 2001. This is an excellent college-type textbook on all aspects of jazz improvisation. The chapter on Coltrane substitutions contains a description of the Coltrane formula, an analysis of Coltrane's solo on "Giant Steps," and a transcription of the first four choruses of the solo.

Books

Joe Diorio, *Giant Steps: An In-Depth Study of John Coltrane's Classic*. Warner Bros. Publications, 1997. This is a book for guitarists. It presents a wealth of solo and chord-melody ideas for "Giant Steps." A bonus is the accompanying CD. This is important because you can hear how the exercises are supposed to sound. These examples are so difficult to play that even the CD plays them at medium tempo. There is very little explanation given for each example, however. Examples are written in notation and tab.

Walt Weiskopf and Ramon Ricker, *Coltrane: A Player's Guide to His Harmony*. Jamey Aebersold, 1991. This is a great book that combines an explanation of "Coltrane cycles" with exercises and etudes to practice in all keys.

David Demsey, *John Coltrane Plays Giant Steps*. Hal Leonard, 1996. Complete transcriptions of all 96 recorded choruses of "Giant Steps."

Jerry Bergonzi, *Inside Improvisation, Volume 1: Melodic Structures*. Advance Music, 1992. This is a great book on how to improvise over chord changes. It is especially useful for songs like "Giant Steps," with fast chord changes and multiple key changes. This books focuses on four-note scale patterns. An analysis of "Giant Steps" shows that much of the solo is comprised of arpeggio patterns and four-note scale or "cell" patterns. This book also demonstrates how to solo using permutations of four-note scale patterns.

The Web

http://en.wikipedia.org/wiki/Giant_Steps—A brief overview of information, with related links on the original recording of "Giant Steps."

http://en.wikipedia.org/wiki/Coltrane_changes—Great background information on "Coltrane changes," with several informative links.

http://patmartino.net—This website by guitar virtuoso Pat Martino has a wealth of material for the jazz musician. Included are examples of guitar solos over the "Giant Steps" changes. Each measure contains a wealth of melodic ideas.

Articles

Corey Christiansen, "Conquering 'Giant Steps,'" *Guitar Player*, September 2005, pp. 92–98. This is an excellent article for developing a soloing approach to "Giant Steps." It is concise, with excellent examples of a wide variety of practical approaches, including arpeggios, digital patterns, chromatic notes, and motifs. This article is an excerpt from the author's *Coltrane Changes* book (Mel Bay Publications).

Eric Nemeyer, "Giant Steps," *Jazz Improv*, Winter 1997, pp. 83–91. This is a good measure-by-measure analysis of an alternate take of John Coltrane's solo on "Giant Steps." The transcription and discussion are very useful for analyzing Coltrane's soloing devices. One minor problem is that the transcription is written for sax and therefore starts in D♭ as opposed to B. However, each measure is like a miniature lesson in soloing and is worth going through.

Dave Mosick, "Giant Steps Patterns," *Just Jazz Guitar*, May 2005, pp. 54–56. This brief article presents some very good melodic examples of soloing over measures 5–6 of "Giant Steps."

Jack Grassel, "Mastering John Coltrane's Giant Steps," *http://www.jackgrassel.com/pages/mastering_giant_steps.html*—This brief article gives example solo ideas over two choruses of the song.

David Baker, "Extending the Coltrane Changes," *Downbeat*, March 1994, p. 63. An excellent and concise description of how "Coltrane changes" relate to the ii–V–I chord progression.

Dan Adler, "The Giant Steps Progression & Cycle Diagrams," *Jazz Improv Magazine*, Volume 3, Number 3, pp. 186–189. This article presents an in-depth and theoretical look at the concept of "cycles" as the underlying principle in "Giant Steps."

Guitarist Recordings of "Giant Steps"

Straight-Ahead Jazz:
Jimmy Bruno, *Burnin'*
Mark Elf, *Mark Elf Trio*
Mike Stern, *Give and Take*
John Scofield, *Now* (John Patitucci as bandleader)

Jazz Bossa:
Pat Metheny, *Trio Live*
Howard Roberts, *The Magic Band II*

Solo Guitar:
Joe Pass, *Virtuoso 2*
Jimmy Bruno, *Solo*

Jazz Fusion:
Greg Howe, *A Guitar Supreme: Giant Steps in Fusion Guitar*
Jennifer Batten, *Above, Below and Beyond*
Scott Henderson, *Vital Tech Tones*

Instructional CD:
Joe Diorio, *Giant Steps: An In-Depth Study of John Coltrane's Classic*

BIBLIOGRAPHY

David Baker, *How to Play Bebop 1*, Alfred, 1987

Jerry Bergonzi, *Inside Improvisation: Volume 1 Melodic Structures*, Advance Music, 1992

Jerry Bergonzi, *Inside Improvisation Series: Vol. 2 Pentatonics*, Advance Music, 1994

Joe Diorio, *Giant Steps: An In-Depth Study of John Coltrane's Classic*, Warner Bros. Publications, 1997

Dan Greenblatt, *The Blues Scales: Essential Tools for Jazz Improvisation*, Sher Music Co., 2004

Ramon Ricker, *Pentatonic Scales for Jazz Improvisation*, CPP/Belwin, 1978

Adelhard Roikinger, *Jazz Improvisation & Pentatonic*, Advance Music, 1987

George Russell, *Lydian Chromatic Concept of Tonal Organization*, Concept Publishing Co., 1959

Bruce Saunders, *Jazz Pentatonics: Advanced Improvising Concepts for Guitar*, Mel Bay, 2004

TRACK LISTING

ABOUT THE AUTHOR

Dr. Ronald S. Lemos is a professor of Information Systems at California State University, Los Angeles. He received his M.B.A and Ph.D. in Information Systems from UCLA.

Dr. Lemos has held positions as Dean of the School of Business and Economics at California State University, Los Angeles, Assistant Vice Chancellor for Academic Affairs for the California State University System, and Dean of the School of Management at California State University, Dominguez Hills.

Dr. Lemos has played guitar professionally since 1967. He still performs weekly with various musical groups, playing a wide range of styles, including pop, Latin, and jazz. For duo jazz performances, he plays a 16" blond archtop (25½" scale, 1¾" nut), custom made by Victor Baker (http://www.victorbaker.com). For jazz combo performances, Dr. Lemos plays a 1997 Gibson L-5 Custom. For popular and Latin performances, he uses a Line 6 Variax 300 modeling guitar.

In addition to writing articles for *Just Jazz Guitar* and *Fingerstyle Guitar*, Dr. Lemos has published articles and presented papers on a wide range of topics, including computing, management, teacher education, and diversity in education.

He is currently authoring forthcoming books on solo chord-melody arrangements and a new system for using arpeggios in jazz improvisation.

He can be contacted at: *rlemos@calstatela.edu*

GUITAR NOTATION LEGEND

Guitar music can be notated three different ways: on a *musical staff*, in *tablature*, and in *rhythm slashes*.

RHYTHM SLASHES are written above the staff. Strum chords in the rhythm indicated. Use the chord diagrams found at the top of the first page of the transcription for the appropriate chord voicings. Round noteheads indicate single notes.

THE MUSICAL STAFF shows pitches and rhythms and is divided by bar lines into measures. Pitches are named after the first seven letters of the alphabet.

TABLATURE graphically represents the guitar fingerboard. Each horizontal line represents a string, and each number represents a fret.

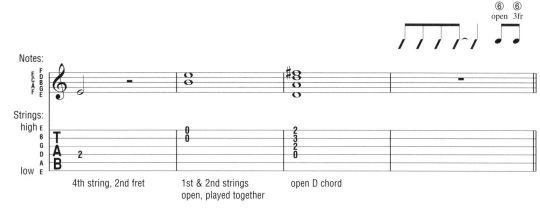

4th string, 2nd fret | 1st & 2nd strings open, played together | open D chord

DEFINITIONS FOR SPECIAL GUITAR NOTATION

HALF-STEP BEND: Strike the note and bend up 1/2 step.

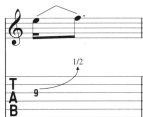

WHOLE-STEP BEND: Strike the note and bend up one step.

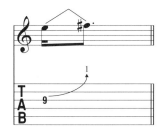

GRACE NOTE BEND: Strike the note and immediately bend up as indicated.

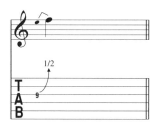

SLIGHT (MICROTONE) BEND: Strike the note and bend up 1/4 step.

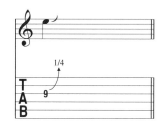

BEND AND RELEASE: Strike the note and bend up as indicated, then release back to the original note. Only the first note is struck.

PRE-BEND: Bend the note as indicated, then strike it.

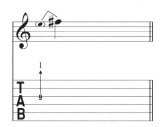

PRE-BEND AND RELEASE: Bend the note as indicated. Strike it and release the bend back to the original note.

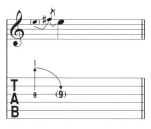

UNISON BEND: Strike the two notes simultaneously and bend the lower note up to the pitch of the higher.

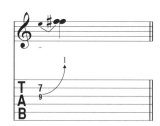

VIBRATO: The string is vibrated by rapidly bending and releasing the note with the fretting hand.

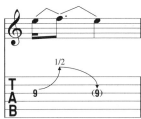

WIDE VIBRATO: The pitch is varied to a greater degree by vibrating with the fretting hand.

HAMMER-ON: Strike the first (lower) note with one finger, then sound the higher note (on the same string) with another finger by fretting it without picking.

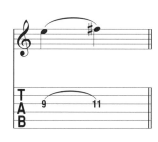

PULL-OFF: Place both fingers on the notes to be sounded. Strike the first note and without picking, pull the finger off to sound the second (lower) note.

LEGATO SLIDE: Strike the first note and then slide the same fret-hand finger up or down to the second note. The second note is not struck.

SHIFT SLIDE: Same as legato slide, except the second note is struck.

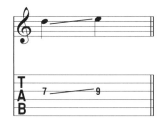

TRILL: Very rapidly alternate between the notes indicated by continuously hammering on and pulling off.

TAPPING: Hammer ("tap") the fret indicated with the pick-hand index or middle finger and pull off to the note fretted by the fret hand.

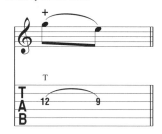

253

NATURAL HARMONIC: Strike the note while the fret-hand lightly touches the string directly over the fret indicated.

PINCH HARMONIC: The note is fretted normally and a harmonic is produced by adding the edge of the thumb or the tip of the index finger of the pick hand to the normal pick attack.

HARP HARMONIC: The note is fretted normally and a harmonic is produced by gently resting the pick hand's index finger directly above the indicated fret (in parentheses) while the pick hand's thumb or pick assists by plucking the appropriate string.

PICK SCRAPE: The edge of the pick is rubbed down (or up) the string, producing a scratchy sound.

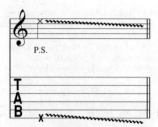

MUFFLED STRINGS: A percussive sound is produced by laying the fret hand across the string(s) without depressing, and striking them with the pick hand.

PALM MUTING: The note is partially muted by the pick hand lightly touching the string(s) just before the bridge.

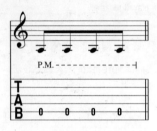

RAKE: Drag the pick across the strings indicated with a single motion.

TREMOLO PICKING: The note is picked as rapidly and continuously as possible.

ARPEGGIATE: Play the notes of the chord indicated by quickly rolling them from bottom to top.

VIBRATO BAR DIVE AND RETURN: The pitch of the note or chord is dropped a specified number of steps (in rhythm), then returned to the original pitch.

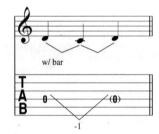

VIBRATO BAR SCOOP: Depress the bar just before striking the note, then quickly release the bar.

VIBRATO BAR DIP: Strike the note and then immediately drop a specified number of steps, then release back to the original pitch.

ADDITIONAL MUSICAL DEFINITIONS

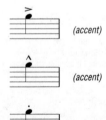

(accent) • Accentuate note (play it louder).

(accent) • Accentuate note with great intensity.

(staccato) • Play the note short.

• Downstroke

∨ • Upstroke

D.S. al Coda • Go back to the sign (𝄋), then play until the measure marked "*To Coda*," then skip to the section labelled "**Coda**."

D.C. al Fine • Go back to the beginning of the song and play until the measure marked "*Fine*" (end).

Rhy. Fig. • Label used to recall a recurring accompaniment pattern (usually chordal).

Riff • Label used to recall composed, melodic lines (usually single notes) which recur.

Fill • Label used to identify a brief melodic figure which is to be inserted into the arrangement.

Rhy. Fill • A chordal version of a Fill.

tacet • Instrument is silent (drops out).

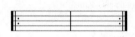

• Repeat measures between signs.

• When a repeated section has different endings, play the first ending only the first time and the second ending only the second time.

NOTE: Tablature numbers in parentheses mean:
1. The note is being sustained over a system (note in standard notation is tied), or
2. The note is sustained, but a new articulation (such as a hammer-on, pull-off, slide or vibrato) begins, or
3. The note is a barely audible "ghost" note (note in standard notation is also in parentheses).

254